Nelson Advanced Science

Respiration and Coordination

revised edition

John Adds • Erica Larkcom • Ruth Miller

Series Editor: Martin Furness-Smith

Endorsed by

Published in 2001 by:
Nelson Thornes Ltd
Delta Place
27 Bath Road
CHELTENHAM
GL53 7TH
United Kingdom

This edition published in 2003

03 04 05 06 07 / 10 9 8 7 6 5 4 3 2 1

A catalogue record for this book is available from the British Library

ISBN 0 7487 7489 0

Illustrations by Hardlines and Wearset
Page make-up by Hardlines and Wearset

Printed in Croatia by Zrinski

Acknowledgements

The authors and publisher are grateful for permission to include the following copyright material:

The examination questions are reproduced by permission of London Examinations, a division
of Edexcel Foundation.

Artwork:
Dean Madden, National Centre for Biotechnology Education, Reading University: figure 4.9
(original appeared in NCBE's 'The lambda protocol'); figures 8.1, 8.2 (originals appeared in
EIBE, Unit 1).
John Schollar, National Centre for Biotechnology Education, Reading University: figure 5.4.

Photographs:
Allsport: 1.14;
English National Hop Association: 6.9;
Erica Larkcom: 6.1, 6.13, 9.1, 9.2, 9.7, 10.3, 10.5;
Geoscience Features Picture Library: 2.11;
Getty Telegraph Colour Library: Greg Pease cover;
Greene King: 6.6;
J Allen Cash: 6.8;
John Adds: 1.2, 2.4 top, 2.6, 3.6, 3.10, 11.1 top, 11.7c, 11.14, 13.1, 13.2, P1, P2, P3;
Neil Thompson: 5.2, 5.3, 6.16, 12.2;
Novara: P4;
Planet Earth Pictures: 2.1;
Rex Features: 7.7, 7.9 Chat, 7.10 SIPA Press;
Science Photolibrary: 2.9 bottom, Alex Bartell 6.10, Barry Dowsett 4.8, Department of Clinical
Radiology, Salisbury District Hospital 11.4 bottom, Dr Kari Lounatama 4.1 top, 4.4, Eamonn
McNulty 11.4 top, Eye of Science 4.1a middle, Manfred Kage 4.7b, Professor P M Motta &
M Castellucci 2.4 bottom, St Mary's Hospital Medical School 6.14, Biophoto Associates 7.8,
Dr Linda Stannard, UCT 4.1b;
Topham Picturepoint: 7.6 Associated Press.

Contents

CONTENTS

CONTENTS

Introduction

This series has been written by Chief Examiners and others involved directly with the Edexcel Advanced Subsidiary (AS) and Advanced (A) GCE Biology and Biology (Human) specification and its assessment.

Respiration and Coordination is one of four books in the Nelson Advanced Science (NAS) series. These books have been developed to match the requirements of the Edexcel specification, but they will also be useful for other Advanced Subsidiary (AS) and Advanced (A) courses.

Respiration and Coordination covers Unit 4 of the Edexcel specification for Advanced GCE Biology and Biology (Human), including the Options. The common material involves:

- a study of metabolic pathways, with emphasis on the central role played by adenosine triphosphate (ATP)
- an understanding of the way in which responses are made to changes in the external environment in order to maintain a constant internal environment
- the role of the mammalian kidney in osmoregulation and nitrogenous excretion
- the control of blood glucose levels
- the involvement of hormones and the central nervous system.

The book also covers the specifications for the following options: Option A *Microbiology and Biotechnology*, Option B *Food Science* and Option C *Human Health and Fitness*. These options build on common material in the specification and give some insight into the applications of biology.

In *Microbiology and Biotechnology*, an indication of the diversity of microorganisms is gained through a study of representative bacteria, fungi and viruses. The requirements for growth and culture techniques are described, together with reference to the use of microorganisms in the food and drink industry and in the production of penicillin.

Food Science covers aspects of food and diet, over- and under-nutrition, food additives, postharvest changes, short- and long-term storage, packaging and some examples of the use of biotechnology in food production.

In *Human Health and Fitness*, the cardiovascular, pulmonary, musculoskeletal and lymphatic systems are studied in more detail, in order to understand training and exercise physiology. In addition, some of the disorders associated with these systems are covered.

Only one of the three options can be studied during the course. The same options are available to both Biology and Biology (Human) students.

The other student books in the series are:

- *Molecules and Cells*, covering Unit 1 and containing the Appendix, which provides the physical science background for the complete course

- *Exchange and Transport, Energy and Ecosystems*, covering Units 2B, 2H and 3
- *Genetics, Evolution and Biodiversity*, covering Units 5B and 5H.

In *Molecules and Cells*, there is an **Appendix**, which provides the **physical science background** that you need in the study of the Biology and Biology (Human) specifications. Much of the information in the appendix is particularly relevant to the topics covered in Unit 1, but it is a useful reminder of some basic scientific concepts that may need to be referred to throughout the course.

Other resources in this series

NAS *Tools, Techniques and Assessment in Biology* is a course guide for students and teachers. For use alongside the four student texts, it offers ideas and support for practical work, fieldwork and statistics. Key Skills opportunities are identified throughout. This course guide also provides advice on the preparation for assessment tests (examinations).

NAS *Make the Grade in AS Biology with Human Biology* and *Make the Grade in A2 Biology with Human Biology* are Revision Guides for students and can be used in conjunction with the other books in this series. They help students to develop strategies for learning and revision, to check their knowledge and understanding, and to practise the skills required for tackling assessment questions.

Features used in this book – notes to students

The NAS Biology student books are specifically written to help you understand and learn the information provided, and to help you to apply this information to your coursework.

The **text** offers complete and self-contained coverage of all the topics in each Unit. Key words are indicated in bold. The headings for sub-sections have been chosen to link with the wording of the specification wherever possible.

In the margins of the pages, you will find:
- **definition boxes** where key terms are defined. These reinforce and sometimes expand definitions of key terms used in the text.
- **questions** to test your understanding of the topics as you study them. Sometimes these questions take the topic a little further and stimulate you to think about how your knowledge can be applied.

Included in the text are boxes with:
- **background information** designed to provide material which could be helpful in improving your understanding of a topic. This material could provide a link between knowledge gained from GCSE and what you are required to know for AS and A GCE. It could be more information about a related topic or a reminder of material studied at a different level.
- **additional** or **extension** material which takes the topic further. This material is not strictly part of the Edexcel specification and you will not be examined on it, but it can help you to gain a deeper understanding, extending your knowledge of the topic.

In the specification, reference is made to the ability to recognise and identify the general formulae and structure of biological molecules. You will see that we have included the structural chemical formulae of many compounds where we think that this is helpful in gaining an understanding of the composition of the molecules and appreciating how bond formation between monomers results in the formation of polymers. It should be understood that you will not be expected to memorise or reproduce these structural chemical formulae, but you should be able to recognise and reproduce the general formulae for all the molecules specified.

The chapters correspond to the sections of the specification. At the end of each of chapters 1, 2 and 3 and each option, you will find the **practical investigations** linked to the topics covered. These practical investigations are part of the specification and you could be asked questions on them in the Unit tests. Each practical has an introduction, putting it into the context of the topic, and sufficient information about materials and procedure to enable you to carry out the investigation. In addition, there are suggestions as to how you should present your results and questions to help you with the discussion of your findings. In some cases, there are suggestions as to how you could extend the investigation so that it would be suitable as an individual study.

At the end of the book, there are **assessment questions**. These have been selected from past examination papers and chosen to give you as wide a range of different types of questions as possible. These should enable you to become familiar with the format of the Unit Tests and help you to develop the skills required in the examination. **Mark schemes** for these questions are provided so that you can check your answers and assess your understanding of each topic.

Note to teachers on safety

When practical instructions have been given we have attempted to indicate hazardous substances and operations by using standard symbols and recommending appropriate precautions. Nevertheless teachers should be aware of their obligations under the Health and Safety at Work Act, Control of Substances Hazardous to Health (COSHH) Regulations, and the Management of Health and Safety at Work Regulations. In this respect they should follow the requirements of their employers at all times. In particular, they should consult their employer's risk assessments (usually model risk assessments in a standard safety publication) before carrying out any hazardous procedure or using hazardous substances or microorganisms.

In carrying out practical work, students should be encouraged to carry out their own risk assessments, that is, they should identify hazards and suitable ways of reducing the risks from them. However they must be checked by the teacher. Students must also know what to do in an emergency, such as a fire.

Teachers should be familiar and up to date with current advice on safety, which is available from professional bodies.

INTRODUCTION

Teachers are strongly advised to refer to Safety Codes of Practice and Guidelines produced by Education Authorities or by Governing Bodies of schools and colleges. This is particularly important in practical work on students, such as investigations into the effects of exercise, in which students should be sufficiently fit and willing to participate. Some practical activities, in particular those involving measurement of body fat and comparisons of fitness, should be approached with sensitivity and understanding.

Acknowledgements

The authors would like to thank Sue Howarth and David Hartley for their help and support during the production of this book, as well as John Schollar and Dean Madden, The National Centre for Biotechnology Education, The British Nutrition Foundation and Sainsburys plc.

About the authors

John Adds is Chief Examiner for AS and A GCE Biology and Biology (Human) for Edexcel and Head of Biology at Abbey College, London.

Erica Larkcom is Deputy Director of Science and Plants for Schools at Homerton College, Cambridge, and a former Subject Officer for A level Biology.

Ruth Miller is a former Chief Examiner for AS and A GCE Biology and Biology (Human) for Edexcel and former Head of Biology at Sir William Perkins's School, Chertsey.

Metabolic pathways

Metabolism is the sum total of all the reactions occurring in cells. It consists of hundreds of linked chemical reactions that make up metabolic pathways, such as the breakdown of glucose to produce carbon dioxide and water. Other metabolic pathways include the series of reactions involved in the synthesis of urea in the liver and in the synthesis of cellulose, from glucose, in flowering plants.

These reactions usually take place in a series of small steps, rather than in one overall reaction. The following diagram represents a metabolic pathway, where each letter represents one substance in the pathway.

$$A + B \rightarrow C \rightarrow D \rightarrow E \rightarrow F \rightarrow G + H$$

In this pathway, A and B represent the **reactants** and G and H are referred to as the **products**. Substances C, D, E and F are referred to as **intermediates**. Each reaction in the sequence is catalysed by a specific enzyme so the product of one step provides the substrate for the enzyme that catalyses the next step, and so on. The products of a metabolic pathway may exert control on the overall pathway, for example, ATP (adenosine triphosphate) produced in respiration acts as an inhibitor for one of the enzymes involved in respiration, so that ATP controls its own production. This is an example of non-active site-directed (or allosteric) inhibition (Unit 1), in which ATP inhibits the enzyme phosphofructokinase, one of the enzymes involved in glycolysis (Figure 1.1).

Metabolic pathways include:
- **catabolism** – the breakdown of complex molecules into simple molecules; for example, the breakdown of glucose into carbon dioxide and water in respiration, with the release of energy
- **anabolism** – the synthesis of complex molecules from simple molecules; for example, joining amino acids together to form a polypeptide, or the synthesis of glycogen from glucose.

Catabolism generally results in the production of ATP, and ATP is used as an energy source in anabolism.

Metabolic reactions take place within cells, and the cell has two ways of controlling metabolic reactions internally:
- by compartmentalisation (that is, that specific reactions occur within particular parts of the cell)
- through enzymes, which may be inhibited by their products, so exerting an overall control on the pathway.

Enzymes involved in metabolic pathways include **oxidoreductases** and **hydrolases**. Oxidoreductases are enzymes that catalyse oxidation or reduction reactions, that is, the removal of hydrogen (oxidation) from a substrate, or the addition of hydrogen (reduction) to a substrate. One example of an oxidoreductase is succinate dehydrogenase, one of the enzymes involved in the Krebs cycle (page 5). Hydrolases catalyse hydrolysis reactions, that is, breaking molecules by the addition of water. Hydrolases include many enzymes involved in digestion, including amylase, maltase, lactase and sucrase.

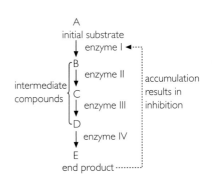

Figure 1.1 Diagram to illustrate end product inhibition by negative feedback in a metabolic pathway. In the metabolic pathway A to E, if E accumulates it acts as an inhibitor of enzyme I, preventing the conversion of A to B. For example, in respiratory pathways concentrations of ATP inhibit phosphofructokinose, an enzyme involved in glycolysis.

In this chapter, we look at cellular respiration as an example of a metabolic pathway.

Cellular respiration

All living organisms require an input of free energy for three major purposes: i) to be able to perform mechanical work, such as muscle contraction and cell movement; ii) the active transport of ions and other substances across cell surface membranes; and iii) for the synthesis of macromolecules. This free energy is obtained from the environment. Chemotrophic organisms obtain this energy by oxidising organic foodstuffs, such as glucose, whereas phototrophic organisms obtain it by trapping light energy (Figure 1.2).

The oxidation of foodstuffs to obtain free energy is known as **cellular respiration**. Cellular respiration occurs as a series of linked, enzyme-catalysed reactions. These reactions can be grouped into three main stages: **glycolysis**, the **Krebs cycle** and **oxidative phosphorylation**.

The most important product of cellular respiration is **adenosine triphosphate** (**ATP**). A molecule of ATP consists of adenine (a nucleotide base) linked to ribose (a five-carbon sugar). The sugar is, in turn, linked to three inorganic phosphate groups. The structure of ATP is shown in Figure 1.3.

ATP is often described as the 'universal currency' of free energy in cells. It is important because the phosphoanhydride bonds, when hydrolysed, yield a relatively large amount of free energy. ATP can be hydrolysed to adenosine diphosphate (ADP) and inorganic phosphate (P_i), as shown below:

$$ATP + H_2O \rightarrow ADP + P_i + H^+ \qquad \Delta G = -30 \text{ kJ mol}^{-1}$$

Notice that, because ΔG is negative, this reaction is **exergonic**, in other words, it yields free energy. This free energy can be used to drive reactions that require an input of free energy, such as active transport. ATP is rapidly resynthesised from ADP and P_i when foodstuffs are oxidised in chemotrophic organisms or when light energy is trapped by phototrophic organisms.

ATP functions as an *immediate* source of free energy in living cells, rather than as a long-term energy store. The rate of production and use of ATP is very high. In a typical cell, 1 ATP molecule is used within one minute of its formation.

Figure 1.2 Green plants are phototrophic organisms: they obtain free energy by trapping light energy.

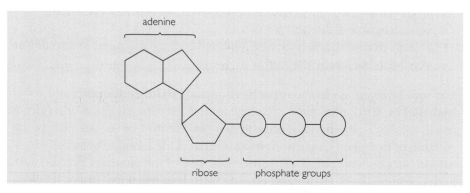

Figure 1.3 Simplified structure of ATP (adenosine triphosphate).

The energy derived from the hydrolysis of ATP to ADP + Pi as shown above is used in cells as a source of energy for a number of processes including:

- the synthesis of macromolecules, including starch, cellulose, proteins and DNA
- active transport
- muscle contraction
- fixation of carbon dioxide during the light-independent reactions of photosynthesis (Unit 5B)
- phosphorylation of glucose at the start of glycolysis (described below).

The link between the hydrolysis of ATP (an exergonic reaction) and the synthesis of a macromolecule from simple molecules (an endergonic reaction) is shown in Figure 1.4.

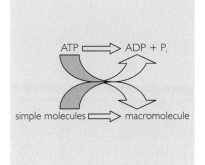

Figure 1.4 The link between the hydrolysis of ATP and the synthesis of a macromolecule.

Electron carriers

Many reactions in metabolic pathways involve the oxidation of a substrate by the removal of electrons (e^-) or hydrogen atoms (H). Electrons are transferred to a group of special substances known as *electron carriers* (also known as hydrogen carriers, or coenzymes). The reduced forms of these carriers eventually transfer their electrons to oxygen by means of a chain of electron carriers situated in the inner mitochondrial membrane. ATP is formed from ADP and P_i as a result of this flow of electrons.

One of the most important electron carriers is nicotinamide adenine dinucleotide (NAD^+). When a substrate is oxidised, NAD^+ accepts a hydrogen ion (H^+) and two electrons. The reduced form of this carrier is called NADH. This reaction is shown below.

$$NAD^+ + 2H^+ + 2e^- \rightarrow NADH + H^+$$

One hydrogen atom from the substrate is transferred to NAD^+, the other appears in solution. Both electrons are transferred to part of the NAD^+ molecule.

Other electron carriers include flavin adenine dinucleotide (FAD) and nicotinamide adenine dinucleotide phosphate ($NADP^+$). The importance of reduced electron carriers is that the change from the reduced form back to the oxidised form of the carrier is linked to the synthesis of ATP.

Glycolysis

Glycolysis occurs in the cytoplasm of cells and it consists of a series of enzyme-catalysed reactions in which each molecule of glucose is converted step-by-step into two molecules of pyruvate. Pyruvate is a compound that contains three carbon atoms and links glycolysis with the reactions that follow.

Initially, glucose is phosphorylated by ATP to form glucose 6-phosphate:

$$\text{glucose} + \text{ATP} \xrightarrow{\text{hexokinase}} \text{glucose 6-phosphate} + \text{ADP} + H^+$$

Each of the six carbon atoms in the glucose molecule is numbered according to a conventional system. The number 6 in the equation above refers to a

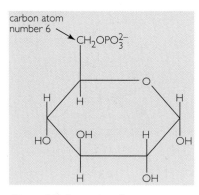

Figure 1.5 Structure of glucose 6-phosphate, produced in the reaction catalysed by hexokinase.

particular carbon atom in the glucose molecule. Figure 1.5 shows the structure of glucose 6-phosphate.

Similarly, in the other compounds that follow, the numbers refer to particular carbon atoms in the compounds.

Phosphorylation of glucose serves two purposes:
  i it prevents glucose from leaving the cell, because the membrane is impermeable to sugar phosphates; and
  ii phosphorylation makes glucose more reactive, so that it can be readily converted into phosphorylated three-carbon compounds.

Figure 1.6 shows all the individual steps of glycolysis, but we can simplify it to show just a few important stages (Figure 1.7). The numbers in square brackets

EXTENSION MATERIAL

Details of the glycolytic pathway

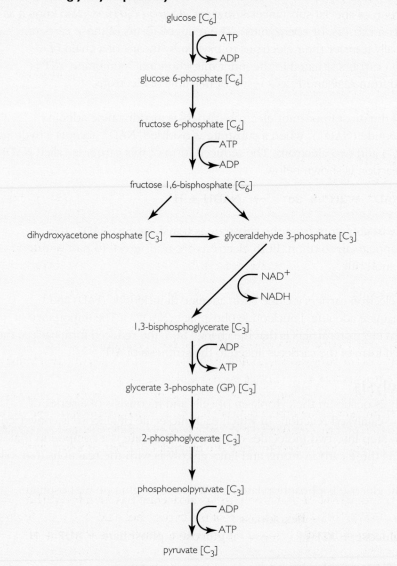

Figure 1.6 Stages in glycolysis, in which one molecule of glucose is broken down into two molecules of pyruvate, with the net generation of two molecules of ATP.

indicate the number of carbon atoms in each compound.

Remember that two three-carbon compounds are produced from each molecule of glucose, so although two molecules of ATP are used in glycolysis, four molecules are produced, giving a net production of two molecules of ATP per molecule of glucose. This is summarised in Table 1.1.

Table 1.1 *Consumption and generation of ATP in glycolysis*

Reaction	ATP change per molecule of glucose
glucose $\rightarrow$ glucose 6-phosphate	−1
fructose 6-phosphate $\rightarrow$ fructose 1,6-bisphosphate	−1
2 × 1,3-bisphosphoglycerate $\rightarrow$ 2 × 3-phosphoglycerate	+2
2 × phosphoenolpyruvate $\rightarrow$ 2 × pyruvate	+2
	net +2

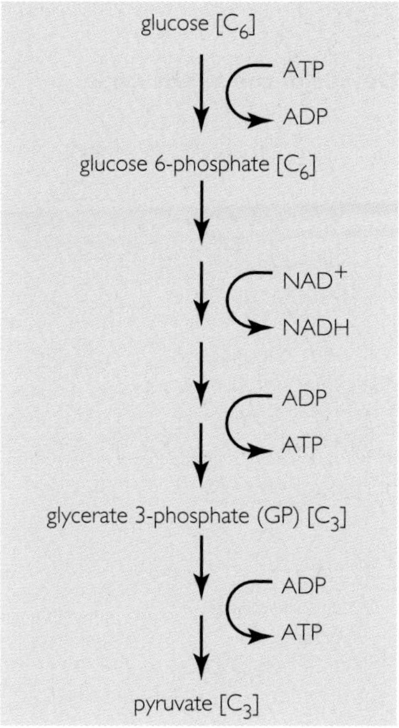

glucose [C_6]

ATP
ADP

glucose 6-phosphate [C_6]

NAD^+
NADH

ADP
ATP

glycerate 3-phosphate (GP) [C_3]

ADP
ATP

pyruvate [C_3]

Figure 1.7 Summary of the essential stages in glycolysis.

The products of glycolysis are, therefore, pyruvate, ATP and NADH. If oxygen is present, pyruvate passes into a mitochondrion and the sequence of reactions known as the **Krebs cycle** occurs.

Aerobic respiration
The Krebs cycle

In aerobic respiration only, the pyruvate, which was produced by glycolysis, passes into the matrix of a mitochondrion. Here the link reaction occurs, in which pyruvate is converted into acetate and combined with a compound called coenzyme A, to form acetyl coenzyme A. This is often abbreviated to *acetyl CoA*. During this reaction, NADH and carbon dioxide are also formed:

pyruvate + NAD^+ + CoA $\rightarrow$ acetyl CoA + NADH + CO_2

The Krebs cycle (also known as the tricarboxylic acid cycle, or TCA cycle) is named after Sir Hans Krebs who, in 1937, pieced together this series of reactions. In the Krebs cycle, a four-carbon compound, oxaloacetate, combines with the two-carbon acetyl unit from acetyl CoA, to form a six-carbon compound, citrate. A sequence of reactions occurs, all of which are catalysed by enzymes present in the mitochondrial matrix, in which citrate is converted back to oxaloacetate. The complete Krebs cycle is shown in Figures 1.8 and 1.9. The numbers in square brackets indicate the number of carbon atoms in each compound.

Since citrate has six carbon atoms and oxaloacetate has four, two carbon atoms must be lost during one turn of the cycle. These exit the cycle in the form of carbon dioxide. Also, several reactions result in the removal of hydrogen from intermediates and both NAD and FAD are reduced (see *Practical: Use of a redox indicator to show dehydrogenase activity,* page 10). One molecule of ATP is also synthesised.

Details of the Krebs cycle

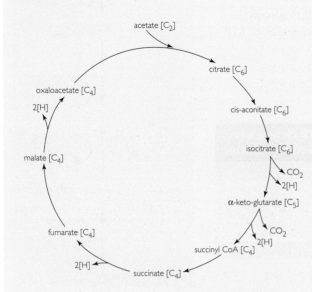

Figure 1.8 *Stages in the Krebs cycle, in which pyruvate is progressively oxidised and decarboxylated, releasing carbon dioxide and hydrogen atoms, which are taken up by hydrogen carriers.*

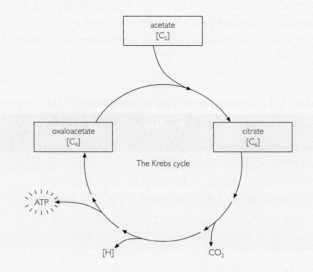

Figure 1.9 *Outline of the Krebs cycle, which results in the release of carbon dioxide and hydrogen atoms, which are picked up by hydrogen carriers (coenzymes). The Krebs cycle also produces some ATP.*

QUESTION

How many molecules of ATP, NADH and $FADH_2$ will be produced from one molecule of glucose? Hint: remember that each glucose molecule produces two molecules of pyruvate.

We can summarise the overall reaction of the Krebs cycle as follows:

- Two carbon atoms enter the cycle and two carbon atoms are lost as carbon dioxide.
- One molecule of ATP is synthesised.
- Four pairs of hydrogen atoms are removed, three NAD^+ molecules are reduced to NADH and one FAD molecule is reduced to $FADH_2$.

All the molecules of reduced electron carriers produced by both glycolysis and the Krebs cycle are reoxidised in the electron transport chain (ETC). During this process, a large amount of free energy is liberated, which can be used to generate ATP. The enzymes for this process are fixed in the folded inner membrane of the mitochondrion.

Oxidative phosphorylation

Oxidative phosphorylation is the process by which ATP is formed when electrons are transferred from NADH or $FADH_2$ to oxygen, by a series of electron carriers. This is the major source of ATP in aerobic organisms. The oxidation of each NADH molecule produces three molecules of ATP and the oxidation of each $FADH_2$ molecule produces two molecules of ATP.

Each hydrogen atom [H] splits into a proton [H^+] and an electron [e^-]. The inner mitochondrial membrane contains numerous electron carriers, such as cytochromes. The transfer of electrons to oxygen through these carriers leads to protons (H^+) being pumped out of the mitochondrial matrix into the intermembrane space. When the protons flow back into the matrix, the free energy made available is used to make ATP from ADP and P_i. Electrons are transferred from NADH to oxygen through a sequence of large protein complexes, including the cytochromes, situated in the inner mitochondrial membrane. These complexes are called NADH-Q reductase, cytochrome reductase and cytochrome oxidase. These are shown diagrammatically below.

NADH → NADH-Q reductase → cytochrome reductase →
             (I)   (II)

cytochrome oxidase → oxygen
(III)

Figures 1.10 and 1.11 show the movement of protons (H^+) back into the mitochondrial matrix and ATP synthesis. The three groups of electron carriers are labelled I, II and III, as in the reaction shown above.

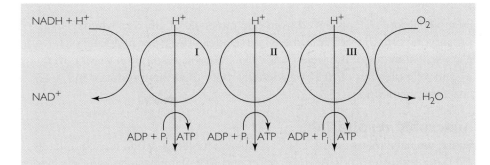

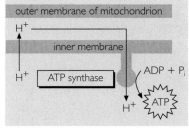

Figure 1.11 Oxidative phosphorylation.

Figure 1.10 Simplified scheme for oxidative phosphorylation, in which hydrogen ions (protons) are transported by a series of carrier molecules – the electron transport chain – across the inner mitochondrial membrane, accompanied by generation of ATP and water.

Oxygen acts as the final electron acceptor and is reduced to form water as shown in the equation below:

$$O_2 + 4H^+ + 4e^- \rightarrow 2H_2O$$

Water is therefore the final product of oxidative phosphorylation.

Yield of ATP from complete oxidation of glucose

We can now work out the total yield of ATP from the complete oxidation of glucose (see Extension Material, page 8).

The complete oxidation of glucose, under standard laboratory conditions, yields 2870 kJ mol^{-1}. The total free energy stored in 36 ATP is 1100 kJ, so the overall efficiency of ATP formation from glucose is

$$(1100 \div 2870) \times 100 = 38\%$$

The total yield of ATP produced in aerobic respiration varies according to the precise conditions. In a eukaryotic cell, such as a liver cell, the total is

EXTENSION MATERIAL

Sources of ATP in aerobic respiration

Source of ATP	ATP yield per glucose molecule
Glycolysis	+2
Krebs cycle	+2
2 × NADH formed in glycolysis	+4
2 × NADH formed in link reaction	+6
2 × FADH$_2$ formed in Krebs cycle	+4
6 × NADH formed in Krebs cycle	+18
	Total +36

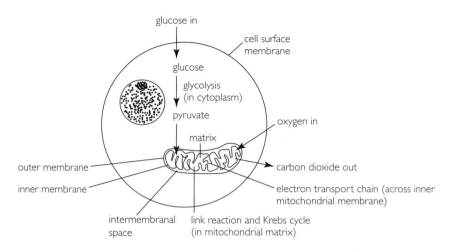

Figure 1.12 Summary diagram to show the sites of glycolysis, the link reaction, Krebs cycle and the electron transport chain in a eukaryotic cell.

36 molecules of ATP produced from one molecule of glucose, whereas in a prokaryotic cell, the yield may be 38 molecules of ATP per molecule of glucose. Estimates of the yield of ATP from aerobic respiration vary between 31 and 39 molecules of ATP, considerably more than that produced in anaerobic respiration.

Anaerobic respiration

So far, we have followed the fate of a glucose molecule when it is completely oxidised, to form carbon dioxide, water and ATP. Many bacteria can only live without oxygen and some organisms, such as yeast, can live with or without oxygen. If oxygen is present, yeast respires aerobically, but in the absence of oxygen, yeast respires **anaerobically**.

Without oxygen, the electron transport chain cannot function, so you would expect reduced electron carriers to accumulate in the cell. Eventually, all the NAD$^+$ would be converted to NADH and all the FAD to FADH$_2$ and metabolism would stop. So organisms that respire anaerobically are faced with the problem of how to reoxidise the reduced electron carriers.

Anaerobic respiration in yeast

Yeast cells solve this problem by using a compound formed from pyruvate to reoxidise the NADH formed during glycolysis. In this way, NAD$^+$ is regenerated and glycolysis can continue. Pyruvate is first converted to ethanal (acetaldehyde) by a decarboxylase enzyme, which removes carbon dioxide from pyruvate. Ethanal is then reduced by NADH to give ethanol and NAD$^+$. The anaerobic breakdown of glucose by yeast is also known as **fermentation** and is the process responsible for producing beer and wine. Anaerobic respiration in yeast is summarised in Figure 1.13.

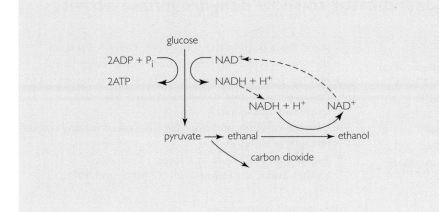

Figure 1.13 Anaerobic respiration in yeast, in which pyruvate is reduced to ethanol instead of entering the Krebs cycle.

Anaerobic respiration in muscle

Anaerobic respiration can also occur in our muscles. This provides additional ATP, which enables muscles to contract even when they have used all their supplies of oxygen, such as during a brief period of vigorous physical exertion. In muscle tissue, pyruvate is reduced directly to lactate and NAD^+ is regenerated, so glycolysis can continue. The reduction of pyruvate to lactate is shown below:

$$\text{pyruvate} + \text{NADH} + \text{H}^+ \rightarrow \text{lactate} + \text{NAD}^+$$

The lactate accumulates in the muscle and, when the exercise is over, lactate is oxidised back to pyruvate. This requires additional oxygen, referred to as the oxygen debt. This additional oxygen is provided by deep and rapid breathing, which continues after the exercise.

To summarise, anaerobic respiration in yeast results in the formation of ethanol and carbon dioxide, whereas in muscle tissue, lactate is the final product. In both cases, the yield of ATP is the same as in glycolysis, that is, two molecules of ATP per molecule of glucose.

Figure 1.14 In the hard-working muscles of this athlete, pyruvate is reduced to lactate in the absence of oxygen, and can build up in the muscles, causing cramp.

QUESTION

Compare the yields of ATP from one molecule of glucose under aerobic and anaerobic conditions. What percentage of the total ATP available can be obtained via anaerobic respiration?

| PRACTICAL | Use of a redox indicator to show dehydrogenase activity |

Introduction

Triphenyl tetrazolium chloride (TTC) is an example of an artificial hydrogen acceptor, or redox indicator. TTC is colourless when oxidised, but forms red, insoluble compounds called formazans when reduced. TTC can therefore be used to show the presence of active dehydrogenase enzymes by a colour change. This experiment investigates the effect of temperature on the activity of dehydrogenases in yeast cells.

Materials

- Actively respiring yeast suspension. This should be prepared by adding 100 g of dried yeast to 1 dm^3 of water and mixing in 50 g glucose. This mixture should be allowed to stand in a large beaker for about 2 hours before the experiment
- Triphenyl tetrazolium chloride solution, 0.5%
- Distilled water
- Test tubes and rack
- Graduated pipettes, or syringes
- Glass rods
- Crushed ice
- Beakers or water baths
- Thermometer
- Stopwatch.

triphenyl
tetrazolium
chloride
HARMFUL

Method

1 Set up a water bath at 30 °C.
2 Pipette 10 cm^3 of yeast suspension into one test tube and 1 cm^3 of TTC solution into another test tube and stand them both in the water bath. Leave for several minutes to reach the temperature of the water bath.
3 Mix the yeast suspension and TTC solution together and return the test tube to the water bath. Start the stopwatch immediately.
4 Observe carefully and note the time taken for any colour changes to develop.
5 Repeat this procedure at a range of suitable temperatures, for example 20 °C, 40 °C and 50 °C.

Results and discussion

1 Explain why the yeast suspension and TTC solution were placed in the water bath before mixing together.
2 Plot a graph to show the relationship between temperature and the rate of activity of dehydrogenases.
3 If possible, try to find the optimum temperature for yeast dehydrogenases.
4 The effect of a 10 °C rise in temperature on the rate of a reaction can be expressed as the Q_{10} value. This is a ratio of the rate of a reaction at, for example, 30 °C to the rate of reaction at 20 °C. The Q_{10} value can be expressed as

$$Q_{10} = \frac{\text{rate at } (t + 10) \text{ °C}}{\text{rate at } t \text{ °C}}$$

Determine the Q_{10} value for yeast respiration between the range of, for example, 30 °C and 40 °C.
5 What are the sources of error in this experiment? How could it be improved?
6 Outline the roles of dehydrogenases in cell respiration.

Regulation of the internal environment

The ability of an organism to control its internal environment is referred to as **homeostasis**. The concept of homeostasis was first described by Claude Bernard, a French physiologist, in 1857. Bernard realised that it is the ability of mammals, in particular, to regulate their internal environment (that is, the composition of their body fluids) which makes it possible for them to survive in widely fluctuating external conditions. Factors such as body temperature, body water content and blood glucose concentration are controlled by physiological mechanisms so that they stay precisely within narrow limits.

If we contrast the distribution of algae and cnidarians (such as seaweeds and jellyfish) with the distribution of flowering plants and mammals, it is clear that flowering plants and mammals are widely distributed in both aquatic and terrestrial habitats, from the tropics to the Arctic and Antarctic regions. Their ability to survive in harsh conditions is entirely due to the regulation of their internal environments (Figure 2.1).

The mammalian kidney

The kidneys are important organs with several homeostatic functions, including controlling the water and salt content of the body and the pH of the blood. They are also organs of nitrogenous excretion, removing excretory products such as urea. Urea is formed in the liver from deamination of excess amino acids. Deamination involves the removal of the —NH_2 part of amino acids; this is combined with carbon dioxide to form urea in a sequence of reactions known as the ornithine cycle.

Figure 2.1 Polar bears are adapted to survive in the harsh conditions of the Arctic.

QUESTION

Describe the ways in which a polar bear is adapted to its Arctic environment.

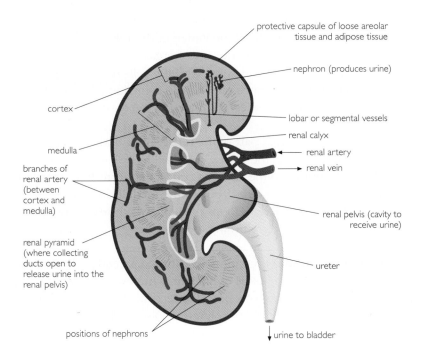

Figure 2.2 Internal structure of the kidney.

REGULATION OF THE INTERNAL ENVIRONMENT

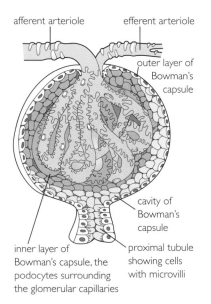

Figure 2.3 *Bowman's capsule and the glomerular capillaries.*

afferent arteriole *efferent arteriole*

outer layer of Bowman's capsule

cavity of Bowman's capsule

inner layer of Bowman's capsule, the podocytes surrounding the glomerular capillaries

proximal tubule showing cells with microvilli

The main functions of the kidneys are to filter blood plasma and to excrete urine. They are situated on the posterior wall of the abdomen on either side of the vertebral column. Each human kidney is about 10 cm long, 5 cm wide and 3 cm thick and weighs about 100 g. In section, each kidney is seen to consist of an outer **cortex** and an inner **medulla** forming about 12 wedge-shaped structures, known as renal pyramids (Figure 2.2).

The apex of each renal pyramid projects into a calyx. The calyces join together to form the renal pelvis which narrows as it leaves the kidney to become the **ureter**. The ureter is a narrow, muscular tube which conveys urine from the kidney to the bladder. The bladder acts as a reservoir for urine before it is expelled via the **urethra**.

Structure of the kidney

Each kidney consists of about 1 million microscopic functional units, the **nephrons**. Nephrons carry out the processes of osmoregulation and excretion and each consists of the following structures: renal corpuscle (Bowman's capsule and glomerulus), proximal convoluted tubule, loop of Henle, distal convoluted tubule and collecting duct.

The **Bowman's capsule** consists of a single layer of flattened epithelial cells and contains a tightly coiled network of capillaries, the **glomerulus**. These capillaries are surrounded by specialised epithelial cells, known as podocytes (Figures 2.3 and 2.4). Each podocyte has long cytoplasmic processes which in turn give rise to short foot processes, or pedicels. The pedicels are packed closely together, with narrow spaces between them of about 25 nm. These spaces are known as slit pores, through which ultrafiltration, the initial stage of urine formation, occurs.

The **proximal convoluted tubule** is the first part of the renal tubule (Figure 2.5). The wall of the proximal convoluted tubule consists of a single layer of cuboidal epithelial cells. These cells have a brush border of long microvilli, which almost completely fill the lumen of the tubule. The cytoplasm of the cells stains darkly due to a high density of organelles, chiefly mitochondria. These features are consistent with the cells having a high metabolic activity. The proximal convoluted tubule is the longest part of the nephron and, like the renal corpuscles, is situated in the cortex of the kidney.

The **loop of Henle** is the second part of the renal tubule and consists of a descending limb which arises in the cortex, followed by a sharp turn and an ascending limb which returns to the cortex. Cortical nephrons have loops of Henle which are restricted to the outer zone of the medulla, whilst juxtamedullary nephrons have longer loops of Henle which reach into the inner zone of the medulla before returning to the cortex.

The **distal convoluted tubule** is continuous with the ascending limb of the loop of Henle and consists of cuboidal epithelium with few, scattered microvilli. In microscopic sections of kidney tissue, distal convoluted tubules can be distinguished from proximal convoluted tubules by the absence of a brush border, a larger, clearly defined lumen and more nuclei as the cells are smaller than those of the proximal convoluted tubule.

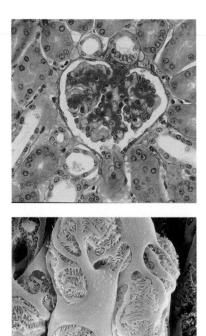

Figure 2.4 *(top) Light micrograph of Bowman's capsule surrounding glomerular capillaries; (bottom) scanning electronmicrograph showing podocytes.*

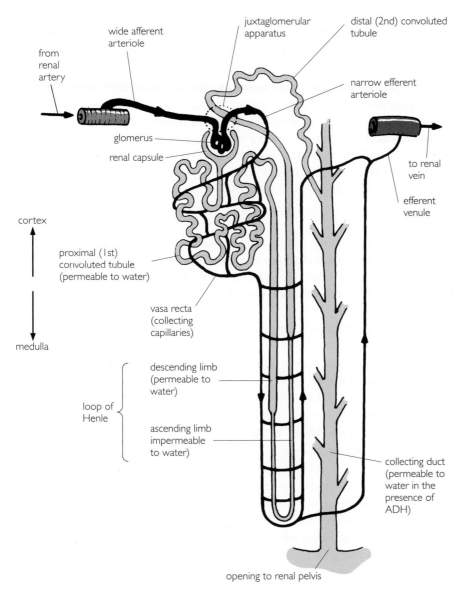

Figure 2.5 *Structure of the nephron.*

The **collecting duct** (Figure 2.6) is a straight tubule that joins the distal convoluted tubules of several nephrons. Collecting ducts converge into larger ducts (known as the ducts of Bellini) which open into one of the calyces.

The function of the nephrons

The kidneys are the most important organs in the body for maintaining water, solute and pH balances. They are able to do this by varying the volume of water and the concentration of solutes which are lost in the urine, thus maintaining a balance of these substances in the body. If the kidneys fail, for example as a result of disease, homeostatic mechanisms also fail and, unless treated, the condition is inevitably fatal.

Urine is formed in the nephron as a result of three major processes: ultrafiltration, reabsorption and secretion.

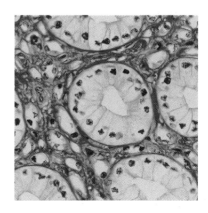

Figure 2.6 *Collecting ducts, tranverse section.*

REGULATION OF THE INTERNAL ENVIRONMENT

Ultrafiltration

Ultrafiltration is a physical process that occurs in the renal corpuscles. Large volumes of blood, approximately 1.2 dm^3, flow through the kidneys each minute. About one tenth of this volume is filtered through the glomerular capillaries and into the Bowman's capsule. The membranes of the glomerular capillaries are normally impermeable to solutes with a molecular mass over 70 000 and the filtrate is essentially a filtrate of plasma, containing virtually no protein and no cells. One reason for the rapid rate of filtration is the fact that the efferent arteriole has a smaller diameter than the afferent arteriole. This increases the resistance to blood flow out of the glomerulus and increases the pressure within the glomerular capillaries. It is this high blood pressure that provides the necessary force for ultrafiltration.

The capillaries have many pores, which increase their permeability. Ultrafiltration takes place through these pores and through the basement membrane of the capillary cells. The basement membrane contains glycoproteins and a network of collagen fibres.

The total rate of formation of glomerular filtrate is about 170 to 180 dm^3 per day in humans, but the volume of urine produced is obviously very much less than this. It is clear that most of the filtrate must be reabsorbed as it passes through the renal tubules.

Reabsorption

Over two-thirds of the volume of filtrate entering the renal tubule from the Bowman's capsule is reabsorbed in the **proximal convoluted tubule**. Sodium ions (Na$^+$) are transported actively out of the lumen of the tubule and then diffuse into the capillaries which surround the proximal convoluted tubule (the peritubular capillaries). The microvilli on the epithelial cells greatly increase the surface area for the uptake of ions and other solutes. As sodium ions are taken up, an electrochemical gradient and negatively charged ions, such as chloride (Cl$^-$), and phosphate (PO$_4^{3-}$), are attracted to the positive ions. The concentration of ions in the capillaries therefore increases and this creates an osmotic gradient, causing water to move out of the proximal tubules by osmosis.

Reabsorption of glucose and amino acids also occurs in the proximal convoluted tubule (Figure 2.7). Reabsorption of glucose involves a special type of active transport, known as **sodium cotransport**. In this mechanism, both sodium ions and glucose bind to a carrier molecule in the epithelial cell surface membrane, which then passively transports both substances into the interior of the cell. Once inside the cell, the substances dissociate from the carrier molecule and diffuse to the basal end of the cell. Here, sodium is actively transported out of the cell and then diffuses into a peritubular capillary; glucose follows by passive diffusion. Normally, all of the glucose which has been filtered out of the glomerular capillaries is reabsorbed by the sodium cotransport mechanism and none is lost in the urine.

After the reabsorption of water, sodium ions, chloride ions, glucose and other solutes, the fluid remaining in the tubule has a relatively high concentration of

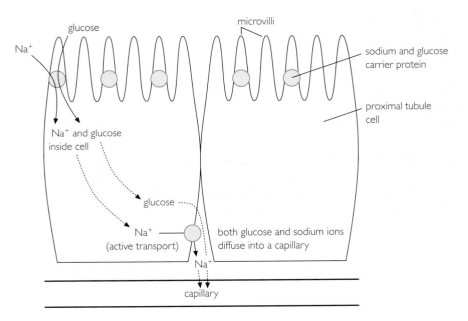

Figure 2.7 Mechanism of glucose reabsorption in the proximal convoluted tubule.

urea. However, since the concentration of urea is higher in the tubule than in the surrounding capillaries, urea passively diffuses into the blood. Approximately half of the urea present in the tubular fluid is reabsorbed in this way.

Reabsorption in the proximal convoluted tubule can be summarised as follows:
- sodium ions are actively reabsorbed
- glucose and amino acids follow the reabsorption of sodium by means of the sodium cotransport mechanism
- chloride and other negatively charged ions are reabsorbed into the blood following an electrochemical gradient
- movement of solutes out of the tubule creates an osmotic gradient and water is reabsorbed by osmosis
- urea is reabsorbed by passive diffusion
- the volume of the filtrate is reduced by 75 to 80 per cent.

Control of water retention

The relatively small volume of filtrate remaining in the proximal convoluted tubule passes into the **loop of Henle**, a structure which enables the kidney to produce concentrated urine. The loop of Henle, and its surrounding capillaries, known as the vasa recta, form a **countercurrent mechanism**. A countercurrent structure is a set of parallel tubes in which the contents flow in opposite directions. In the loop of Henle, the contents of the descending limb flow in the opposite direction to the contents of the ascending limb. The structure of the loop of Henle and the mechanism for the formation of concentrated urine are shown in Figure 2.8.

It appears that cells in the ascending limb of the loop of Henle actively pump chloride ions out of the filtrate and into the surrounding fluid. Since sodium ions follow the chloride ions, we often refer to active transport of sodium

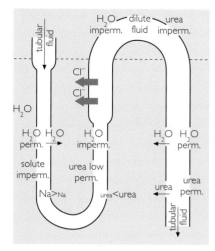

Figure 2.8 The concentrating mechanism in the loop of Henle (perm. = permeable imperm. = impermeable).

chloride. The descending limb is permeable to water, but impermeable to solutes. As the chloride pump has made the fluid surrounding the loop of Henle more concentrated, water is drawn out of the descending limb of the loop so that its contents become more concentrated. The fluid within the loop passing to the ascending limb has therefore become more concentrated, so more chloride ions are pumped out, more water is withdrawn from the descending limb, and so on. The water which is removed passes into the capillaries of the vasa recta (there is an osmotic gradient due to the plasma proteins). The fluid that flows from the ascending limb of the loop of Henle into the distal convoluted tubule has had sodium chloride removed from it and its concentration is lower than that of blood plasma. However, although the concentration of sodium chloride is low, the concentration of urea is relatively high. The presence of these solutes in the medulla of the kidney means that there is an increasingly negative water potential surrounding the loop of Henle and the collecting duct. The water potential becomes more negative (due to the increasing solute concentrations) towards the tip of the loop of Henle; that is, deeper in the medulla. Cells in the collecting duct are permeable to both water and urea. Remember that the concentration of sodium chloride in the fluid surrounding the loop of Henle and the collecting duct is high and therefore water is drawn out of the collecting duct, by osmosis. As water moves out, the urea becomes more concentrated and moves out of the collecting duct by diffusion. The urea contributes to the osmotic effect and the high concentration of solutes in the medulla, derived from both urea and sodium chloride, enables the kidney to produce a concentrated urine.

The ability of the mammalian kidney to produce a concentrated urine is closely related to the length of the loop of Henle. Desert mammals, such as the gerbil, *Meriones* sp., produce highly concentrated urine and have nephrons with exceptionally long loops of Henle. Indeed, so efficient is the mechanism for reabsorption of water that some desert rodents can live indefinitely on dry food and never need to drink.

The main functions of the loop of Henle are summarised below:
- water is reabsorbed from the tubular fluid in the descending limb
- sodium and chloride ions are reabsorbed in the ascending limb
- reabsorption of sodium and chloride ions creates a high solute concentration in the medulla.

The **distal convoluted tubule**, like the proximal convoluted tubule, also reabsorbs sodium ions (Na^+), but in much smaller amounts. Cells in the distal convoluted tubule also secrete substances, including potassium ions (K^+), hydrogen ions (H^+) and ammonia (NH_3), into the lumen of the tubule. Here, ammonia combines with hydrogen ions to form ammonium ions (NH_4^+), which are excreted in the urine.

Cells in the **collecting ducts** are relatively impermeable to water, but their permeability is markedly increased by **antidiuretic hormone (ADH)**, which is secreted by the posterior pituitary gland. ADH is involved in the regulation of water loss by the kidneys. It acts on cells in the collecting ducts and causes

QUESTION

On a hot day, would you expect your circulating levels of ADH to be high or low? Explain your answer.

them to become more permeable to water. The more ADH present, the more water will be reabsorbed and, consequently, the more concentrated the urine will be.

The secretion of ADH depends on the concentration of solutes in plasma and extracellular fluids. If this is raised by about 1 per cent, the secretion of ADH is increased. If the concentration decreases, ADH secretion will also decrease. Changes in the concentration of plasma and extracellular fluid are detected by specialised nerve cells, known as **osmoreceptors**, situated in the hypothalamus. Increased activity of the osmoreceptors results in an increased ADH secretion and, therefore, increased reabsorption of water.

Regulation of blood glucose

The normal level of glucose in the blood is about 5 to 5.5 mmol dm^{-3}. It is vital that this level is maintained so that all the tissues of the body receive a constant supply of glucose for respiration. It is also important that the level of glucose in the blood does not rise too high, as this would affect the water content of the body. Under normal circumstances, all the glucose that is removed from the blood by ultrafiltration in the kidneys is reabsorbed in the first proximal tubule, so that none appears in the urine. If glucose is present in the urine – a condition known as **glycosuria** – the water potential gradient between the renal filtrate and the blood could be affected and water reabsorption would be reduced. If the glucose concentration of the tissue fluid is abnormally high, water would be lost from the tissue cells by osmosis.

A blood glucose level of below 3 mmol dm^{-3} results in a condition known as **hypoglycaemia**, inducing feelings of nausea, loss of concentration and cold sweats, leading eventually to loss of consciousness (coma). **Hyperglycaemia** results if the blood glucose level rises above 10 mmol dm^{-3} and glucose appears in the urine. This is accompanied by a fall in the pH of the blood and eventually leads to coma as well. Both hypoglycaemia and hyperglycaemia can occur in people with diabetes mellitus.

Variations in blood glucose level occur for a number of reasons. In humans, the level of blood glucose will show slight variations over a 24-hour period, rising slightly after meals but dropping again to a more or less constant level. The fall in level overnight or after a period of fasting is only slight.

Insulin

Insulin is secreted from the β cells of the islets of Langerhans in the pancreas in response to an *increase* in the level of glucose in the blood. It is a peptide molecule, consisting of 51 amino acids. The primary structure was worked out by Sanger in 1950. Insulin is secreted into the blood where it circulates in the plasma and affects all organs of the body. It binds to receptors on cell surface membranes, altering the permeability of the membrane to glucose and affecting enzyme systems within the cells. There are three main target organs for insulin:
- the liver, where **glycogenesis** (conversion of glucose to glycogen) is stimulated
- muscle tissue, where glycogenesis is also stimulated
- adipose (fat storage) cells, where breakdown of lipids is prevented.

In addition, **glycogenolysis** (breakdown of glycogen to glucose) in the liver is inhibited and the uptake of amino acids into cells is promoted. All these events lead to a *reduction* in the level of glucose in the blood.

During glycogenesis (the building up of glycogen from glucose), glucose is first phosphorylated and glycogen is then formed by a condensation process. The effect of insulin is to activate the phosphorylase and **glycogen synthetase** in the liver and muscle cells. Overall, insulin promotes the building up of proteins, lipids and glycogen.

It is interesting to note that glucose is not the only stimulus for insulin release. The presence of food in the stomach stimulates the **vagus nerve**, which results in insulin release before the blood glucose level increases after a meal.

Glucagon

Glucagon is a peptide made up of 29 amino acids and is produced by the α cells in the islets of Langerhans in the pancreas (Figure 2.9). It is antagonistic to insulin and is secreted in response to a *fall* in the level of glucose in the blood (Figure 2.10). The release of glucagon is inhibited by insulin and, if insulin is absent, more glucagon is released. A balance between the two hormones exists, ensuring that glucose is released when levels in the blood are low. Glucagon affects the liver cells, promoting the breakdown of glycogen by activating the relevant enzymes. Glucagon also stimulates the uptake of amino acids and glycerol into the liver, where conversion to glucose occurs.

The major site of the action of glucagon is in the liver cells where it promotes the breakdown of glycogen to glucose by activating the enzyme **glycogen phosphorylase** and blocking the synthesis of glycogen by deactivating glycogen synthetase. If there is no insulin in the blood, lipids and proteins break down to give fatty acids, glycerol and amino acids. Glucagon stimulates the uptake of amino acids and glycerol by the liver cells, where they are converted to glucose by gluconeogenesis.

The hormone **adrenaline**, secreted from the medulla of the adrenal gland, also has an effect on blood glucose. Adrenaline prepares the body for physical exertion and increased mental performance, such as might be needed in a

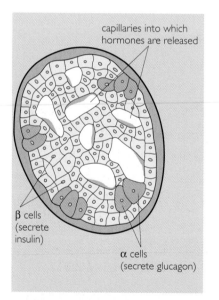

capillaries into which hormones are released

β cells (secrete insulin)

α cells (secrete glucagon)

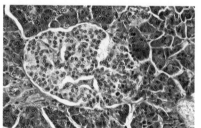

Figure 2.9 (top) Diagram to illustrate the structure of an islet of Langerhans in the pancreas; (bottom) photomicrograph of an islet of Langerhans in the pancreas.

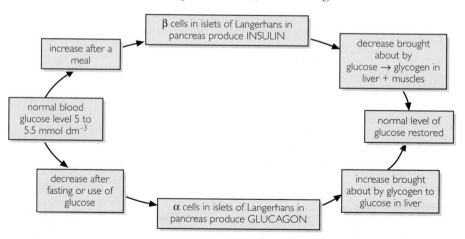

Figure 2.10 The control of the blood glucose level by insulin and glucagon.

stressful situation. One of the effects of this hormone is to increase blood glucose levels by stimulating the breakdown of glycogen in the liver into glucose (**glycogenolysis**).

Response to changes in the external environment

Linked with the ability to regulate the internal environment, there is a need for organisms to detect and respond to external stimuli in order to be able to survive. In animals, all cells are sensitive to changes in their environment, but some cells are specialised to detect stimuli and respond by producing an action potential which can be passed on to the nervous system. These sensory cells, or sensory receptors, usually respond to one type of stimulation, such as light, touch or heat, and may be located in sense organs. The responses are usually rapid movements or changes in behaviour. In contrast, as they lack specialised sense organs and a nervous system, plant responses to external stimuli usually involve growth or turgor movements, which are much slower.

Detection of light in flowering plants

Photoreception is the detection of light and usually involves the absorption of light by a pigment known as a **photoreceptor**. Light is an important factor in the growth of plants as it not only provides the energy for photosynthesis and influences the direction of plant growth, but also has a direct effect on plant development. Some seeds need the stimulus of light before germination can occur. Light affects the formation of chlorophyll and the initial stages of growth, and it also affects the time of flowering in many plants.

If a plant is grown entirely in the dark, the whole plant appears yellowish-white in colour because no chloroplasts develop, the stem elongates more rapidly than normal, the leaves do not expand and the tip of the stem often remains in a hooked position. Such plants are described as **etiolated** (Figure 2.11): they are fragile and die as soon as all the food reserves in the seed are used up. In the early stages of seedling growth after germination, it is possible that etiolated plants are more suited to pushing their way through the soil, as sturdy stems and fully expanded leaves would offer more resistance. In addition, the rapid growth upwards towards a light source would be a competitive advantage.

Figure 2.11 Etiolated cress seedlings (right) alongside normal plants.

Some seeds require exposure to light before germination can occur. Imbibition, involving the uptake of water, must occur first, then the seeds become sensitive to light and need only a brief exposure to bring about the initiation of germination. Experiments carried out in 1937 on lettuce seeds showed that exposure to red light of wavelengths between 600 and 700 nm promoted germination, but exposure to far-red light of wavelengths between 720 and 760 nm inhibited germination. Subsequent investigations showed that the effect of exposure to red light was not reversed by putting the seeds in the dark, but the effect appeared to be cancelled by exposure to far-red light.

In an experiment, using a variety of lettuce called 'Grand Rapids', batches of seeds were soaked in the dark and then exposed to alternating periods of red and far-red light. The percentage germination was determined. Each period of exposure to light lasted for 5 minutes. As can be seen from the results, shown

Table 2.1 *Effect of alternating periods of red and far-red light on the germination of lettuce seeds*

Treatment	Percentage germination
red	70
red (R) / far-red (FR)	6
R / FR / R	74
R / FR / R / FR	6
R / FR / R / FR / R	76
R / FR / R / FR / R / FR	7
R / FR / R / FR / R / FR / R	81
R / FR / R / FR / R / FR / R / FR	7

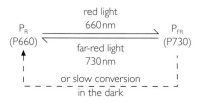

Figure 2.12 The diagram shows the interconversion of the two forms of phytochrome P$_R$ and P$_{FR}$

in Table 2.1, the wavelength of light to which the seeds were last exposed has the greatest effect on the percentage germination.

From these experiments, it was deduced that the light was detected by a photoreceptor, called **phytochrome**, later isolated and identified by Borthwick and Hendrick. Phytochrome is a blue-green pigment, present in very small quantities in the leaves of plants. It exists in two interconvertible forms, P$_R$ and P$_{FR}$, which have different absorption spectra. P$_R$, otherwise known as P$_{660}$, absorbs red light of wavelengths in the region of 660 nm, and P$_{FR}$, otherwise known as P$_{730}$, absorbs far-red light of wavelengths in the region of 730 nm. When P$_R$ absorbs red light it is converted to P$_{FR}$ and when P$_{FR}$ absorbs far-red light it is converted to P$_R$. So red light converts P$_R$ into P$_{FR}$ and the absorption of far-red light reverses the effect of red light. Exposure to natural daylight on a sunny day is equivalent to exposure to red light, so there will be more P$_{FR}$ than P$_R$ in plants. P$_{FR}$ is converted slowly back to P$_R$ in the dark (see Figure 2.12).

Investigations on the phototropic responses of seedlings have shown that phytochrome is not involved. Experiments have indicated that the wavelengths of light which stimulate the phototropic response are in the blue region of the spectrum. However, there is evidence to suggest that phytochrome is involved in the unbending of the plumule hook in the stems of seedlings of French beans after germination and also in the initial expansion of leaves. These responses are similar to germination in that they appear to be triggered by a high level of P$_{FR}$.

As mentioned earlier, only a short exposure to light of the right wavelength is necessary to trigger germination in lettuce seeds, but much longer periods of illumination are required for leaves to expand fully and for the synthesis of chlorophyll. From a number of investigations, it has been shown that red light is more effective at inducing rapid responses, whereas far-red light is more effective in stimulating long-term responses. The explanation for this apparently paradoxical state may be that long-term responses require high levels of P$_R$ or low levels of P$_{FR}$, or possibly that the level of P$_{FR}$ has to be maintained within certain limits.

The length of the photoperiod (that is, day length) has an effect on the initiation of flowering in many plants. Experiments have shown that exposure to red light, resulting in an accumulation of P$_{FR}$, inhibits flowering in short-day plants but will promote flowering in long-day plants. This topic is discussed in more detail in *Genetics, Evolution and Biodiversity*.

QUESTION

Design an experiment which you could carry out to determine how long seeds need to be exposed to the correct wavelength of light before germination is initiated.

Detection of light in animals

Light is detected by the pigments in the retinal cells of the mammalian eye.

BACKGROUND

The eyes are spherical structures located and held in bony sockets, called the orbits, of the skull. They are held in place by rectus and oblique muscles, which also control the eye movements. The wall of the eye is composed of three distinct layers, the composition and functions of which are summarised in Table 2.2.

Table 2.2 *The layers of the wall of the mammalian eye*

Layer	Location and composition	Function
sclera	tough outer covering containing collagen fibres; front part is transparent forming the cornea	protects the eye and maintains the shape of the eyeball; cornea allows light into the eye and the curved surface refracts the light on to the retina
choroid	found between the retina and the sclera; contains numerous blood vessels and pigment cells; modified to form the pigmented iris at the front, which contains radial and circular muscles	supplies retina with blood; pigment prevents reflection of light within the eye; iris controls amount of light entering by altering the size of the pupil
retina	innermost layer containing photoreceptors, the rods and cones, together with neurones supplying the optic nerve	respond to stimulus of light by producing action potential, leading to production of impulses which are transmitted to the brain via the optic nerve

Inside the eye is a biconvex, crystalline lens, located behind the pupil and held in place by suspensory ligaments attached to the ciliary body, which contains smooth muscle. The lens separates the eye into two chambers: the anterior chamber at the front, containing a colourless, watery fluid called aqueous humour, and the posterior chamber, which is filled with transparent, gelatinous mucoprotein called vitreous humour. Both the aqueous and vitreous humours contribute to the maintenance of the shape of the eye. (See Figure 2.13.)

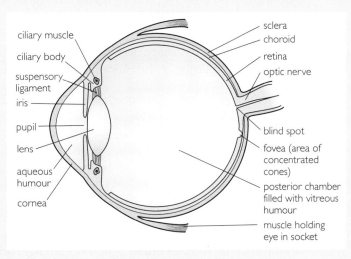

Figure 2.13 Vertical section through the mammalian eye.

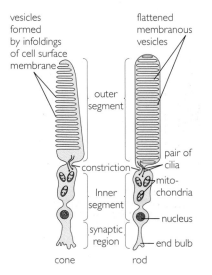

Figure 2.14a Rod and cone cells.

The **retina** is made up of three layers of cells:
- the outermost, photoreceptor layer, contains **rods** and **cones**, both of which are partly embedded in pigmented epithelial cells of the choroid
- the intermediate, middle layer, contains bipolar neurones, which have synapses with the rods and cones in the photoreceptor layer and also with the ganglion cells in the inner layer
- the inner layer, called the internal surface layer, contains ganglion cells and axons of the optic nerve.

Light entering the eye has to pass through the inner layer and the intermediate layer before it reaches the photoreceptor cells. Both the rods and cones are transducers, that is, they convert one form of energy into another form of energy. In this case, light energy is converted into the electrical energy of a nerve impulse. Their functioning depends on the light stimulus being detected by a photosensitive pigment: **rhodopsin** in the rods and **iodopsin** in the cones.

Rods

Rods are distributed more or less evenly throughout the retina, but are absent from the fovea. They are sensitive to different intensities of light and are involved in vision at low light intensities. Their structure is shown in Figure 2.14a. The outer segment contains the pigment rhodopsin, sometimes called **visual purple**, in flattened membranous vesicles called **lamellae**. There may be up to 1000 of these vesicles in each outer segment, enclosed by an outer membrane. The outer segment is connected to the inner segment by a narrow region containing cytoplasm and a pair of cilia. The inner segment contains large numbers of mitochondria, polysomes and a nucleus. The mitochondria provide ATP for the resynthesis of the rhodopsin. The synthesis of proteins for the production of visual pigment and the formation of the vesicles occurs at the polysomes. At the base of the inner segment is the synaptic region where the cell forms a synapse with a bipolar neurone.

- In the *light*, Na$^+$ pumped out, cannot diffuse in because membrane becomes impermeable. Inside of rod becomes increasingly negatively charged (hyperpolarisation)

- in the *dark*, Na$^+$ pumped out, diffuses back in

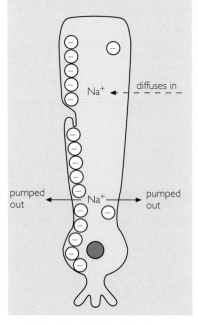

Figure 2.14b Hyperpolarisation in a rod cell.

Rhodopsin consists of a protein, **opsin**, combined with **retinal**, which is a derivative of vitamin A. Retinal can exist in two forms: a *cis* isomer and a *trans* isomer. Light causes the *cis* isomer to change into the *trans* isomer, which has a different shape and can no longer bind tightly to the opsin. This results in the splitting of the rhodopsin molecule into retinal and opsin.

A generator potential is produced, which causes an impulse to be transmitted along a sensory neurone. The initial stimulus in the rod cell causes hyperpolarisation, rather than depolarisation, because the outer segment membrane has a decreased permeability to sodium ions (Figure 2.14b). Sodium ions continue to be pumped out by the inner segment and the rod cell becomes increasingly negatively charged (hyperpolarisation).

Rhodopsin has to be resynthesised, using energy from ATP, but this takes time. Rhodopsin breaks down quite rapidly in bright light and there is not much of it stored in the rods. In bright light, eyes are light-adapted as the cones are used for vision and the rhodopsin in the rods is '**bleached**', in other words in the form of retinal and opsin. If a person goes from bright light into dim conditions, vision is poor until enough rhodopsin has been resynthesised and the eyes become dark-adapted.

Cones

Cones differ from rods in the following ways:
- the outer segment is cone-shaped
- there are fewer membranous vesicles and they are formed from infoldings of the outer membrane
- they contain the visual pigment **iodopsin**, which is thought to occur in three different forms, each responding to light in a narrow range of wavelengths.

There are fewer cones than rods and they are more concentrated at and around the fovea. They are less sensitive to light, but more sensitive to the wavelength of light. There are three different types, one responding to red wavelengths, one to blue and one to green, involving different forms of iodopsin. According to the **trichromatic theory** of colour vision, different colours are perceived according to the degree of stimulation of each type of cone by light reflected from objects.

Cones give greater visual acuity by enabling the formation of more accurate images than rods. Each cone synapses with a monosynaptic bipolar neurone, which in turn synapses with one ganglion cell (Figure 2.15). Several rods synapse with one bipolar cell, in this case referred to as a diffuse bipolar cell, giving rise to synaptic convergence. Vision is not as acute but the sensitivity is increased.

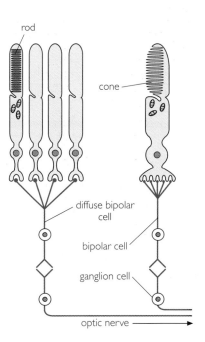

Figure 2.15 Synaptic connections in rods and cones.

Chemical coordination in animals

Mammalian hormones

Hormones are secreted by **endocrine glands**. Unlike exocrine glands, which have special ducts transporting their secretions to the site of action, endocrine glands have no ducts and their secretions pass straight into the blood. The secretions, known as hormones, enter the general circulation, where they are transported to their target organs.

Most mammalian hormones belong to one of three major groups of chemical compounds:
- **amines** – such as adrenaline from the adrenal gland and thyroxine from the thyroid gland
- **peptides** and proteins – such as insulin and glucagon involved in the control of the blood glucose level
- **steroids** – such as oestrogen, testosterone and the corticosteroids.

Hormones may *promote* actions or they may have an *inhibitory* effect. They often affect one specific organ, referred to as the **target organ**, or they may have more widespread, diffuse effects involving several organs. A good example of the latter is **adrenaline**, which can affect the heart, the blood vessels and other glands. The secretions of many endocrine glands are under the influence of the **pituitary gland**, which plays a major role in coordinating the activities of the body.

Hormones are secreted in response to one of three types of stimulus:
- the presence, or change in concentration, of a specific substance in the blood; for example, increase in blood glucose level triggers the release of insulin from the islets of Langerhans in the pancreas

QUESTION

What happens to excess hormones in the blood?

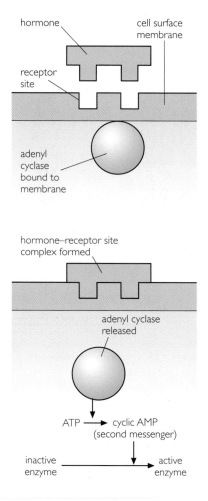

Figure 2.16 Hormone action

involving a second messenger.

- the presence, or change in concentration of another hormone in the blood; for example, thyroid stimulating hormone from the anterior pituitary gland stimulates the thyroid gland to secrete the hormone thyroxine
- nervous stimulation involving neurones of the autonomic system; for example, the release of adrenaline from the adrenal medulla in response to danger.

Hormones circulating in the blood only affect their target organs or cells because these will have the appropriate receptor sites or receptor molecules on their cell surface membranes. Protein and polypeptide hormones combine with receptor sites on the cell surface membrane and, once a hormone–receptor site complex is formed, another substance inside the cell, called the **second messenger**, becomes activated and has an effect within the cell. In many cases the second messenger is the nucleotide **cyclic adenosine monophosphate (AMP)**. The hormone–receptor site complex causes the release of adenyl cyclase from the membrane. This enzyme catalyses the formation of cyclic AMP from ATP. Cyclic AMP activates specific enzymes within the cell (Figure 2.16).

The steroid hormones work slightly differently by combining with the receptor molecules on the cell surface membrane and then, being lipid-soluble, the hormone–receptor complex is able to diffuse through the cell surface membrane and into the nucleus of the cell, where the steroid hormone activates a specific gene (Figure 2.17).

Some hormones, such as insulin, affect the permeability of the cell surface membrane to other molecules. Insulin causes the cell surface membrane to become more permeable to glucose molecules.

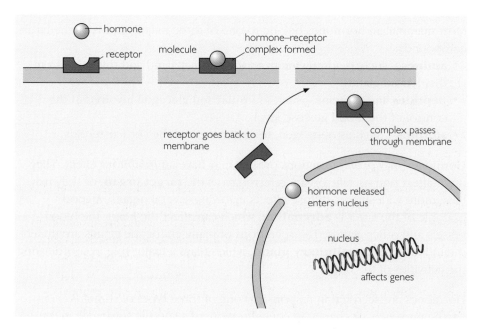

Figure 2.17 Action of steroid hormones.

The secretion of hormones in response to the presence, or increase in concentration, of another substance or another hormone is under the control of **feedback mechanisms**. In most cases, **negative feedback** operates, where an increase is detected, and a response is triggered which brings the level of the substance back to normal. This is shown clearly with the control of blood glucose level, where an increase in the level of glucose in the blood triggers the release of insulin, which causes the uptake of glucose into cells and leads to the conversion of glucose to glycogen, resulting in a decrease in the level of glucose in the blood (Figure 2.18). In some cases, **positive feedback** may occur: in the menstrual cycle, increasing levels of oestrogen cause the release of luteinising hormone from the pituitary gland.

Another example of negative feedback is shown by the secretion of **ADH (antidiuretic hormone)** and osmoregulation (Figure 2.19). When the solute potential of the body fluids becomes more negative, due to increased sweating, little intake of water or a large intake of salt in the diet, osmoreceptors in the hypothalamus detect the change and trigger the release of more ADH from the posterior pituitary gland. The ADH is released into the blood and affects its target organ, the kidney. ADH increases the permeability of the walls of the collecting ducts, so more water is reabsorbed by osmosis and passed back into the blood capillaries, leaving the urine more concentrated. The reabsorption of water from the filtrate results in the solute potential of the body fluids becoming less negative and the secretion of ADH decreases. The walls of the collecting ducts become less permeable to water and less water is reabsorbed, resulting in a greater volume of less concentrated urine.

Reproduction is a cyclic process and involves a number of hormones. In both males and females, the pituitary gland secretes two gonadotropins: luteinising hormone (LH) and follicle stimulating hormone (FSH). These are both glycoproteins and their target organs are the gonads, the ovaries and testes, where they regulate the secretion of steroid and peptide hormones and are involved in the maturation of the tissues. By means of feedback loops, these hormones control the release of the gonadotropins. In females, the control of the menstrual cycle is achieved by interaction of the hormones and by negative feedback mechanisms. For more details of the reproductive hormones, reference should be made to *Exchange and Transport, Energy and Ecosystems*, Chapter 10, Reproduction in humans.

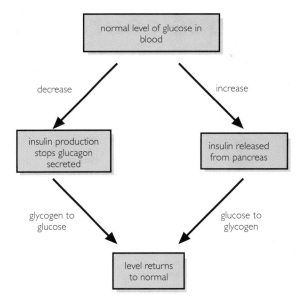

Figure 2.18 Negative feedback in the control of the blood glucose level.

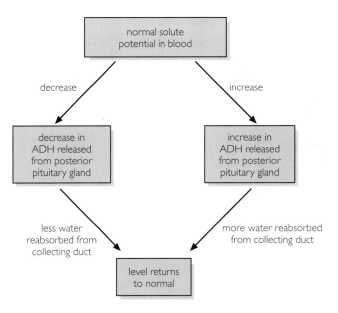

Figure 2.19 Negative feedback in ADH secretion.

3 Nervous coordination in mammals

The nervous and endocrine systems perform the function of communication and coordinate all the different actions of cells, tissues and organs within the body. Both systems enable animals to detect and make appropriate responses to changes in both their external environment and internal environment. Chemical coordination is achieved by the secretion of hormones, by endocrine glands, into the bloodstream. Hormones are carried in the blood and affect the activity of distant target organs and tissues. Nervous coordination involves the transmission of nerve impulses, along specialised cells, or **neurones**, either towards the spinal cord and brain, or from the brain to an effector organ, such as a gland or muscle. In general, responses brought about by nervous coordination are much more rapid than those brought about by hormones. Furthermore, nervous responses may be relatively short term but hormonal responses can be long lasting. The nervous system consists of the brain, spinal cord and peripheral nerves, and is organised to detect changes in both the external and the internal environment, to evaluate this information, and to make the appropriate responses. In this chapter we look at the organisation of the nervous system and transmission of the nerve impulse, and focus on the structure and functions of the central nervous system

The nervous system

The nervous system is very complex and, in order to help to understand the way in which it functions, it can be subdivided into several smaller systems, as shown in Figure 3.1.

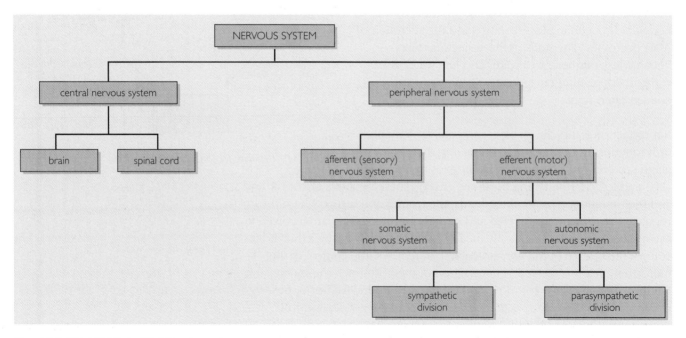

Figure 3.1 Organisation of the nervous system.

The **central nervous system** consists of the **brain** and **spinal cord**. It integrates sensory information from various receptors and initiates the appropriate responses. The **peripheral nervous system** consists of paired **nerves**, which arise either directly from the brain, known as cranial nerves, or from the spinal cord, called the spinal nerves. It is convenient to divide the peripheral nervous system into the afferent nervous system, which consists of all the afferent, or sensory, nerve pathways, and the efferent nervous system, which consists of the efferent, or motor, nerve pathways. The efferent nervous system is further divided into the somatic and autonomic systems. Somatic nerves carry impulses to skeletal muscles, whereas autonomic nerves carry impulses to smooth muscle, the heart and glands.

Sensory, relay and effector neurones

The entire nervous system consists of two main types of cells: **neurones** and **neuroglia**. Neurones are cells which are adapted to carry nerve impulses; neuroglia, which include Schwann cells, are cells which provide structural and metabolic support to the neurones. Neurones show considerable variation in size and shape, but they all have the same basic structure, as shown in Figure 3.2.

Each neurone consists of:
- a cell body, containing the nucleus, which is surrounded by granular cytoplasm, known as the perikaryon. The granules in the cytoplasm are referred to as Nissl substance and consist of dense clusters of rough endoplasmic reticulum.
- cytoplasmic processes which branch from the cell body – a single axon and one or more dendrites. The axon conducts impulses *away* from the cell body, either to other neurones or to effectors, such as muscles. Dendrites are highly branched processes which carry impulses from specialised receptors, or from adjacent neurones with which they form synapses.

Although there is considerable variation in the size and shape of neurones, they can be classified into three main groups according to the arrangement of dendrites and axons. These groups are known as multipolar neurones, bipolar neurones and pseudo-unipolar neurones (Figure 3.2).

- **multipolar neurones** are the most numerous type and have many dendrites branching from the cell body. Typical effector (motor) neurones are multipolar.
- **bipolar neurones** have only a single dendrite which arises directly from the cell body opposite the axon. These are relatively unusual neurones and act as receptors for the senses of sight, smell and balance.
- **pseudo-unipolar neurones** have a single dendrite which, with the axon, branches from a common stem from the cell body. Typical sensory neurones are pseudo-unipolar.

In the mammalian peripheral nervous system, most axons are surrounded by specialised **Schwann cells**. During fetal development, the axon becomes enclosed by the cytoplasm of a Schwann cell, which progressively wraps itself around the axon. By this process, the axon becomes enclosed in a spiral layer of Schwann cell cytoplasm (Figure 3.3). The covering formed by the Schwann cell is referred to as the **myelin sheath**, and axons which are covered in this

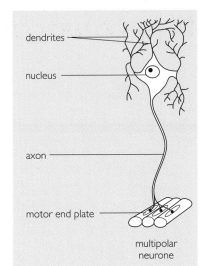

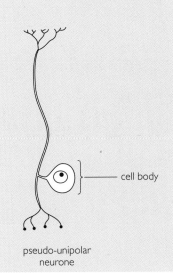

Figure 3.2 The three main types of neurone.

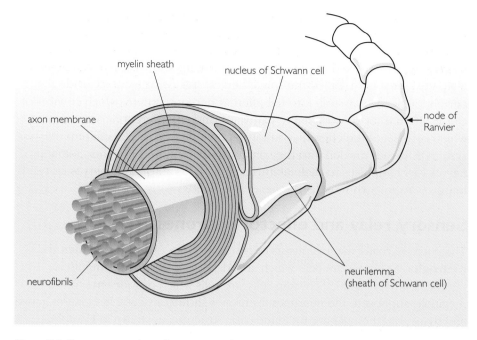

Figure 3.3 Transverse section of an axon and its coverings formed by the Schwann cell.

way are said to be **myelinated**. Between adjacent Schwann cells, there are short gaps where the axon is not covered by myelin. These gaps are known as the **nodes of Ranvier** (Figure 3.3).

The speed of conduction of the nerve impulse – the conduction velocity – is proportional to the diameter of the axon, which varies between about 1 and 20 μm. As a general rule, as the diameter increases, the conduction velocity also increases. However, in a myelinated axon, the conduction velocity is considerably faster than in a non-myelinated axon of the same diameter.

The nerve impulse

In order to understand the nature of the nerve impulse, we need to look at the concentrations of different ions inside and outside the axon. Each nerve impulse involves the movement of ions through the axon membrane. During the passage of an impulse, sodium ions move into the axon and potassium ions move out. When a neurone is not conducting an impulse, it is said to be in the **resting state**, and the inside of the axon membrane has a negative electrical charge – the resting potential – relative to the outside. However, when positively charged sodium ions enter, the inside briefly becomes positive, or **depolarised**, generating an action potential. When potassium ions move out, the inside becomes negative again and the resting potential is restored.

In the resting state, the resting potential is due to the overall effect of differences in the concentrations of ions across the axon membrane. These ions include sodium, potassium, chloride and large negatively charged organic ions. The concentration of sodium ions is much greater outside than inside, but in the case of potassium ions, the reverse is true. Chloride ions are more concentrated outside than inside and the large negatively charged organic ions are exclusively on the inside. These differences in the concentrations of ions are due to the permeability of the axon membrane to these ions. In the resting state, the permeability of the membrane to potassium is relatively high, due to the presence of protein channels, or 'gates', in the membrane which allow potassium ions to pass through. However, there are no gates that allow the negatively charged organic ions to pass through, so these remain trapped on the inside. The large ions are the main source of the negative charge on the inside of the axon. Although potassium ions can escape, relatively few of them do so. The tendency for potassium to move out, by diffusion, is countered because they will be attracted back in by the overall negative charge on the inside. This results in most of the potassium remaining on the inside. The concentration gradient for chloride is inwards, but remember that, since the inside is negatively charged, chloride ions will be repelled. Sodium ions have a high concentration on the outside and would be expected to be attracted inwards by the negative internal potential. However, the permeability of the axon membrane to sodium is relatively low and, although there is a slow inward movement of sodium ions, through **sodium channels**, they are captured by ion pumps and expelled to the outside.

When a nerve impulse is generated, the permeability of the membrane to sodium ions briefly increases, by the opening of more sodium channels, and sodium ions enter faster than they can be expelled by the ion pumps. As these positively charged ions flow in, the potential difference inside the axon rises to a positive value, known as the **action potential**. The permeability of the membrane to sodium then decreases, but this is followed by an increase in permeability to potassium ions, as more potassium channels open. This allows potassium ions to flow out and, as they do so, the potential difference inside the axon decreases to its negative resting value. The potassium channels remain open as the resting potential is restored, and there is a slight 'potassium overshoot' which causes the membrane potential to become slightly lower than its normal resting value. This is known as **hyperpolarisation**, but the resting potential is gradually restored as sodium and potassium ions return to their resting concentrations. These changes in membrane permeability and membrane potential are shown in Figure 3.4.

> ### DEFINITION
> **Action potential** is the maximum positive charge generated within the axon as a result of a nerve impulse.

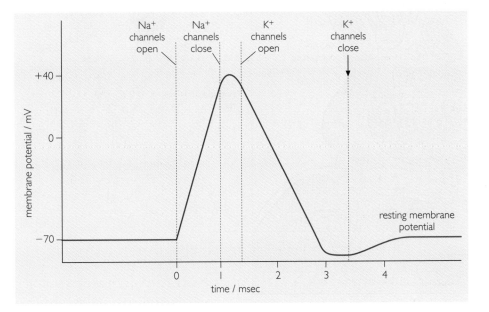

Figure 3.4 The action potential.

A **nerve impulse** is a propagated action potential, or wave of depolarisation, which travels along the axon membrane. The ion channels in the membrane are referred to as 'voltage-dependent ion channels' and open in response to depolarisation of the membranes, which sets up a current. The current spreads from the region of the membrane occupied by the action potential to the region of the membrane just ahead of it, stimulating sodium ion channels to open.

The changes described occur in a small segment on the axon membrane, but remember that a nerve impulse is a propagated action potential, which moves at a constant velocity along the axon membrane. In a myelinated axon, however, the action potential 'jumps' from one node of Ranvier to the next. This type of conduction is known as **saltatory conduction** and greatly increases the conduction velocity.

During the passage of a nerve impulse, the axon has gained sodium ions and lost potassium ions. These ions are re-exchanged by sodium–potassium pumps, which actively pump sodium ions out and potassium ions into the axon.

The synapse

It has been estimated that there are over 10^{12} neurones in the human central nervous system, yet none of these neurones is in direct contact with other neurones. The impulse passes from one neurone to another across specialised junctions, known as **synapses**. There are two main types of synapses in nervous systems: electrical and chemical (see Figure 3.5). In an electrical synapse, the membranes of the two adjacent neurones are so close, approximately 2 nm, that

> ### QUESTION
>
> Examine Figure 3.5, showing the structure of a chemical synapse, and identify the following structures:
> - the plasma membrane of the presynaptic cell
> - vesicles containing transmitter substance
> - the synaptic cleft
> - the plasma membrane of the postsynaptic cell
> - receptors on the postsynaptic membrane.

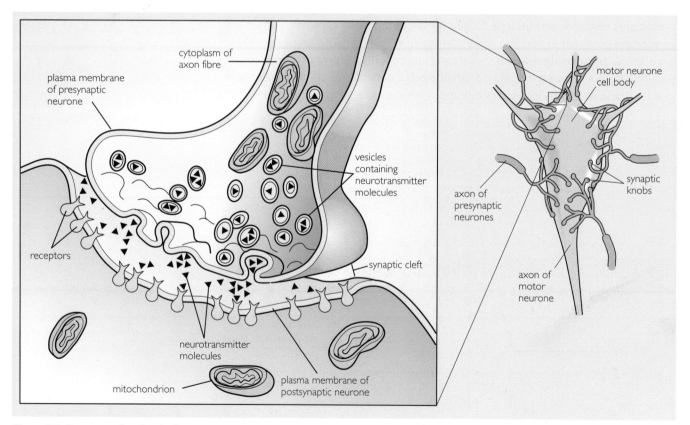

Figure 3.5 Structure of a chemical synapse.

the wave of electrical excitation can pass directly from one neurone to the next. However, in most synapses, the gap is about 20 nm; this is too large for direct electrical excitation. In these chemical synapses, the arrival of an impulse in the presynaptic neurone triggers the release of a chemical transmitter substance.

The mechanism of chemical synaptic transmission is summarised below.
- An action potential reaches the synaptic knob of the presynaptic neurone and calcium channels in its membrane open to allow calcium ions to diffuse into the knob.
- The increase in the intracellular concentration of calcium stimulates the movement of vesicles, which contain a transmitter substance, towards the presynaptic membrane.
- These vesicles fuse with the membrane and release their transmitter substance, by exocytosis, into the synaptic cleft. Each vesicle contains about 10 000 molecules of transmitter substance.
- The transmitter substance rapidly diffuses across the synaptic cleft and binds to receptors on the postsynaptic membrane, which causes specific ion channels in the membrane to open.
- The subsequent movement of ions, such as Na^+, K^+ or Cl^-, in or out of the postsynaptic neurone results in the generation of a **postsynaptic potential**. Depending upon which ions move, the postsynaptic membrane may be temporarily depolarised, or the inside of the membrane may become more negative than its normal resting value, in which case it is said to be **hyperpolarised**. Depolarisation of the membrane results in the development of an **excitatory postsynaptic potential**; hyperpolarisation results in the development of an **inhibitory postsynaptic potential**.
- The transmitter substance is quickly removed from the receptors, partly by diffusion and partly by enzyme action which, breaks down the transmitter substance into inactive products.

There are many different transmitter substances within the nervous system, and they can be classified into four main groups according to their chemical nature. Examples of some of these transmitter substances and their functions are shown in Table 3.1.

Effect of drugs on synaptic transmission
Many drugs and other substances act directly on the synapse and affect synaptic transmission. Such substances include **nicotine**, caffeine and opiates.

EXTENSION MATERIAL

Opiates are a group of substances which includes morphine, codeine and heroin. The effects of these substances are outlined below.
- **Caffeine** inhibits the action of an enzyme, phosphodiesterase, resulting in an increased intracellular concentration of cyclic AMP. This can result in the release of increased amounts of excitatory transmitter substances in the brain and has a mild stimulatory effect, increasing alertness.
- **Opiates** act on the brain by binding to specific receptors, thus reducing the response to painful stimuli.

Table 3.1 *Examples of transmitter substances*

Transmitter substance	Function
acetylcholine	transmitter substance at neuromuscular junctions and in many parts of the brain
amines, e.g. noradrenaline	transmitter in the sympathetic division of the autonomic nervous system and in several parts of the central nervous system
amino acids, e.g. glycine	an inhibitory transmitter substance in nerve pathways in the spinal cord
neuropeptides, e.g. endorphins	present in several regions of the brain, act like opiates to block pain

Nicotine has a similar effect to acetylcholine at some synapses, having an excitatory effect on the postsynaptic cell. In large concentrations, nicotine can block synaptic transmission after initial stimulation.

The central nervous system

The brain

Table 3.2 *Main adult derivatives of the early brain. The brainstem comprises the midbrain, pons and medulla oblongata*

Early brain	Adult derivatives
forebrain	left and right cerebral hemispheres, hypothalamus
midbrain	midbrain
hindbrain	pons, cerebellum and medulla oblongata

Table 3.3 *Functions of the main areas of the brain*

Part of brain	Main functions
cerebral hemispheres	The two cerebral hemispheres make up the **cerebrum**, the largest part of the human brain. The two hemispheres are connected by a mass of nerve fibres known as the **corpus callosum**. Functions of the cerebrum include: • receiving impulses from sensory receptors associated with the senses of heat, cold, touch, sight, hearing, taste and smell • initiating and controlling the contraction of skeletal muscles for voluntary movement • mental activities associated with consciousness, language and speech, emotions and memory.
hypothalamus	• synthesises hormones secreted by the posterior pituitary gland • has an essential role in osmoregulation and maintaining body temperature • contains some neurones that function as endocrine glands.
midbrain	• conducts impulses between the hindbrain and midbrain • contains centres associated with visual and auditory reflexes.
cerebellum	• acts with the cerebrum to produce skilled, coordinated movement of groups of skeletal muscles • coordinates activities associated with the maintenance of balance and posture of the body.
pons	• consists mainly of nerve fibres which make a bridge between the two main parts of the cerebellum • contains nerve fibres passing between the cerebrum and the spinal cord • contains centres associated with the control of breathing (the pneumotaxic centres).
medulla oblongata	• contains nerve fibres passing between the brain and spinal cord • contains reflex centres associated with controlling the rate and force of the heart beat, the rate and depth of breathing and the diameter of blood vessels • contains centres associated with the reflexes of coughing, sneezing and vomiting.

QUESTION

Examine Figure 3.6, which shows a midline section of a human brain and, using Figure 3.7 to help you, identify the structures named in Table 3.2.

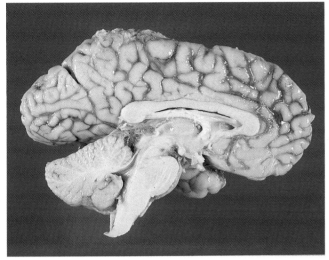

Figure 3.6 Midline section of a human brain.

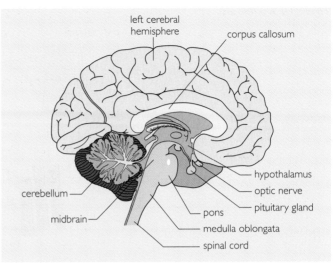

Figure 3.7 Diagram of a section of a brain to show the major structures.

The brain develops from a structure in the early embryo known as the **neural plate**, from which folds arise, fuse and form the **neural tube**. The anterior end of this tube expands to form the three main parts of the brain, referred to as the **forebrain**, **midbrain** and **hindbrain**.

These three main areas subdivide to form the different regions of the adult brain, as shown in Table 3.2.

The detailed structure and organisation of the brain is very complex, but we can summarise the functions of the major parts, as shown in Table 3.3.

The spinal cord and spinal reflexes

The spinal cord is continuous with the medulla oblongata and lies within the vertebral canal of the vertebral column, or backbone. Thirty-one pairs of spinal nerves arise from the spinal cord and leave the vertebral column through spaces between adjacent vertebrae. In transverse section, the spinal cord is seen to consist of a central area of **grey matter** and an external layer of **white matter**. In the centre of the spinal cord, there is a canal, the central canal, containing cerebrospinal fluid (Figure 3.8).

The grey matter consists of the cell bodies of nerve cells, for example, **effector neurones**, which transmit impulses to skeletal muscles, and unmyelinated **connector (or relay) neurones**, hence its grey appearance. The white matter contains columns of nerve fibres conducting impulses to and from the brain.

Spinal reflexes are the type of reflex action in which the effector neurone is stimulated by another neurone which originates in the spinal cord. This is called a relay neurone, as it provides a link between a **sensory neurone** and an effector neurone. The arrangement between the sensory neurone, the relay neurone and the effector neurone forms the basis of a reflex arc, illustrated in Figure 3.9.

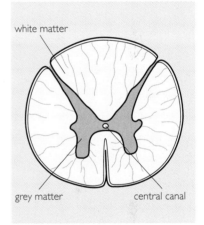

Figure 3.8 Structure of the spinal cord as seen in transverse section.

> **DEFINITION**
>
> A **sensory neurone** carries a nerve impulse from a receptor into the central nervous system.
> A **relay neurone** carries a nerve impulse from the central nervous system to a motor neurone.
> A **motor effector (motor neurone)** carries a nerve impulse from the central nervous system to a skeletal muscle.

33

NERVOUS COORDINATION IN MAMMALS

Figure 3.9 A reflex arc.

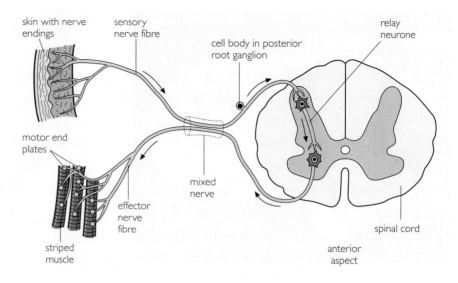

In this particular case, the diagram shows the arrangement between neurones involved in a reflex such as the response to a painful stimulus, arising from stimulation of receptors in the skin. This is an example of a **withdrawal reflex**, which rapidly moves the hand, for example, away from a potentially harmful stimulus, such as a hot or sharp object. Withdrawal reflexes generally have a protective function. **Muscle stretch reflexes**, including the knee jerk and ankle jerk reflexes, involve only two neurones, sensory and effector; there is no relay neurone. Tapping the tendon just below the knee cap stimulates stretch receptors in the quadriceps muscle of the thigh. These receptors initiate impulses which pass into the spinal cord along sensory neurones. These neurones form synapses directly with effector neurones. Impulses arising in these effector neurones are conducted to the same muscle, which contracts, causing the foot to kick forward.

Measuring reaction time

Introduction

This investigation uses a simple technique to measure your reaction time, that is, the time taken to respond to a stimulus. A meter rule is dropped between your thumb and forefinger and the distance it drops before you catch it is then measured. This method is also known as the stick-drop test.

Materials

- Metre rule.

Method

1 Your partner holds the metre rule vertically at the zero end, between your thumb and forefinger, with the 50 cm mark level with the top of your forefinger.
2 Without any warning, the rule is dropped and you catch it between thumb and forefinger. Note the distance just above your forefinger.

Results and discussion

1 Record your results in a table.
2 Compare your results with the ratings shown in Table 3.4.

Table 3.4 *Ruler-drop test ratings*

Distance measured on rule / cm	Rating
> 42.5	Excellent
37.1 to 42.5	Good
29.6 to 37.0	Average
22.0 to 19.5	Fair
< 22.0	Poor

Further work

1 Investigate the variation in reaction times within a group of students of the same age.
2 Investigate the relationship between age and mean reaction time. Are there any differences in reaction times of males and females?
3 Investigate the effect of circadian rhythms on reaction time, for example, by measuring reaction time at different times of the day.
4 Investigate the effect of a controlled dose of caffeine (such as a standardised cup of coffee) on reaction time.
5 Are the differences in reaction times statistically significant?

You can convert the distance dropped to the time taken to catch the rule using the formula below:

$$t = \sqrt{\frac{2s}{g}}$$

where t = time (in seconds), s = distance dropped (in metres), g = 9.81 (acceleration due to gravity).

Note: More accurate timing can be achieved by using electronic millisecond timers, which can be externally switched.

NERVOUS COORDINATION IN MAMMALS

Histology of the spinal cord

Introduction

The aim of this practical activity is to familiarise you with the histology of the spinal cord, as seen using a light microscope. Before looking at the sections of the spinal cord, it will be helpful to refer to your theory notes and any other pictures of the spinal cord. When seen in transverse section, the appearance of the spinal cord varies along its length, but basically it consists of a central H-shaped area of grey matter surrounded by an outer zone of white matter.

Materials

- Prepared microscope slide of spinal cord (transverse section)
- Microscope.

Method

1 Examine the slide using the low power of the microscope ($\times 40$) first.
2 Identify the anterior (or ventral) aspect and the posterior (or dorsal) aspect of the section.
3 Examine the anterior part of the grey matter using high power ($\times 400$). You may see the cell bodies of effector (motor) neurones, as shown in Figure 3.10.

Results and discussion

1 Make a labelled, low-power plan of your section to show the grey matter (anterior and posterior horns), white matter and central canal.
2 Include a scale on your drawing, to show the actual size of the specimen.
3 Write a brief description of the structure of the spinal cord, including a reference to the neurones involved in a simple, spinal reflex arc.

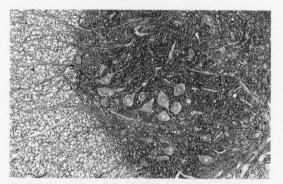

Figure 3.10 Cell bodies of effector neurones in the anterior horn of the spinal cord.

Option A: Microbiology and Biotechnology

4 Diversity of microorganisms

The term **microorganism** is widely used to describe an organism which is too small to be seen without using a microscope. It is an imprecise term, as such organisms do not possess any other features in common, apart from the fact that they are usually single-celled. They are found within a range of taxonomic groups, many of which also include larger, multicellular organisms. It is generally agreed that all the **bacteria** (kingdom **Prokaryotae**) are microorganisms.

The term can, however, also be applied to the unicellular, heterotrophic **protozoa**, to the unicellular **algae** found within the kingdom **Protoctista**, and to members of the kingdom **Fungi**, such as filamentous moulds and the yeasts.

Viruses fulfil some of the criteria, in that they are very small, but differ in lacking a cellular structure with no organised nucleus (**akaryote**) and being dependent on other cells for their reproduction. The effect of viruses on other living organisms is often profound, although some viral infections of plants seem to have little effect.

If we include viruses as microorganisms, then three levels of organisation, or cell structure, can be distinguished:
- **prokaryotic** – as shown by bacteria
- **eukaryotic** – as shown by the protoctistans (unicellular protozoa and unicellular algae) and the fungi (yeasts and moulds)
- **viruses** – consisting only of nucleic acid and proteins, sometimes referred to as akaryotic.

A more detailed comparison of prokaryotes and eukaryotes is given in *Molecules and Cells*, Chapter 4.

Microorganisms range in size from those which are just about visible to the naked eye, such as some of the larger protoctistans, to those which can only be seen using an electron microscope. Most eukaryotic cells have a diameter between 10 and 30 μm (micrometres), whereas the diameter of bacterial cells may range from 0.2 to 2.0 μm and viruses from 20 to 300 nm (nanometres).

The internal structure of bacterial cells and the structure of viruses are only visible using electron microscopy. The sizes of a range of microorganisms are shown in Table 4.1.

Table 4.1 *The sizes of some microorganisms (in micrometres)*

Type of microorganism	Size in μm
Amoeba sp. (Protoctista, protozoan)	150 to 200
Chlorella sp. (Protoctista, alga)	20
Saccharomyces sp. (Fungi, yeast)	10
Escherichia coli (Prokaryotae, bacterium)	1.0
poliomyelitis virus	0.02
tobacco mosaic virus	0.015

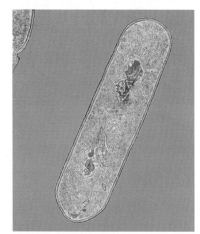

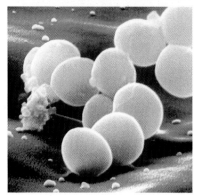

Figure 4.1a Representatives of bacteria: (top) Bacillus licheniformis, *which can be isolated from soil or air and produces an antibiotic called bacitracin; (bottom)* Staphylococcus aureus, *which causes skin infections in humans.*

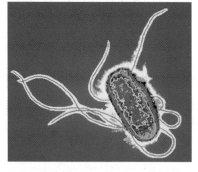

Figure 4.1b Electronmicrograph of Escherichia coli, *showing flagellae.*

Bacteria

When bacteria are viewed using light microscopy, it is impossible to discern any details of their structure apart from their shape (Figure 4.1). For this reason, the earliest attempts at a classification grouped the bacteria into the following categories:

- **bacilli** (singular: **bacillus**) – rod-shaped, for example, *Bacillus*
- **cocci** (singular: **coccus**) – spherical, for example, *Staphylococcus*
- **spirilla** (singular: **spirillum**) – spiral, for example, *Spirillum*
- **vibrio** – comma-shaped, for example, *Vibrio.*

This system was extended by determining whether the cells remained single, or formed chains or clusters, and whether or not flagella were present.

Structure of bacterial cells

All bacteria possess:

- a rigid cell wall
- a cell surface membrane
- cytoplasm
- a double-stranded loop of DNA (the bacterial chromosome)
- small (70S) ribosomes
- storage granules of glycogen and liquid droplets.

Many bacteria can alter their shape as a result of ageing, or an environmental shock such as a rapid change in temperature – a phenomenon known as **pleomorphy**. This can cause confusion in the identification of species if only morphological features are used, but with the development of the electron microscope, it has been possible to determine the internal organisation of bacterial cells. Their structure is remarkably similar.

In some bacteria the outer surface of the cell wall may be coated with a **glycocalyx**, which can take the form of a **slime layer** or a thicker, more structured **capsule**. Slime layers form loose, soluble coverings that are easily washed off, whereas capsules, which may be composed of polysaccharides, polypeptides or a mixture of both, are bound more tightly to the cell wall and have a more 'gummy' consistency. Any gelatinous covering will reduce the chances of desiccation and cause the cells to stick together. In pathogenic bacteria, the capsule prevents antibodies and phagocytic blood corpuscles from binding to the cell wall. The bacterial cell walls are not destroyed and the bacteria are able to multiply within the host and infect the body tissues.

Many bacteria possess **flagella** (singular: **flagellum**) (see Extension Material, Figure 4.2). These may occur singly, all over the cell, or be limited to a group at one or both ends.

Pili and **fimbriae** are projections from the cell surface membrane through the cell wall (Figure 4.3). They occur in some bacteria and differ from flagella, both in their structure and their function. They are more rigid than flagella, are concerned with attachment to other bacteria or to host cells, rather than with locomotion. They are both antigenic and attachment often involves interaction with the molecules of host-cell membranes. In pathogenic bacteria, the presence of large numbers of fimbriae may help to prevent phagocytosis by host cells. The longer pili are found in some (Gram negative) bacteria, where they are associated with the process of **conjugation**, in which exchange of genetic material occurs.

The bacterial cell wall is largely composed of a mixed polymer of hexose sugars and amino acids called **peptidoglycan**, sometimes referred to as **mucopeptide** or **murein**. The peptidoglycans provide a strong but flexible framework, supporting the cell contents and protecting the bacterial cell from lysis. The effectiveness of certain drugs in the treatment of bacterial infections depends on their ability to destroy or prevent the synthesis of peptidoglycan, thus weakening the cell wall and enabling lysis to occur. **Lysozyme**, a naturally occurring enzyme present in tears and saliva, hydrolyses peptidoglycan and provides defence against some bacteria. Damage to bacterial cell walls can also be caused by some disinfectants.

The **Gram stain**, which depends on differences in cell wall structure, is an important staining technique for bacterial cells. It was developed in 1884 by Hans Christian Gram and is still a useful technique for the classification of bacteria. It also provides a rapid means for the initial identification of pathogenic species (see *Practical: The Gram stain,* page 74). Bacteria described as **Gram positive** have thick peptidoglycan walls which retain the crystal violet stain when washed with alcohol. Counterstaining with safranin has no effect. **Gram negative** bacteria have thinner walls, containing less peptidoglycan. Washing with alcohol dissolves the lipids on the surface then removes the dye from the peptidoglycan layer. Counterstaining with safranin leaves the cells stained pink. Differences in cell structure, as revealed by electron microscopy, are summarised in Figure 4.3 and Table 4.2. Gram positive bacteria include *Lactobacillus*, *Bacillus* and the majority of cocci, such as *Staphylococcus*. Gram negative bacteria include *Escherichia coli* (*E. coli*), *Salmonella* and some cocci.

In Gram negative bacteria, the outer membrane forms an extra barrier, making them more impervious to disinfectants and dyes, although alcohol can dissolve the lipids.

QUESTION

Draw a prokaryotic cell showing structures always present and structures sometimes present, and write down the functions of these structures.

EXTENSION MATERIAL

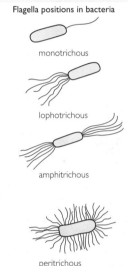

Flagella positions in bacteria

(a)

monotrichous

lophotrichous

amphitrichous

(b)

peritrichous
e.g. *Escherichia coli*

Figure 4.2 Different positions in which flagella occur in bacteria: (a) polar attachment – flagella attached at one or both ends; (b) peritrichous attachment – flagella dispersed randomly over surface of cell.

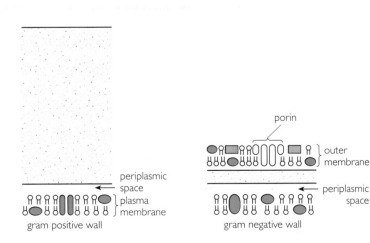

porin

outer membrane

periplasmic space

plasma membrane

gram positive wall

periplasmic space

gram negative wall

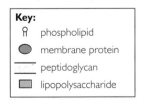

Key:

ዩ	phospholipid
⬤	membrane protein
—	peptidoglycan
▨	lipopolysaccharide

Figure 4.3 Differences in cell wall structure between Gram positive and Gram negative bacteria.

Table 4.2 *Differences in cell wall structure between Gram positive and Gram negative bacteria*

Feature	Gram positive bacteria	Gram negative bacteria
overall thickness	20 to 80 nm	8 to 11 nm
thickness of peptidoglycan layer	20 to 80 nm	1 to 2 nm
outer membrane with lipoprotein and protein lipopolysaccharides present	no	yes
channels present spanning outer membrane (porins)	no	yes
space between cell surface membrane and cell wall (periplasmic space)	sometimes present	always present

The bacterial cell surface membrane is composed of a lipid bilayer with protein molecules embedded in it. It is very similar to the cell surface membranes of eukaryotic organisms, except that there is a higher ratio of protein to phospholipid molecules. The major functions are control of the transport of substances into and out of the cell, secretion and metabolic activities. Most of the enzymes concerned with respiration are located here, as are enzyme systems concerned with the synthesis of structural molecules. The membrane also secretes enzymes and toxins into the outside environment.

In some Gram positive bacteria, it can be seen quite clearly that the cell surface membrane is extensively infolded (invaginated) forming a **mesosome** (Figure 4.4). Although there is some debate as to the precise nature of such structures, it is generally agreed that there is an increase in the surface area available for metabolic activities. It is thought that the mesosomes may be involved with cell wall synthesis and that they may play a role in cell division, in addition to increasing the surface area available for the generation of ATP. Mesosomes may also be present in Gram negative bacteria, but they are less easily seen due to their small size. In photosynthetic bacteria, the cell surface membrane is invaginated to form **thylakoids**, on which are found pigment molecules and associated enzymes.

The cytoplasm of bacterial cells is largely composed of water, together with sugars, amino acids and salts. Also present are inclusions such as glycogen granules, lipid droplets and polyhydroxybutyric acid (PHB), all of which are energy-rich storage molecules.

Large numbers of **ribosomes** are present in bacterial cells. They are either scattered singly in the cytoplasm or arranged in chains, forming polysomes. These ribosomes are the sites of protein synthesis and function in exactly the same way as the ribosomes in eukaryotic organisms, but they are smaller and lighter (70S as opposed to 80S).

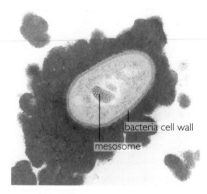

Figure 4.4 Transmission electron micrograph through a skin bacterium showing the mesosome.

EXTENSION MATERIAL

Bacterial **DNA** is in the form of a ring, called the **chromatin body**, or **bacterial chromosome**. The DNA molecule is very long and tightly coiled around basic protein molecules. There are no histone proteins associated with the DNA and there is no nuclear envelope surrounding it. The genes present on this bacterial chromosome are those necessary for growth and maintenance. In addition, many bacteria contain smaller, circular pieces of extra-chromosomal DNA called **plasmids**. These may either be free in the cytoplasm or attached to the bacterial chromosome, but they are independent and self-replicating. The genes on the plasmids are not essential for the growth or metabolism of the bacterial cell, but may be concerned with the production of sex pili, or confer resistance to drugs or produce toxins and enzymes. When the bacterial cell undergoes binary fission, the plasmids are duplicated and passed on to the daughter cells. Modern techniques in gene (DNA) technology enable such plasmids to be manipulated in the laboratory and they provide a valuable means of introducing additional genetic information into bacterial cells.

As indicated earlier in this chapter, identification and classification of bacteria are difficult. We have considered some of the morphological features which are used, but precise identification may require the use of other characteristics. Some of the additional ways which may be used to identify and classify bacteria are summarised in the Extension Material below.

EXTENSION MATERIAL

Methods of identification and classification of bacteria

Method	Description and comments
macroscopic morphology	appearance of colony in broth or on solid media; texture, size, rate of growth, pigmentation
microscopic morphology	use of cell shape, size, Gram staining; presence of flagella, pili, fimbriae, capsules, endospores
biochemical characteristics	ability to ferment certain sugars; breakdown specific proteins or polysaccharides; produce gases, for example
chemical characteristics	presence of certain compounds in the cell wall and membrane
presence of specific antigens	antibodies are produced in response to specific antigens; useful in the identification of pathogens in specimens and cultures
use of genetic probes	small single-stranded fragments of DNA (probes), labelled with a dye or a radioactive isotope, are mixed with unknown DNA; if there is a match, hybridisation occurs; probes become attached to unknown DNA and can show up

DIVERSITY OF MICROORGANISMS

QUESTION

How do microorganisms gain entry to the human body?

Bacteria as agents of infection

Pathogenic bacteria generally cause disease by invasion of host tissues, but a few do so by producing poisonous chemical compounds called **toxins**.

An infection is caused when pathogenic microorganisms penetrate the defences of a host organism, enter the tissues and begin to multiply. Damage to the tissues results in a disease. In order to gain entry, it is necessary for the pathogenic organism to bind, or adhere, to its host in some way. Structures such as fimbriae, pili, flagella and slime capsules may enable adhesion to the host organism. It must then penetrate the host's tissues.

Many pathogenic microorganisms secrete **exoenzymes** that break down and damage host tissues, thus providing a means of entry. For example, staphylococci can produce the enzyme **hyaluronidase**, which digests hyaluronic acid, the main ground substance causing animal cells to stick together. Fungal plant pathogens may produce **pectinases** which break down the middle lamellae of plant cell walls, allowing entry to the host. In addition, toxins may be produced and these interfere with the host's metabolic processes.

Bacterial pathogens

Both *Salmonella* and *Staphylococcus* produce **enterotoxins**, which are active in the human gut. *Staphylococcus* produces **exotoxins**, which are soluble compounds secreted by the cells into their immediate environment. Only small quantities of such toxins are needed to give rise to symptoms in the host organism. *Salmonella* and other genera of Gram negative bacteria also produce toxins, but these are not released from the bacteria until the cell wall is damaged or lysis occurs. These toxins are referred to as **endotoxins** and need to be present in large amounts to have any effect, such as causing a fever, inflammation or diarrhoea, in the host. Endotoxins are lipopolysaccharides and form part of the outer membrane of the Gram negative cell wall.

Food poisoning can be caused by a number of pathogenic bacteria, but it is interesting to compare the onset of symptoms due to *Staphylococcus aureus* with that of *Salmonella enteritidis*. With *Staphylococcus*, the onset of vomiting and diarrhoea occurs from 1 to 6 hours after the ingestion of the exotoxin in foods such as cream, cooked meats and poultry. With *Salmonella*, the onset of diarrhoea does not occur until 1 or 2 days after eating infected eggs or undercooked poultry. In this case, the bacteria from the infected food stick to the surface of epithelial cells lining the intestine. The bacteria are taken up into the cells by phagocytosis. Cell damage occurs when the bacteria multiply and produce endotoxins, which cause fever and inflammation of the tissue.

Mycobacterium tuberculosis is the organism responsible for the disease **tuberculosis** in humans. The spread of the disease is due to the inhalation of the organism into the respiratory tract. When the bacteria reach the alveoli of the lungs, they are engulfed by macrophages. The bacteria are able to survive and multiply within the macrophages. Other macrophages are attracted to the site of infection, ingest the bacteria and then carry the bacteria to lymph nodes, where a cell-mediated immune response is stimulated (more details of this can be found in Option C, Chapter 11). T-cells become sensitised and produce lymphokines which activate macrophages to destroy the bacteria. The body reacts to the invasion by forming 'tubercles', which are small granular nodules that surround the bacteria, thus isolating them. The bacteria do no direct damage to the tissues and there is no damage due to toxins. Primary infections due to these bacteria are usually mild and go no further, but secondary infections, due to the activation of dormant bacteria from a previous infection, may occur in about 10 per cent of cases. If the bacteria are not contained within the tubercles, they may invade the bloodstream and spread to other areas of the body. An affected person may show fatigue, weight loss, weakness and fever. If the infection occurs in the lungs, there is a characteristic, chronic cough with blood-stained sputum. Tissue destruction occurs in the lungs and blood vessels can rupture causing haemorrhage.

The cell wall of *Mycobacterium* contains peptidoglycans and stains Gram positive, but it also contains lipids, giving it a thick waxy outer coat which is highly resistant to chemicals and dyes. This waxy outer coat prevents desiccation and enables the bacteria to survive for long periods of time in the air and in house dust. Infected people cough up large numbers of the bacteria, so strict measures have to be taken to prevent the spread of infection.

Fungi: yeasts and moulds

Fungi are eukaryotic organisms that:
- form spores
- lack flagella at any stage in their life cycle
- do not possess chlorophyll
- usually have chitin in their cell walls.

They may be single-celled, as in the **yeasts** (*Saccharomyces*) or more usually filamentous, as in **moulds** such as *Penicillium*. The kingdom is divided into phyla, which differ from each other in the nature of their spore-producing structures. Both *Saccharomyces* and *Penicillium* belong to the phylum Ascomycota.

In the **filamentous moulds**, individual filaments are called **hyphae** (singular: **hypha**) and develop directly from spores (Figure 4.5). The hyphae grow together, forming a loose network of threads called a **mycelium**. The hyphal walls are normally chitinous and divided into cell-like compartments by cross-walls, or **septa** (singular: **septum**). The hyphae contain cytoplasm in which are situated one or two nuclei per 'cell'. Each nucleus is surrounded by a nuclear envelope; organelles typical of eukaryotic organisms (such as mitochondria, ribosomes and Golgi bodies) are also present in the cytoplasm. There are pores in the septa so that the cytoplasm is continuous in each hypha, making cell-to-cell communication possible.

Most fungi are terrestrial and saprobiontic, feeding on the dead and decaying remains of plants and animals. When grown in the laboratory, fungi need to be supplied with organic sources of carbon and nitrogen, together with inorganic ions and one or more vitamins. Digestive enzymes are secreted from the hyphae onto the food material and the soluble products of this **extracellular digestion** are absorbed. Growth of the mycelium is concentrated at the tips of the hyphae where the cytoplasm is dense and most metabolic activity is

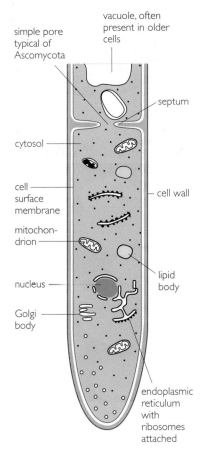

Figure 4.5 Structure of fungal hypha.

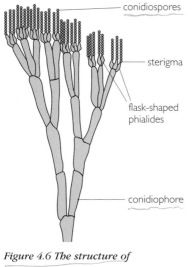

conidiospores

sterigma

flask-shaped
phialides

conidiophore

Figure 4.6 The structure of
Penicillium *sp.*

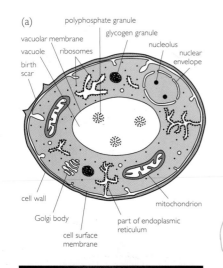

(a)

polyphosphate granule

glycogen granule

vacuolar membrane

nucleolus

vacuole ribosomes

nuclear
envelope

birth
scar

cell wall

mitochondrion

Golgi body

part of endoplasmic
reticulum

cell surface
membrane

(b)

Figure 4.7 (a) Electronmicrograph
drawing of a section of a yeast cell;
(b) scanning electronmicrograph of
yeast cells.

occurring. In the older parts of the mycelium, vacuoles develop and the cytoplasm is restricted to the periphery of the hyphae.

The genus *Penicillium* is a filamentous mould in which septate hyphae are produced, forming a typical mycelium. Members of this genus are responsible for the familiar blue and green moulds which cause spoilage of citrus fruits and other stored products such as cheese and bread. The genus is of economic importance as *Penicillium roquefortii* is used in the production of blue-veined cheeses, and *P. notatum* and *P. chrysogenum* are used in the production of the antibiotic penicillin.

Penicillium species can be distinguished from other moulds by the characteristic appearance of the asexual spores, the **conidiospores**, which are formed on special aerial branches of the mycelium called **conidiophores** (Figure 4.6). The conidiospores develop in chains from **sterigma** at the tips of the conidiophores and, as they are very light, they are easily dispersed in air currents when dislodged.

The yeasts are single-celled fungi, which do not usually form hyphae. The genus *Saccharomyces* is of economic importance in the fermentation processes associated with the baking and brewing industries.

Yeast cells are ellipsoidal to spherical in shape (Figure 4.7). Each is surrounded by a wall containing polymers of the sugars glucose and mannose. In the cytoplasm, the nucleus is usually situated to one side of a large central vacuole. In addition to the other membrane-bound organelles, typical of eukaryotic cells, there are usually storage granules of glycogen and the vacuole may contain lipid droplets and polyphosphate granules. *Saccharomyces* reproduces asexually by budding, during which process a daughter cell develops as an outgrowth from one end of a parent cell. When the daughter cell detaches, a scar is left, which is visible as an indentation on the parent cell wall.

Viruses

Most viruses are less than 0.2 μm in diameter, which means an electron microscope is necessary to determine their fine structure. They contain a **core** of nucleic acid, either DNA or RNA, often with some protein, surrounded by an outer covering of protein called a **capsid**. There may be an external **envelope**, consisting of a piece of cell surface membrane derived from the previous host cell. In this envelope, some or all of the host cell membrane proteins may be replaced by special viral proteins. There may be exposed glycoproteins on the outside of the envelope, forming **spikes**, which enable the virus to attach to its next host cell. Classification of viruses is based on their structure and nucleic acid type.

The functions of the capsids and envelopes are to:
- protect the nucleic acid of the virus from enzymes and chemicals when the virus is outside its host cell
- bind to the surface of the host cell

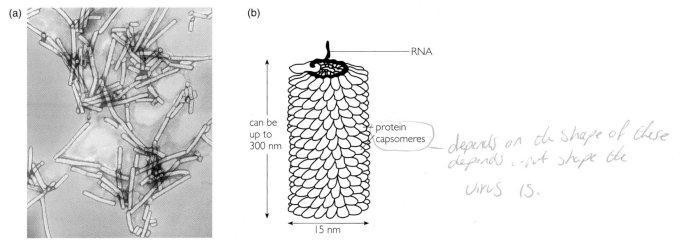

(a)

(b)

RNA

can be up to 300 nm

protein capsomeres

15 nm

Figure 4.8 Tobacco mosaic virus: (a) electronmicrograph; (b) diagrammatic structure.

depends on the shape of these depends - not shape the virus is.

- assist in the penetration of the host cell and the introduction of the viral nucleic acid.

The capsid is composed of sub-units called **capsomeres**, each consisting of protein molecules. The shape and arrangement of the capsomeres determines whether the virus is classified as:

- **helical**, as in the tobacco mosaic virus (TMV)
- **polyhedral**, as in the herpes virus and the human immunodeficiency virus (HIV)
- **complex**, where there is a polyhedral head and a helical tail, as in the λ (lambda) phage.

Helical capsids are composed of rod-shaped capsomeres which bond together, forming a continuous helix, inside which the nucleic acid strand is coiled.

Tobacco mosaic virus (TMV) has a helical capsid, with a single strand of RNA coiled inside (Figure 4.8). The particles of this virus are rod shaped and 15 nm in diameter but can be up to 300 nm in length.

The λ **(lambda) phage** consists of a head, containing a double-stranded DNA molecule wrapped around a core of protein surrounded by a polyhedral capsid, and a helical tail (Figure 4.9). The λ phage is an example of a bacteriophage, a virus that uses a bacterium as its host. It invades the bacterium *Escherichia coli*, where it can destroy the host cells or insert its DNA into the bacterial chromosome and remain dormant for several generations (Figure 4.10).

In polyhedral viruses, the capsid is usually a 20-sided polygon with 12 corners, called an **icosahedron**. Two types of capsomeres are involved in its construction: triangular ones form the flat faces of the polygon and round ones form the corners. The nucleic acid is packed into the centre. In the **human immunodeficiency virus** (**HIV**), the icosahedral capsid, containing single-stranded RNA, is surrounded by an envelope (Figure 4.11).

HIV is an RNA **retrovirus**. It carries the enzyme **reverse transcriptase**, which

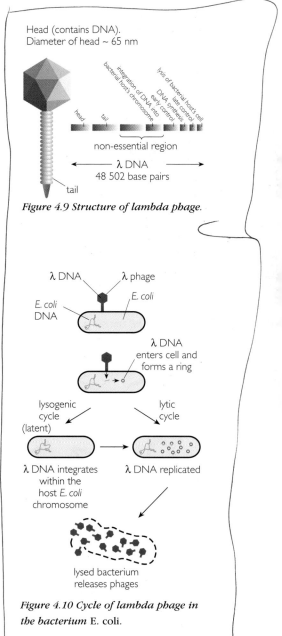

Head (contains DNA).
Diameter of head ~ 65 nm

head   tail

integration of DNA into
bacterial host's chromosome

lysis of bacterial host's cell
late control
DNA synthesis
early control

non-essential region

λ DNA
48 502 base pairs

tail

Figure 4.9 Structure of lambda phage.

λ DNA   λ phage

E. coli
DNA   E. coli

λ DNA
enters cell and
forms a ring

lysogenic
cycle
(latent)

lytic
cycle

λ DNA replicated

λ DNA integrates
within the
host E. coli
chromosome

lysed bacterium
releases phages

Figure 4.10 Cycle of lambda phage in the bacterium E. coli.

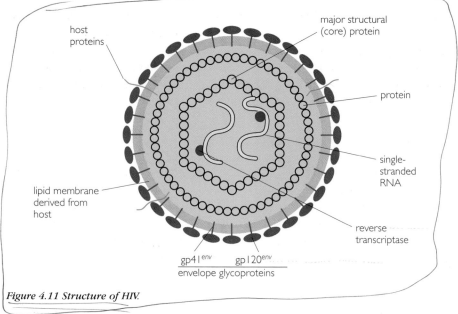

Figure 4.11 Structure of HIV.

can synthesise a single strand of DNA from the viral RNA and then direct the formation of a complementary double strand of DNA. The double-stranded DNA is inserted into a chromosome in the host cell, where it codes for the synthesis of viral proteins.

Certain features of the three types of viruses are summarised in Table 4.3.

Table 4.3 *Summary of relevant virus features*

Feature	λ phage	TMV	HIV
nucleic acid	DNA	RNA	RNA retrovirus
capsid / envelope	complex	helical	polyhedral
size	head diameter ~ 65 nm	diameter ~15 nm	diameter ~ 0.1 μm

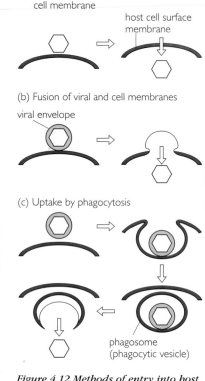

Figure 4.12 Methods of entry into host cells shown by viruses.

Viruses as agents of infection

All viruses are parasitic, so they must enter the cells of a living organism in order to reproduce (Figure 4.12). As parasites, they are usually pathogenic, causing symptoms in the host organisms. Virus particles are incapable of independent movement, so they have to be transmitted between hosts in some way. The commonest forms of transmission of viruses affecting humans are by:

- droplet inhalation
- contaminated food or water
- insect bites
- sexual transmission.

Plant viruses may be transmitted by insect vectors or gain entry to plants by mechanical means, such as physical damage during cultivation.

A specific interaction must occur between molecules on the surface of the pathogen and receptors on the host cells. In some cases, the molecules are proteins which form part of the capsid of the virus and in others, the molecules are present in the external envelope.

Viruses show **host specificity**, usually infecting only a restricted range of host species. Once inside the host organism, the virus particles attach to specific host cells by means of interactions between molecules on the capsid or the envelope and receptor molecules in the host cell membrane. Once attachment has been achieved, the virus can enter the host cell in one of three ways:

- by direct translocation across the cell surface membrane
- by fusion of the viral and cell surface membranes
- by uptake into a special vesicle or phagosome.

Once inside the host cell, the capsid is shed and the viral nucleic acid is released. Viral messenger RNA is formed and the host cell's ribosomes are used to synthesise viral protein molecules for the formation of new capsids. In addition, new viral nucleic acid is replicated, usually in the nucleus of the host cell. New virus particles are assembled, with the capsids forming around the nucleic acid. This process may take place in the cytoplasm or the nucleus of the host cell.

In viruses that lack envelopes, lysis of the host cell results in the release of the new virus particles and the host cell is destroyed in this process. The cycle of infection, replication and release by lysis is referred to as a **lytic cycle** and results in a **lytic infection** (Figure 4.13).

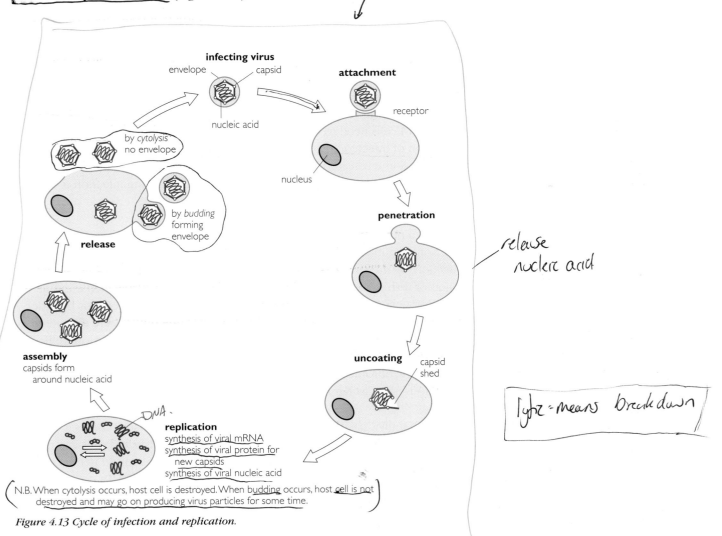

Figure 4.13 Cycle of infection and replication.

In viruses with envelopes, viral envelope proteins and glycoproteins are inserted into specific areas of the host cell surface membrane. The new virus particles are attracted to these regions and the host membrane becomes extended, forming buds around the virus particles. The buds become pinched off, and each virus particle is now surrounded by a modified portion of the host cell surface membrane containing viral proteins and glycoproteins. In this process, the host cell is not destroyed, so infected cells can bud off new virus particles for long periods, often at a slow rate, giving rise to a **persistent infection** (Figure 4.13). This type of infection is characteristic of diseases such as hepatitis B, in which an infected person may act as a symptomless carrier capable of passing on the condition to other people.

In **latent infections**, the viral genetic material may become incorporated in the genome of the host cell, as in the retroviruses and bacteriophage, or it may remain in the cytoplasm, as in herpes. Replication does not take place until some signal, such as stress or cell damage, triggers a release from latency.

The **human immunodeficiency virus (HIV)** has an envelope containing glycoproteins, designated gp41 and gp120. As the virus enters the bloodstream, it infects T-helper cells (otherwise known as T4 lymphocytes or T4 cells), monocytes and macrophages, which have a surface protein CD4. This protein molecule acts as a binding site for the viral glycoprotein gp120. The virus particles are then either taken into the cells in vesicles formed by the T4 cell membrane or enter by fusion with the membrane. Once inside the cells, the genetic material of the virus, in the form of single-stranded RNA, is converted into double-stranded DNA and incorporated into the genome of the host cell. Replication of the virus and cell destruction does not occur straight away as infected T4 cells need to be activated, so the virus is said to be **latent**. Activation of infected T4 cells may be triggered as a result of a secondary infection. Some research workers, however, consider that the HIV disease is not usually latent but that the disease-free period following infection is better described as the **asymptomatic period**.

There is a poor response by the immune system of the body to infection by HIV. Some antibodies may be produced, but these fail to eliminate the infection, so the virus persists. There are functional changes in affected cells, together with some destruction of T4 cells, leading to a depressed immune response generally and an increased liability to secondary infections by other microorganisms. Gradually the number of T4 cells decreases, there is an increase in replication of the virus and the secondary infections become more difficult to control. Eventually the infected person may develop AIDS (acquired immune deficiency syndrome). The lymph glands become enlarged and more malignant conditions, such as Kaposi's sarcoma, develop with inevitably fatal results.

Within an individual, the virus spreads by cell-to-cell transmission as a result of the fusion of infected cells with uninfected ones, and infected cells can pass from one body system to another. Transmission from person to person can occur via infected blood or by sexual intercourse. Babies of HIV positive mothers can become infected before birth by transmission of the virus across the placenta or after birth through breast-feeding.

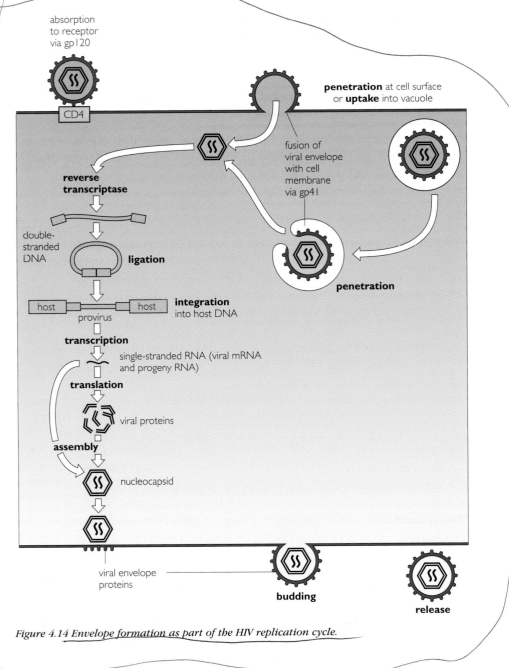

Figure 4.14 Envelope formation as part of the HIV replication cycle.

Some drugs, such as AZT (azidothymidine, also called zidovudine), have been shown to prolong survival and quality of life in AIDS sufferers, but at present, there is no known cure. Much research is being carried out to develop a vaccine and to identify vulnerable stages in the infection and replication cycle of the virus. The best available methods of prevention and control are the education and counselling of the public in the avoidance of transmission of the virus.

5 Culture techniques

Requirements for growth

Like all living organisms, microorganisms require an energy source, a carbon source and a range of nutrients for metabolism and cell growth. Microorganisms can be divided into two main groups on the basis of the source of energy they use. Microorganisms that use light as their energy source are referred to as phototrophs, and organisms that use chemicals as energy sources are referred to as chemotrophs.

Most of the organisms you will encounter in microbiology use **organic** chemical substances, such as glucose, as their energy source. These microorganisms can be considered to be **heterotrophic** and are sometimes referred to as **chemoorganotrophs**. These microorganisms include bacteria such as *Escherichia coli* (*E. coli*) and fungi such as *Penicillium* and *Saccharomyces*.

Heterotrophic microorganisms require an organic source of carbon, usually in the form of a carbohydrate, a nitrogen source, and mineral salts, including potassium, magnesium and iron. Various other growth factors, such as vitamins, amino acids and nucleic acid bases, may also be required.

The nutrients which are required by microorganisms can be divided into two groups:
- **macronutrients**, which are required in relatively large amounts
- **micronutrients**, which are required in small quantities.

Macronutrients include carbon, hydrogen, oxygen, nitrogen, sulphur, magnesium and iron (Table 5.1). All nutrients have to be provided in a suitable form in the culture media in which the microorganisms are grown. Carbon is often provided in the form of organic substances, including glucose, organic acids, fatty acids or amino acids. Phototrophic microorganisms, such as *Chlorella*, use carbon dioxide as their carbon source. Nitrogen is available to microorganisms either in organic substances, such as amino acids or nucleotide bases, or as inorganic substances including ammonia or nitrate ions. Many bacteria are able to use ammonia as their only source of nitrogen; the nitrogen fixing bacteria, such as *Rhizobium*, use nitrogen gas.

Micronutrients (also known as trace elements) are metals and are essential for normal cell function. They are required in very small quantities and it is not normally necessary to add these separately to culture media as they will often be present in sufficient quantities in other ingredients. Micronutrients include copper, manganese, vanadium and zinc. These may function as enzyme activators or as constituents of enzyme molecules. Iron is sometimes considered to be a micronutrient, although it is required in larger quantities than the other metals.

In addition to these micronutrients, microorganisms may also require certain organic growth factors in very small amounts. Such factors include amino

Table 5.1 *Macronutrients required by microorganisms and the forms in which they are supplied in culture media*

Elements	How supplied
carbon (C)	glucose, organic acids, yeast extract, peptone
hydrogen (H)	water, organic compounds
oxygen (O)	water, oxygen gas, organic compounds
nitrogen (N)	nitrogen gas, ammonium ions, nitrate ions, amino acids, nucleotide bases
phosphorus (P)	inorganic phosphates
sulphur (S)	sulphates, sulphur-containing amino acids
magnesium (Mg)	magnesium salts such as magnesium sulphate
sodium (Na)	sodium chloride
calcium (Ca)	calcium chloride
iron (Fe)	iron salts such as iron sulphate
potassium (K)	potassium salts such as potassium chloride

acids, vitamins, purines and pyrimidines. These compounds can be synthesised by the majority of microorganisms, but some microorganisms may require one or more of these to be present in their culture media.

All the nutrients required by microorganisms must be provided in the media in which they are grown. There are two main types of culture media used in microbiology: **defined** and **undefined** (or complex) media. Defined media are made up using pure chemical substances, dissolved in distilled water so that the exact chemical composition is known. Undefined media contain mixtures of substances such as yeast extract, peptone, or casein hydrolysate, in which the exact composition is unknown. To illustrate these types of culture media, Table 5.2 shows examples of culture media for *Escherichia coli*.

Environmental influences on growth of microorganisms

As well as the nutrients required, several environmental factors influence growth. These include temperature, availability of oxygen, light (for photoautotrophic microorganisms) and pH.

Temperature

In general, as temperature increases, enzyme activity within the cells also increases and growth becomes faster. However, above a certain temperature, proteins – including enzymes – will be denatured. Therefore, growth increases up to a point above which enzymes become denatured and inactivated. Above this point, growth rate falls rapidly to zero. For every microorganism, there is a minimum temperature below which there is no growth, an optimum temperature where growth occurs at the most rapid rate, and a maximum temperature above which growth will not occur (Figure 5.1).

The optimum temperature for microorganisms varies widely; some have optima between 5 and 10 °C, whereas at the other extreme, some have optima at 80 °C or above. On the basis of their temperature optima, microorganisms can be divided into four groups:

- **psychrophiles** have low optima, for example, *Flavobacterium*, optimum 13 °C
- **mesophiles** have mid-range optima, for example, *Escherichia coli*, optimum 39 °C
- **thermophiles** with high optima, for example, *Bacillus stearothermophilus*, optimum 60 °C
- **hyperthermophiles** with very high optima, for example, *Thermococcus celer*, optimum 88 °C.

Oxygen

Microorganisms vary in their requirements for oxygen. Some grow only in the *presence* of oxygen, whereas others grow only in the *absence* of oxygen. To the latter group of microorganisms, oxygen is actually toxic, probably because they are unable to remove toxic products of oxygen metabolism, such as hydrogen peroxide.

Table 5.2 *Examples of culture media for* Escherichia coli

Defined culture medium for *E. coli*	
K$_2$HPO$_4$	7 g
KH$_2$PO$_4$	2 g
(NH$_4$)$_2$SO$_4$	1 g
MgSO$_4$	0.1 g
CaCl$_2$	0.02 g
glucose	4 to 10 g
micronutrients (Fe, Co, Mn, Zn, Cu, Ni, Mo)	2 to 10 μg each
distilled water	1 dm^3

Undefined culture medium for *E. coli*	
glucose	15 g
yeast extract	5 g
peptone	5 g
KH$_2$PO$_4$	2 g
distilled water	1 dm^3

QUESTION

Identify each of the nutrients present in these two types of media (defined and undefined, Table 5.2) and find out the function of each nutrient.

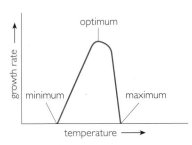

Figure 5.1 Temperature and the growth rate of a microorganism.

On the basis of their requirements for oxygen, microorganisms can be separated into four groups, as outlined below:
- **obligate aerobes** grow only in the presence of oxygen, for example, *Micrococcus luteus*
- **facultative aerobes** can grow in the absence of oxygen, but grow better if oxygen is supplied, for example, *Escherichia coli*
- **microaerophilic aerobes** require oxygen at lower concentrations than atmospheric, for example, *Spirillum volutans*
- **obligate anaerobes** grow only in the absence of oxygen, for example, *Desulphovibrio*.

Figure 5.2 An anaerobic jar for the incubation of cultures under anaerobic conditions. Air in the jar is replaced with an oxygen-free gas mixture, such as hydrogen and carbon dioxide, or a chemical catalyst is placed in the jar which removes oxygen from the atmosphere.

In small-scale culture, such as on agar in Petri dishes or in universal containers of broth media, oxygen diffuses directly from the air to the microorganisms. Broth media (or **liquid media**) contain the same nutrients as solid media but do not contain agar. These media therefore remain as liquids and do not set to form a gel. Broth media include **nutrient broth** and **malt extract broth** and are used to culture microorganisms in, for example, universal bottles and laboratory fermenters (page 53) and can be used to study growth rates. If aerobic microorganisms are grown on a larger scale, such as in a laboratory fermenter, it is necessary to aerate the culture, usually by bubbling sterile air through the medium. This supplies the microorganisms with oxygen, where otherwise the rate of diffusion and poor solubility of oxygen in water would mean that insufficient oxygen was available. If it is necessary to culture obligate anaerobes, for example in a hospital laboratory, they are grown on agar plates placed in a special container referred to as an **anaerobic jar** (Figure 5.2), a container which can be filled with a mixture of hydrogen and carbon dioxide to replace the air. The jar contains a catalyst which removes any residual oxygen, to ensure anaerobic conditions.

pH

Most microorganisms have a pH optimum between 5 and 9, but a few species can grow at pH values outside this range. In general, fungi tend to be more tolerant than bacteria of acid conditions, with optima at pH 5 or below. These pH values refer to the extracellular environment, and although this may vary widely, the intracellular pH remains nearly neutral. The pH of culture media is kept relatively constant by the use of buffer solutions, such as phosphate buffers. During the growth of a microorganism, the pH of the medium may change due to the production of acidic or alkaline products of metabolism. This may be regulated by the addition of appropriate sterile buffer solutions during the growth phase.

Methods for culturing microorganisms

If we wish to study a single species of microorganism, it is often necessary to isolate it from a mixed culture of many different species. Microorganisms are present in almost every habitat – soil and water are particularly rich sources. In order to obtain a *pure* culture of a single species, it must be grown in a laboratory in suitable conditions, with all the necessary nutrients provided. It is also essential to avoid contaminating the culture with other, unwanted microorganisms. The medium used to grow the microorganism must be sterile, and it is essential to take precautions in handling the materials used for culture of the organism in order to avoid contamination.

Aseptic technique is the term used describe the proper handling of cultures, sterile apparatus and sterile media to prevent contamination (see *Practical: Preparation and sterilisation of media,* page 73). Preparation is usually carried out in sterile areas, and sometimes in sterile rooms, to prevent contamination. Microbiological **media** are formulated to contain all the nutrients required by particular microorganisms; some different types of media are described below.

Selective media contain substances which selectively inhibit the growth of certain microorganisms, whilst allowing others to grow. These media are particularly important in medical microbiology, as they are used to culture and isolate organisms from clinical specimens such as blood and urine. An example of a selective medium is MacConkey agar, which contains lactose and bile salts. This is used to isolate enteric bacteria, that is, bacteria which grow in the intestinal tract. Bacteria such as *Escherichia coli*, which are able to utilise lactose as an energy source, are able to grow, but the growth of other species of bacteria, including *Staphylococcus* spp., is inhibited.

Some microbiological media contain a coloured pH indicator substance, such as phenol red or bromocresol purple. These are known as **indicator media** (or differential media) and show whether or not a change in pH has occurred as a result of the metabolism of the bacteria during growth. For example, if the bacteria produce acids, then a broth medium containing phenol red changes in colour from red to yellow. Eosin-methylene blue (EMB) agar is an example of a medium which is both selective and an indicator medium and is used to isolate Gram negative enteric bacteria. EMB agar contains lactose and sucrose as energy sources, and the dyes eosin and methylene blue. Methylene blue inhibits the growth of Gram positive bacteria; eosin changes colour according to the pH of the medium, changing from colourless to black in acidic conditions. *E. coli* will grow in EMB agar to produce colonies which are black, with a greenish metallic sheen. *Salmonella* produces colonies which are translucent or pink.

Although selective media are important in the isolation and identification of bacteria, many species can be successfully cultivated using nutrient broth or nutrient agar. The composition of nutrient broth is given on page 73. Broth media may be solidified by the addition of **agar**, a polysaccharide obtained from red algae. Agar is usually added at about 1.5 per cent by weight to the medium, and is dissolved by boiling. On cooling to about 42 °C, the medium will set to produce a clear, firm gel.

Use of fermenters

Microorganisms may be grown on a large scale to produce a wide range of useful products, such as antibiotics, enzymes, food additives and ethanol. Some examples of ways that microorganisms are exploited are described in Chapter 6.

Fermenters are vessels used for the growth of microorganisms in liquid media. These vary in size from small-scale laboratory fermenters containing perhaps 250 cm³ of medium to very large-scale industrial fermenters containing up to 500 000 dm³. The majority of microorganisms grown are

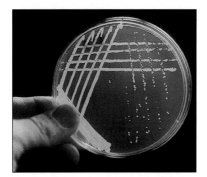

Figure 5.3 Bacterial colonies growing on an agar plate.

aerobic and it is therefore essential to ensure an adequate supply of oxygen to maintain aerobic conditions. Two main systems for culturing microorganisms are used, referred to as **batch culture** and **continuous culture**.

In **batch** culture, growth of the microorganism occurs in a fixed volume of medium and, apart from oxygen, substances are not normally added to the medium during culture. The organism typically goes through the usual phases of growth, that is, lag, exponential and stationary. The organism continues to grow in the medium until conditions become unfavourable. In **continuous** culture, fresh, sterile medium is added to the fermenter at a constant rate and spent medium, together with cells, is removed at the same rate. The number of cells and the composition of the medium in the fermenter therefore remains constant. Continuous culture can, theoretically, run indefinitely but, apart from the production of Quorn™ mycoprotein, few industrial cultures are maintained continuously.

The simple fermenter shown in Figure 5.4 is suitable for use in a school laboratory and can be used to illustrate the principle of a fermenter. This fermenter could be used to grow an organism such as yeast (*Saccharomyces cerevisiae*) under controlled conditions. Before use, the syringes are removed and suitable broth medium is added to the flask. The ends of the tubes are then covered with aluminium foil and the whole apparatus is sterilised by autoclaving. When in use, the fermenter may be kept at a constant temperature by standing it in a water bath at, say, 30 °C. Filter-sterilised air is supplied by means of an aquarium pump, and waste gases are vented through another filter. The small syringe at the top of the apparatus is used to inoculate the sterile medium with a culture of the organism to be grown and samples may be removed at regular intervals using the syringe at the side. In this way, the growth of the organism may be monitored using a suitable counting technique (See *Practical: Counting cells using a haemocytometer*, page 77, and *Counting cells using the pour plate dilution method*, page 78).

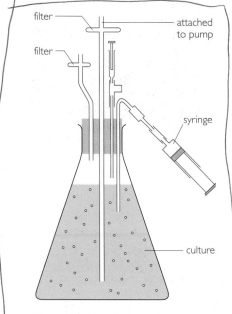

Figure 5.4 A simple fermenter.

Figure 5.5 shows an industrial fermenter and this illustrates how the simple fermenter is scaled up. Industrial fermenters are usually made of stainless steel, which can be sterilised by passing steam, under pressure, through the whole equipment. Industrial fermenters have a number of important features. These include:

- a **cooling jacket** through which cold water is passed to remove excess heat produced by metabolic activities of the microorganisms. If the culture is not cooled in this way, the temperature would increase to a point at which enzymes would start to be denatured and the microorganisms killed.
- an efficient system for the **aeration** of the culture. This includes a **sparger** – a device through which sterile air is pumped under a high pressure, breaking the stream of air into fine bubbles. An **impeller** is used to stir the contents of the fermenter. Stirring mixes air bubbles with the medium, helping oxygen to dissolve and ensures the microorganisms are kept mixed with the medium. This ensures that access to nutrients is maintained.
- systems for monitoring the growth of the culture, controlling the pH by the addition of buffers, and for removing the products when growth is completed.

Using fermenters to produce antibiotics

The production of the antibiotic penicillin can be used to illustrate the principle of an industrial fermenter. The discovery of penicillin is described on page 69. Fleming's original isolate was a strain of *Penicillium notatum*, which yielded about 20 units of penicillin per cm^3 when grown on the surface of a broth medium (1 million units of penicillin G = 0.6 g).

A search for natural variants of *Penicillium* led to the isolation of *P. chrysogenum*, strain NRRL 1951, from a mouldy melon purchased at a market in Peoria, USA. The introduction of this strain, together with a change in culture methods, increased the yield of penicillin to 100 units per cm^3. Repeated steps of mutation and selection have led to the development of the strains of *P. chrysogenum* used today, which produce penicillin at a concentration of about 30 000 units per cm^3. *more efficient*

Industrially, *P. chrysogenum* is grown in large fermenters (with a capacity of up to 200 000 dm^3) similar to that shown in Figure 5.5. Initially the fungus is grown in the laboratory on a small scale to produce an **inoculum** (that is, a pure culture of the microorganism), which is used to inoculate the fermenter (Figure 5.6). In order to obtain a large enough inoculum to ensure rapid growth in the final fermenter, *P. chrysogenum* is grown in stages, from a solid medium, to flask culture in a broth medium, through to 'seed stages' of up to 100 m^3. Media for the production of penicillin often contain corn-steep liquor, a by-product of maize starch production. This contains the nitrogen source and other growth factors.

> ### DEFINITION
> A **culture inoculant** is usually a small quantity of liquid medium, containing actively growing microorganisms, which is added aseptically to a large-scale fermenter.

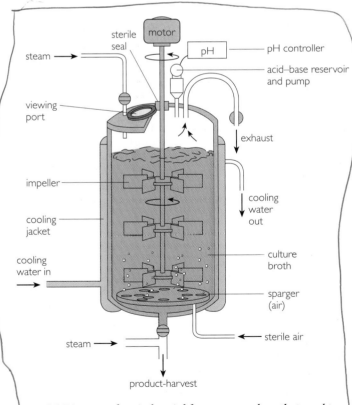

Figure 5.5 Diagram of an industrial fermenter, such as that used to produce the antibiotic penicillin.

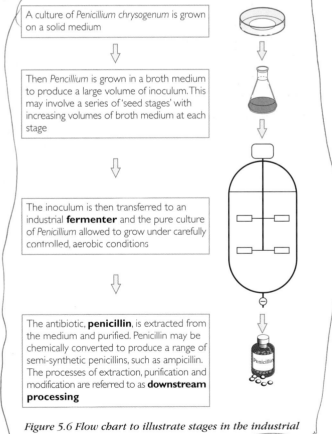

A culture of *Penicillium chrysogenum* is grown on a solid medium

Then *Pencillium* is grown in a broth medium to produce a large volume of inoculum. This may involve a series of 'seed stages' with increasing volumes of broth medium at each stage

The inoculum is then transferred to an industrial **fermenter** and the pure culture of *Penicillium* allowed to grow under carefully controlled, aerobic conditions

The antibiotic, **penicillin**, is extracted from the medium and purified. Penicillin may be chemically converted to produce a range of semi-synthetic penicillins, such as ampicillin. The processes of extraction, purification and modification are referred to as **downstream processing**

Figure 5.6 Flow chart to illustrate stages in the industrial production of penicillin.

CULTURE TECHNIQUES

The structure of some types of penicillin

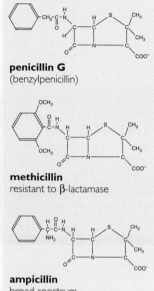

penicillin G
(benzylpenicillin)

methicillin
resistant to β-lactamase

ampicillin
broad-spectrum
acid-resistant

Figure 5.7 The structure of penicillin G and two examples of semi-synthetic penicillins.

Penicillin G is first converted into 6-amino penicillanic acid (6-APA) using the enzyme penicillin acylase. 6-APA is then chemically modified by adding various chemical side groups, to produce a range of substances known collectively as semi-synthetic penicillins, such as amoxycillin, ampicillin and methicillin. The structures of penicillin G and two examples of semi-synthetic penicillins are shown in Figure 5.7.

The energy source is usually lactose. The production of penicillin is stimulated by the addition of phenylacetic acid, but the concentration is critical as it is toxic to the fungus. A supply of oxygen is required, as the growth of *P. chrysogenum* and the production of penicillin require aerobic conditions. Oxygen is supplied by means of filter-sterilised air pumped into the fermenter. The temperature is maintained between 25 and 27 °C and the pH between 6.8 and 7.7.

Penicillin is excreted into the medium and so is in solution with various other substances. The process of extraction, purification and subsequent chemical modification of penicillin is referred to as **downstream processing**. The penicillin is extracted, firstly by filtration, which separates fungal material from the medium, then by using solvent extraction to isolate the penicillin. The pH is first reduced to between 2.0 and 2.5 and the penicillin is extracted into an organic solvent such as amyl acetate. Penicillin is then re-extracted back into an aqueous buffer at pH 7.5, concentrated, and then crystallised. Penicillin produced in this way is known as penicillin G, which may be converted to semi-synthetic penicillins, as a means of overcoming the problems of penicillin-resistant strains of bacteria.

Antibiotics belong to a group of chemical substances referred to as **secondary metabolites**. These are substances which are produced by microorganisms towards the end of the growth phase and into the stationary phase. The synthesis of secondary metabolites is very dependent on the culture conditions, particularly the composition of the medium. It appears that they are not essential for the growth and reproduction of the microorganism, and often accumulate in the growth medium in relatively high concentrations. In order to maximise the production of penicillin, nutrients such as nitrogen sources may be added to the medium towards the end of the growth phase – this is referred to as fed-batch culture.

ADDITIONAL INFORMATION

Plant and animal cell culture

The principles involved in the culture of microorganisms can be applied to the culture of cells and tissues obtained from plants and animals. Essentially, this involves the culture of suitable cells, under aseptic conditions, in complex media which have been specially formulated for this purpose. The maintenance of strict aseptic conditions is essential in cell and tissue culture, as any contaminating microorganisms are likely to grow very much faster than the plant or animal tissue. **Plant tissue culture** is described in *Tools, Techniques and Assessment in Biology*, Chapter 5.

Animal cells that are cultured can be derived from explants of the four basic tissue types: epithelial, connective, nervous or muscular tissues. Some of these cells, such as lymphocytes (derived from connective tissue), can be grown in a suspension culture, similar to bacteria in a liquid medium. Most normal mammalian cells, however, grow attached to a surface and form a single layer of cells, referred to as a **monolayer**.

Growth of cultures

Under favourable conditions, the number of single-celled microorganisms doubles at regular intervals. This is because each of the two daughter cells produced has the same potential for growth as the original parental cell. The time required for the number of cells to double is known as the **mean doubling time**. Table 5.3 shows how the number of cells increases, starting with a single cell, assuming a doubling time of 20 minutes. The table shows both the arithmetic number of cells and the number expressed as a logarithm to the base 10 ($\log_{10}$).

Table 5.3 *Increases in the numbers of bacterial cells with a doubling time of 20 minutes*

Time/minutes	Number of divisions	Number of cells	$\log_{10}$ number of cells
0	0	1	0.000
20	1	2	0.301
40	2	4	0.602
60	3	8	0.903
80	4	16	1.204
100	5	32	1.505
120	6	64	1.806
140	7	128	2.107
160	8	256	2.408
180	9	512	2.709
200	10	1024	3.010

The **experimental growth rate constant (k)** is defined as the number of doublings per unit time, usually expressed as the number per hour. This can be calculated using the formula:

$$k = \frac{\log_{10} N_t - \log_{10} N_0}{t \times \log_{10} 2}$$

where k = exponential growth rate constant
$\log_{10} N_0 = \log_{10}$ of the number of cells at a certain time
$\log_{10} N_t = \log_{10}$ of the number of cells at a later time
t = time
$\log_{10} 2 = 0.301$

Let us consider a specific example. Suppose that the number of bacteria in a population increases from 10^2 cells to 10^9 cells in 8 hours. The exponential growth rate constant can be calculated as follows.

$$k = \frac{\log_{10} 10^9 - \log_{10} 10^2}{0.301 \times 8}$$

$$= \frac{9 - 2}{2.408}$$

$$= 2.91 \text{ generations per hour}$$

The number of **complete** generations in this example is 2.

EXTENSION MATERIAL

How the formula is derived

A graph showing the log number of cells plotted against time is a straight line, as long as the cells are dividing at a steady rate. If N_0 is the size of the population at a certain time, and N_t is the size at a later time (t), then the number of generations which has occurred can be calculated using the following formula:

$$N_t = 2^{kt} \times N_0$$

where k is the exponential growth rate constant, that is, the number of doublings per unit time, usually expressed as the number of doublings per hour.

The exponential growth rate constant, k, can be found using the formula:

$$k = \frac{\log_2 N_t - \log_2 N_0}{t}$$

where $\log_2 N_0$ is the log to the base 2 of the initial population size, and $\log_2 N_t$ is the log to the base 2 of the final population size, after t hours.

Rather than using logarithms to the base 2, the calculation can be made using logarithms of N_0 and N_t to the base 10, and dividing by $\log_{10} 2$, which can be taken as 0.301:

$$k = \frac{\log_{10} N_t - \log_{10} N_0}{0.301 \times t}$$

CULTURE TECHNIQUES

The growth rate is sometimes expressed as the time taken for the population to double, or the **mean doubling time**. This is the reciprocal of the exponential growth rate, that is, $1/k$. In the example above, the mean doubling time is $1/2.91$, 0.34 hours or approximately 21 minutes.

So far, we have considered cells only in the exponential phase of growth. With a limited supply of nutrients, cell growth does not continue indefinitely. The growth of the population is normally limited either by the exhaustion of one or more essential nutrients, or by the accumulation of toxic by-products of metabolism.

Figure 5.8 shows a typical complete growth curve for a microorganism. Four distinct phases of growth can be seen: the lag phase, exponential (or logarithmic) phase, stationary phase and death phase. When fresh, sterile medium is inoculated with a culture of a microorganism, growth may not begin immediately. There is a period of time in which the cells are synthesising the enzymes required for the metabolism of nutrients present in the medium. This period of time is referred to as the **lag phase**, and can be seen as a period of adjustment to the culture conditions. A lag phase does not always occur. If, for example, cells already in the exponential phase are transferred to fresh, identical medium, exponential growth would continue at the same rate.

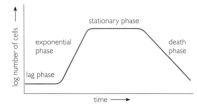

Figure 5.8 Typical growth curve for a bacterial culture. Four distinct phases of growth can be seen.

> ### QUESTION
>
> Identify the phases of growth shown in Figure 5.8 and describe what is happening in each.

We have already described the **exponential phase** as a period of constant growth in the size of the microbial population, during which both cell numbers and cell mass increase in parallel. The growth rate constant is affected by both genetic and environmental factors; it varies from one species to another, and is influenced by such factors as the concentration of nutrients in the growth medium, temperature and pH. The exponential phase is followed by the **stationary phase**, in which the overall growth rate is zero. During this phase, slow growth of some cells continues to occur, but is balanced by the death of others, so that the total number of viable cells remains constant. This phase is followed by the **death phase** in which the number of viable cells progressively decreases. Death of cells may be accompanied by cell lysis so that both the total cell number and the viable cell count decreases.

Diauxic growth is sometimes observed if a microorganism is grown in a medium containing two different carbon sources (Figure 5.9). Diauxic growth is

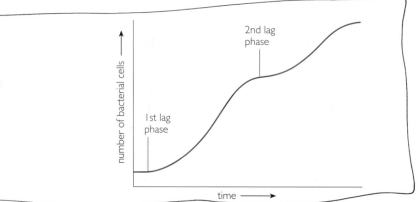

Figure 5.9 Diauxic growth of E. coli *in a medium containing glucose and lactose. Two growth phases are seen, separated by a second lag phase. During the second lag phase, cells synthesise enzymes including lactase (β-galactosidase).*

characterised by two distinct phases of exponential growth, separated by a brief lag phase. For example, if *Escherichia coli* is grown in a medium containing both glucose and lactose, the glucose is metabolised first. Glucose actually inhibits the synthesis of lactase (β-galactosidase). This is referred to as catabolite repression and only after the glucose has been used up will lactase be synthesised. Growth then resumes using lactose as an energy source.

Measuring the growth of microorganisms

We have seen that the growth of a culture of unicellular microorganisms results from an increase in the number of cells, so growth of microbial populations can be measured by determining changes in either the number of cells or the cell mass. The number of cells in a suspension can be determined by counting the number of cells present in an accurately determined, very small volume of culture medium. This is usually carried out using special microscope slides, known as **counting chambers** (see *Practical: Counting cells using a haemocytometer*, page 77). These are slides that are ruled with a grid of squares of known area and are made so that, when correctly filled, they contain a film of liquid of known depth. The volume of liquid overlying each square is therefore known. This method for determining cell numbers is referred to as a **total cell count**, which includes both viable and non-viable cells, as it is not normally possible to distinguish one from another using a microscope.

The number of cells can also be determined using a **plate count** (see *Practical: Counting cells using the pour plate dilution method,* page 78). This method depends on the ability of each single, viable cell to grow in or on an agar medium and produce a visible colony. This method of counting is referred to as a **viable count**, as only those cells which are able to grow in the culture medium are detected. Appropriate dilutions of a bacterial culture are made and are used to inoculate a suitable medium. The number of viable cells present in the original culture is then determined by counting the number of colonies which develop after incubation of the plates and multiplying this number by the dilution factor. Two or three replicate plates of each dilution should be prepared in order to reduce the sampling error. The greatest accuracy is obtained with relatively large numbers of colonies on each plate, but the practical limit is reached with between 300 and 400 colonies per plate.

The only direct method for determining **cell mass** is to measure the dry mass of cells in a known volume of culture medium. This is a suitable method for measuring the growth of a filamentous organism, where cell counting is inappropriate, but it is rarely used for unicellular bacteria because of the relatively insensitive method for weighing. It is difficult to weigh with an accuracy of less than 1 mg, but this represents the dry mass of between 1 and 5×10^9 bacteria.

One useful approach for estimating the number of cells present in a suspension is to use an **optical method**, for example, by determining the amount of light which is scattered by a cell suspension. A suspension of cells appears cloudy, or turbid, to the eye because the cells scatter light passing through the suspension. The cloudiness increases as the cell numbers increase and, within limits, the amount of light scattered by the cells is proportional to

QUESTION

What are the advantages of using the viable count and optical methods for estimating the number of bacterial cells in a culture?

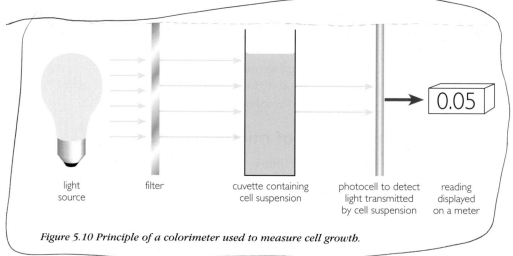

light
source

filter

cuvette containing
cell suspension

photocell to detect
light transmitted
by cell suspension

reading
displayed
on a meter

0.05

Figure 5.10 Principle of a colorimeter used to measure cell growth.

their numbers. A **colorimeter** is an instrument which can be used to measure the amount of light which is transmitted by a cell suspension (Figure 5.10). When a beam of light passes through a cell suspension, the reduction in the amount of light transmitted gives a measure of cell density. A colorimeter can be calibrated by combining measurements of light transmitted with another method for measuring cell growth, such as plate counting.

Use of microorganisms in biotechnology

Biotechnology is a relatively modern word, though its roots lie at the very beginnings of human civilisation. In this chapter, we see how the art of making yoghurt, beer and bread has developed and grown with different human societies through the centuries. Today, at the start of the 21st century, biotechnology is concerned with exploiting the activities of living organisms, especially microorganisms. Applications of biotechnology range from the food and beverage industries to medicine and agriculture, production of fuels and treatment of waste. As well as the traditional fermentations, more recent developments in biotechnology extend into gene technology. Techniques have been developed that enable very precise modification of DNA, to alter the genome within an organism or to transfer genetic information from one organism to another. If we view the whole range of applications for biotechnology, we can see that its future potential is considerable and is likely to escalate as we move through the 21st century. (For further information on gene technology, see *Genetics, Evolution and Biodiversity,* Chapter 9, and for Extension Material on the use of microorganisms in biotechnology, see Chapter 10 of this book.)

Food and drink

The ancient art of modifying raw harvested food has evolved into the modern food and drink industry. Modern processing is highly mechanised, rigorously monitored and controlled to ensure uniformity of end-products, many of which are destined for world-wide distribution. The impact of biotechnology in the modern food and drink industry is illustrated here by the activities of microorganisms in fermentations and harvesting of microorganisms as biomass to be consumed as food for humans or feed for animals.

Fermentations are a significant way of modifying raw fresh food. The fermented product has properties that are different from the original material. The fermentation may enhance the flavour or alter the texture, palatability and digestibility of the food, and there may be changes in the nutritional content. These changes often make the food safer because it is then unsuitable for the growth of other microorganisms. Sometimes toxins are eliminated. Traditionally, fermentation of various foods has provided an important means of preservation, though today other methods, such as freezing, have become more important. (See also Chapter 10, page 123.)

The term **fermentation** is used in two senses. In the narrower, biochemical sense, fermentation is a form of **anaerobic respiration**, and is a means by which organisms, or cells within organisms, obtain energy from an organic substrate in the absence of oxygen. In the broader sense, the term is used to describe a very wide range of processes carried out by microorganisms. Many yield products of commercial importance. Some fermentations involve anaerobic respiration, but many do not.

BACKGROUND

The art of processing food stems from the very beginnings of human civilisation, as humans changed from a hunter-gatherer way of life to more permanent, settled communities. The making of bread, cheese, yoghurt, wine and beer are food-processing practices that are central to many human societies, traditional and modern. The origins of different discoveries were probably accidental, but the benefits were doubtless soon appreciated. Food could be kept longer, transported or stored from one season to the next. A wider range of flavours became part of the diet, and alcoholic liquor, in particular, assumed an importance in ceremonies and social gatherings.

QUESTION

When, historically, did people begin to be aware of the existence of microorganisms, and understand that they are the agents responsible for many of these modifications to food?

USE OF MICROORGANISMS IN BIOTECHNOLOGY

Figure 6.1 Kumiss (fermented mare's milk), being sold by the bucket in a traditional market in Kyrgystan. The fermentation uses a mixture of lactic acid bacteria and lactose fermenting yeasts. Streptococcus lactis *and* Lactobacillus bulgaricus *produce lactic acid with some acetaldehyde and the yeasts* (Candida kefyr *and* Torulopsis *spp.) produce ethanol and carbon dioxide. The result is a fizzy, sweet drink which is both alcoholic and acidic.*

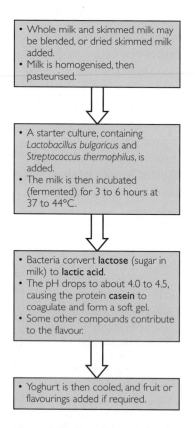

- Whole milk and skimmed milk may be blended, or dried skimmed milk added.
- Milk is homogenised, then pasteurised.

⇩

- A starter culture, containing *Lactobacillus bulgaricus* and *Streptococcus thermophilus*, is added.
- The milk is then incubated (fermented) for 3 to 6 hours at 37 to 44°C.

⇩

- Bacteria convert **lactose** (sugar in milk) to **lactic acid**.
- The pH drops to about 4.0 to 4.5, causing the protein **casein** to coagulate and form a soft gel.
- Some other compounds contribute to the flavour.

⇩

- Yoghurt is then cooled, and fruit or flavourings added if required.

Figure 6.2 A flow diagram showing the main stages in the production of yoghurt.

Lactic acid fermentations are carried out by a range of bacteria, including species of *Lactobacillus*, *Leuconostoc* and *Streptococcus*. These lactic acid bacteria convert carbohydrate to lactic acid, sometimes with other products. The carbohydrate is usually lactose, but other sugars are also utilised. The lowered pH provides an environment unsuitable for the growth of many microorganisms, which is why these fermentations offer a means for reducing spoilage of foods. This gives the foods improved storage properties as well as alterations in flavour and texture. Lactic acid fermentations are the basis of the dairy industry, and are also involved in the production of sauerkraut (fermented cabbage), some sausages and salamis, and sourdough bread.

Yeasts, particularly of the genus *Saccharomyces* and also *Kluyveromyces*, are important in the **alcoholic fermentation** of sugars (mainly glucose), which is the basis of the wine and brewing industries and is also used in bread making.

Lactic acid fermentation of milk in the production of yoghurt

Fermentation of milk into yoghurt is both a very ancient and a widespread practice. In Europe, we are most familiar with yoghurt from cow's milk, or from sheep, but milk from other mammals, including goats, buffalo and camels, is also used. Probably the first yoghurt was from the Middle East. Milk being carried under warm conditions doubtless became sour, developed agreeable flavours and could be kept longer than fresh milk, with obvious advantages to nomadic people. A portion of a successful ferment might have been used again to start the next batch, effectively selecting suitable strains of bacteria.

In the modern preparation of yoghurt, whole milk may be **blended** with skimmed milk or skimmed milk solids. Starch or sugar may be added to give a different flavour or consistency. Sometimes the milk is heated to allow evaporation and make a thicker yoghurt, though on a large scale the viscosity (thickness) of the end-product is controlled by the initial mixture of milk and solids. The fat content can be adjusted by removing fat or by adding cream. The milk is **homogenised** to disperse the fat as small globules, then heated to 88 to 95 °C for between 15 and 30 minutes to **pasteurise** the milk. The high temperature and time used are necessary to kill bacteria, which may be active at relatively high temperatures (described as *thermophilic* bacteria). Milk inevitably carries a microflora from the udder, and these contaminants could act as competitors in the yoghurt-making process.

The starter culture includes two species of bacteria which enhance each other's activities. First, *Lactobacillus bulgaricus* acts on milk protein, converting it to small peptides and amino acids. These stimulate the growth of the second species, *Streptococcus thermophilus*. *S. thermophilus* in turn produces formic acid which stimulates growth of *L. bulgaricus* (Figure 6.3). *L. bulgaricus* is mainly responsible for the conversion of lactose to lactic acid and production of some ethanal (acetaldehyde), which, with other compounds, contributes to the flavour. The culture is incubated at 40 to 45 °C for 3 to 6 hours (or at 32 °C for 12 hours), then cooled rapidly to prevent further bacterial fermentation. At the end of the fermentation, the lactic acid concentration is about 1.4 per cent and the pH is between 4.4 and 4.6. The thickening of the yoghurt is the result of the coagulation of proteins.

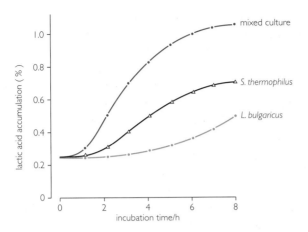

Figure 6.3 Preparation of yoghurt and the effect of different culture organisms. Comparison of two single-strain cultures, Streptococcus thermophilus *and* Lactobacillus bulgaricus, *and a mixed culture of both strains.*

In the set method for making yoghurt, the homogenised milk with starter culture is poured into the final containers and incubated. More commonly, the mixture is stirred during the fermentation then poured into containers at the end of the process (see Figure 6.2, page 62).

EXTENSION MATERIAL

More about making yoghurt

Fruit or other flavours may be added, either at the start of incubation for set yoghurt, or at the end for stirred yoghurt. The fruit may introduce unwanted yeasts or other microbial contaminants into the yoghurt. Fruit yoghurts are often protected by adding sugar, giving a higher osmotic potential and lower pH. At the same time the sugar sweetens the yoghurt.

The popularity of yoghurt comes in part from its improved digestibility. It is particularly valuable for lactose-intolerant people, but if additional milk solids are added to thicken the yoghurt, some lactose may remain in the final product. Variations in the end-product come from using cultures of different organisms.

Fermentation by yeast in brewing

The basic brewing process involves 'malting' of barley grains by soaking in water and allowing them to germinate, followed by fermentation of the sweet liquor by yeasts. The modern brewing industry produces either **ale**, fermented with 'top-fermentation yeast' (see page 65), or **lager**. Lagers are fermented with a 'bottom-fermentation yeast'. Other beers, such as sorghum beer, which is made in Africa mainly from sorghum, millet and maize, are brewed using similar principles.

QUESTION

Skimmed milk is added to milk in making yoghurt, to help thicken it and improve its nutritional value, but this also increases its lactose content. Only about 15 per cent of this lactose sugar is used during the fermentation. Pre-treatment of the milk with lactases reduces the lactose content and the yoghurt sets more rapidly.
Devise a practical investigation that you could carry out to compare the rate of setting of yoghurt, made from lactose-reduced and normal milk. What other benefits might there be in making yoghurt from lactose-reduced milk?

QUESTION

Many different names are used for yoghurt-type preparations throughout the world. Find out where the following fermentations are eaten or drunk, what milk each uses, and how they differ in their processing from the yoghurt described in this chapter:
acidophilous milk, buttermilk, dadih, filmjolk, kefir, kumiss, lassi, raita, yakult, yiaourti.

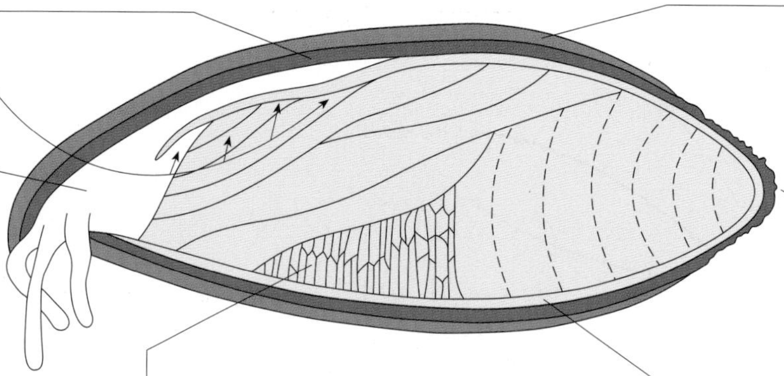

USE OF MICROORGANISMS IN BIOTECHNOLOGY

pericarp-testa
• influences permeability

• route of gibberellin transport

embryo
• produces hormones (e.g. gibberellins)
• produces enzymes (e.g. lipoxidase)
• produces precursors of beer flavour compounds

husk
• protects grain
• forms filter-bed in wort separation

abrasion
• outer layers removed
• added gibberellic acid gains access to distal region of grain

starchy endosperm
• food store – provides substances which are degraded in malting and mashing to give yeast nutrients and components of beer

aleurone
enzyme production including
• endopeptidase
• α-amylase

Figure 6.4 Changes within the barley grain during the malting process.

Barley (*Hordeum vulgare*) is a cereal crop which grows widely in temperate zones as well as in the tropical highlands of Africa. The main stages in the brewing of beer from barley can be summarised as follows:

• malting
• milling and mashing
• addition of hops and boiling
• fermentation
• maturation
• packaging for distribution and sale.

The barley grain contains stored starch in the endosperm (Figure 6.4). Most yeasts cannot utilise the starch so the first stage of the brewing process is the conversion of starch to soluble sugars (Figure 6.5). To prepare the barley **malt**, the grains are **steeped** in water and allowed to **germinate**. The steeping is generally done in a vertical tank for about 2 days. Air is passed through the water to ensure conditions are aerobic. After about 12 hours, the water is drained out to give a period of 'air-rest' which allows oxygen from the surrounding air to dissolve in the film of water around the grain. This gives faster and more uniform germination. The barley is immersed in water again and this process may be repeated several times. Traditionally the barley is then spread out on a malting floor. A wooden shovel is used to turn the germinating barley in order to provide air which allows respiration to continue and accumulated carbon dioxide to be removed. Temperatures should be maintained at about 15 °C. After about 5 days, rootlets appear in the sprouting barley, which is now called **malt**. During the germination process, some degradation of starch and proteins occurs, but the main purpose of malting is to allow development of enzymes which become important in the subsequent stages. This is stimulated by release, from the embryo of the plant, of the growth substance **gibberellic acid** which acts on the aleurone layer (see *Genetics, Evolution and Biodiversity*, Chapter 2). Germination is stopped by heating to between 65 and 80 °C, a process known as **kilning**. This temperature kills the embryo but does not inactivate the enzymes. It also improves the flavour and dries the malt, allowing storage.

EXTENSION MATERIAL

Changes within a barley endosperm cell during the malting process

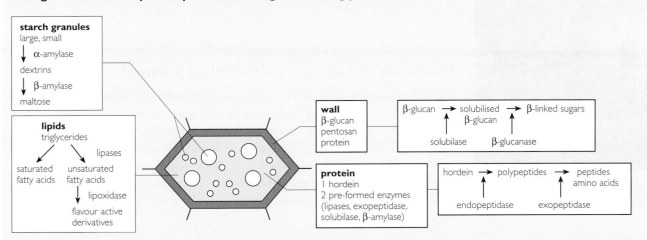

Figure 6.5 Changes within a barley endosperm cell. Note the activities of the different enzymes involved in the breakdown of storage compounds.

The malt is converted to wort which contains sugars and other nutrients and is now ready to be **fermented** by yeasts. Various strains of **brewers' yeasts** are used and added as prepared cultures. The choice depends on the type of beer to be produced. After an initial lag phase, the yeasts grow rapidly then, as the oxygen is used up, the yeasts switch to anaerobic fermentation and the sugars are converted to ethanol and carbon dioxide. Heat is given off so the fermentation vessel must be cooled. *Saccharomyces cerevisiae* is used for ales and this strain of yeast produces a froth on the surface of the fermenting vessel, described as 'top-fermentation'. Fermentation takes about 7 days at 20 °C. For lager, the 'bottom-fermenting' yeast strain *S. carlsbergensis* is used. Fermentation takes between 7 and 14 days at lower temperatures (5 to 15 °C) and, because less froth is produced, the yeast sinks to the bottom. At the end of the fermentation, the yeast is removed, either by skimming from the surface or by collecting the sediment from the bottom. This surplus yeast is used in the food industry, to produce yeast extract and products such as Marmite™.

Figure 6.6 Froth on the surface during beer fermentation.

The wort has now become beer, but requires further conditioning before it is ready to be drunk. Traditionally this has been done in wooden casks, over a period of a few weeks (or months for lagers), in cool temperatures. During this time, there are changes in flavour and some secondary fermentation takes place. In many modern breweries, the maturation takes place in large storage vessels. The beer is then centrifuged to remove cell debris, artificially carbonated with carbon dioxide, filtered, bottled or transferred to small barrels, and often pasteurised to improve the keeping quality. The range of beers available differs in colour, sweetness, flavour and alcoholic strength. See Figures 6.7 (page 65) and 6.11 (page 67).

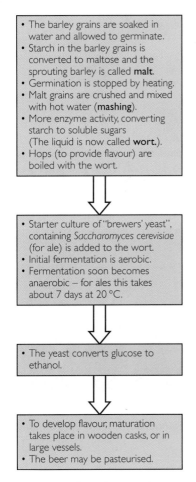

- The barley grains are soaked in water and allowed to germinate.
- Starch in the barley grains is converted to maltose and the sprouting barley is called **malt**.
- Germination is stopped by heating.
- Malt grains are crushed and mixed with hot water (**mashing**).
- More enzyme activity, converting starch to soluble sugars (The liquid is now called **wort**.).
- Hops (to provide flavour) are boiled with the wort.

- Starter culture of "brewers' yeast", containing *Saccharomyces cerevisiae* (for ale) is added to the wort.
- Initial fermentation is aerobic.
- Fermentation soon becomes anaerobic – for ales this takes about 7 days at 20 °C.

- The yeast converts glucose to ethanol.

- To develop flavour, maturation takes place in wooden casks, or in large vessels.
- The beer may be pasteurised.

Figure 6.7 A flow diagram showing the main stages in the production of beer.

EXTENSION MATERIAL

Figure 6.8 Mash tun at Masham Brewery, North Yorkshire.

Figure 6.9 Female flowers (cones) of the hop plant. These give 'bitter' its bitter flavour.

Figure 6.10 Oast houses. Hops were traditionally dried in such buildings.

Production of wort and the role of hops in beer production

The brewing process continues by milling the malt grains to break the starchy endosperm into a gritty flour known as grist. This is then mixed with hot water, usually at about 65 °C, in a large vessel, the mash tun (Figure 6.8). Some other unmalted ground cereals may also be added. During this mashing stage, enzymes from the original barley convert starch into soluble sugars. The resulting extract is a sweet liquor called wort. After 1 to 3 hours, the wort is drained through the bed of husks from the barley and retained. The spent barley grains are removed and have some value as cattle feed.

The female flowers (cones) of hops (*Humulus lupulus*) give the characteristic bitter flavour to beer (Figure 6.9). In Britain, hops are harvested in September then dried in a warm current of air in an oast house or hop kiln (Figure 6.10). Hop picking used to be done by hand and urban families migrated to the countryside for a working 'holiday', but now most picking is done mechanically. The wort and hops (included to give the bitter flavour) are boiled together for about 2 hours in a large vessel, known as a copper, and, if required, some sugar is added. The boiling stops further enzyme activity, provides a means of sterilising the liquid and allows other changes, including extraction of tannins and oils from the hops which contribute to flavour. The boiled wort is cooled and passed to the fermenting vessel. The spent hops are discarded and may be used as a fertiliser.

EXTENSION MATERIAL

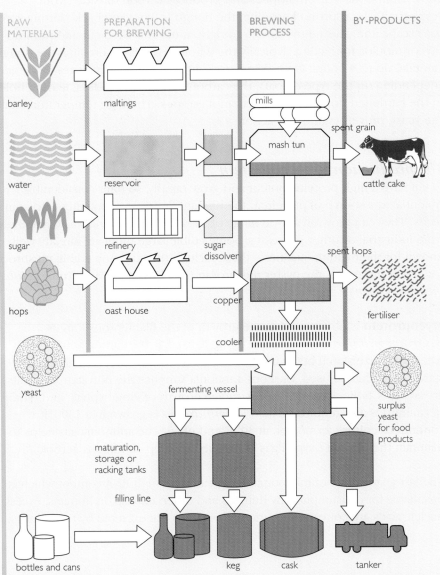

Figure 6.11 Summary of the brewing process, showing inputs and by-products at different stages.

Fermentation by yeast in dough production

Today most bread is made from wheat flour, though rye and other flours can be used (Figure 6.12). A simple, unleavened (flat) bread can be made by mixing flour with water then baking it. Using yeast in the mixture produces the lighter, leavened bread, now consumed widely throughout the world. The yeast used by bakers is a suitably selected strain of *Saccharomyces cerevisiae*. The process requires mixing of flour with water, salt and yeast and often some sugar is added. Enzymes (α- and β-amylases) in the wheat flour hydrolyse amylose and amylopectin in the starch, mainly to maltose and some glucose. The yeast utilises the sugars, converting them to carbon dioxide and some ethanol. The carbon dioxide is responsible for the raising of the bread dough. As the gas expands it becomes trapped in the dough, making it lighter.

Figure 6.12 The basic principles of bread making have changed little. This engraving shows a baker making bread in 1635.

USE OF MICROORGANISMS IN BIOTECHNOLOGY

- Flour, water, sugar, salt and **yeast** thoroughly mixed together (**kneading**).
- Dough left at about 26 °C to rise.

- Dough mixed again, cut into pieces and placed in baking tins.
- Dough left to rise.

- Baked at about 232 °C for 15 minutes or longer.

Figure 6.12a An outline of breadmaking.

QUESTION

Describe the processes which occur during the *mixing* and *rising* of the dough.

Figure 6.13 Mycoprotein – marketed as Quorn™, on sale in the UK.

During the mixing, or **kneading**, the dough is kept at a temperature of about 26 °C. At first the yeast multiplies and produces carbon dioxide (from respiration). In a second kneading, the dough is 'knocked back', letting some gas escape and causing the dough to tighten up. It is then cut and put into tins or moulds for baking. Typically the whole process of 'proving' the dough can take up to 4 hours. On **baking** at about 232 °C for 15 minutes or longer (depending on the type of loaf), the carbon dioxide is expelled, leaving holes in the hardened dough, and the ethanol escapes. The high temperatures kill the yeast, preventing further action.

The production of mycoprotein

Fungi have a high protein content and grow rapidly, so offer considerable potential as a source of protein in the human diet or as supplements to animal feeds. They can grow on a wide range of substrates, including waste materials from industrial or other processes. Some edible large fungi are already well known for their eating qualities – these include the common edible mushroom (*Agaricus bisporus*), the oyster mushroom (*Psalliota* spp.) and truffles (*Tuber melanosporum*).

Mycoprotein is obtained from the growth of the filamentous fungus *Fusarium graminareum*. Glucose syrup is used as the carbon source, with wheat or maize starch being used as the source of glucose, though other starch crops can be used. Gaseous ammonia supplies the nitrogen, and salts are added. Choline is added to encourage growth of long hyphae, and biotin (a vitamin) is also required. The *F. graminareum* is grown in a 1300 litre continuous culture fermenter, at 30 °C and pH 6. The ammonia gas helps to maintain the pH and oxygen gas is supplied to keep conditions aerobic.

The fast growth rate of microorganisms leads to a high RNA content which is unsuitable for consumption by humans and other animals. In humans, excess nucleic acids are converted to uric acid which is not excreted by the kidneys,

BACKGROUND

During the 1950s to 1970s, there was active research into ways of utilising microorganisms as a source of food, to produce **single-cell protein (SCP)**. The term SCP is used to describe protein derived from microbial cells (such as yeasts, other fungi, algae and bacteria), though the microorganism producing the protein is not necessarily 'single-celled'. The whole organism is harvested and consumed, rather than using the products of their fermentations or other processing. Exploitation of SCP production offers a way of increasing the available protein for consumption by humans and by livestock, and could be valuable particularly in areas where the land is infertile or the climate inhospitable. While SCP production may have potential for feeding the ever-increasing world population, in practice only a few schemes have proved to be commercially successful – the most successful for human consumption being **mycoprotein**, marketed under the name of Quorn™ (Figure 6.13).

resulting in the accumulation of uric acid crystals in the joints, giving gout-like symptoms. In the normal production of mycoprotein, after fermentation the RNA content is around 10 per cent, which is too high, but this can be reduced to about 2 per cent by using thermal shock and the action of ribonucleases. After RNA reduction, the mycelium is harvested continuously on a horizontal filter bed and the filter cake which is recovered can be stored at 18 °C for long periods.

The harvested mycoprotein is a mat of interwoven fungal hyphae, which can then be formulated into a range of food products. Its filamentous nature gives it a texture and 'bite' similar to that of meat. Mycoprotein itself tastes bland but can be flavoured to resemble chicken and is added to pies, burgers and cold slicing meats. Its composition compared to that of lean beef is given in Table 6.1.

Table 6.1 *Comparison of mycoprotein and beef*

Feature	Myco-protein	Beef
protein	44.3%	68.2%
dietary fibre	18.3%	0.0%
fat	13.0%	30.2%

Medical applications

At the turn of the 21st century, applications of medical science have assumed a dominant role in modern society. Healthcare and advice now start before conception, continue through pre-natal stages and childhood, and carry on during adulthood through to old age. We are tested, advised, protected or cured for many potential or actual medical conditions. We can appreciate the impact of medical science and hygiene measures by looking at the enormous reduction of infectious disease on a global scale. Biotechnology infiltrates many parts of medical practice and research continues to look for ways of giving relief to non-infectious diseases, including inherited and degenerative diseases. Medical treatments that are dependent upon biotechnology include therapeutic products, such as antibiotics and hormones, and the production of vaccines. Biotechnology is involved in pre-natal diagnosis of genetic diseases and in the development of immunological techniques for clinical diagnosis. At the molecular level, DNA probes can be used for disease identification and there is now considerable interest in the potential for gene therapy. The exploitation of microbial activities in medicine are illustrated here by production of antibiotics.

BACKGROUND

Like so much in biotechnology, the therapeutic properties of some fungal preparations were known from ancient times and used in the treatment of wounds. The benefits, however, tended to be dismissed as folklore, rather than being taken seriously by the medical profession. In 1929, Alexander Fleming discovered penicillin almost accidentally. He was growing plates of pathogenic bacteria and noticed that, when they were contaminated with the mould *Penicillium notatum*, growth of the bacteria was inhibited. Penicillin was isolated from the medium and found to be responsible for the effect. While the potential for medical applications was appreciated at the time, the stimulus for finding a means of purification followed by large-scale production and medical use came during the 1939–1945 war. Since the 1940s, penicillin and other antibiotics of fungal origin have produced a revolution in the history of medicine to the extent that many major infectious diseases have largely been brought under control.

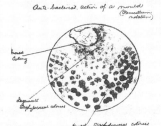

Figure 6.14 Notes on and drawing of the original culture plate of the fungus Penicillium notatum, *made by Alexander Fleming in 1928.*

Production of antibiotics

The term **antibiotic** was originally used to describe substances produced by microorganisms that could be used to kill or inhibit growth of certain other microbes. The term was introduced in the 1940s to distinguish the newly produced **penicillin** from other synthesised chemicals used for chemotherapy. Since that time, the meaning of the term has broadened to include natural antibiotics, which are modified to become semi-synthetic, and other entirely synthetic antimicrobial compounds.

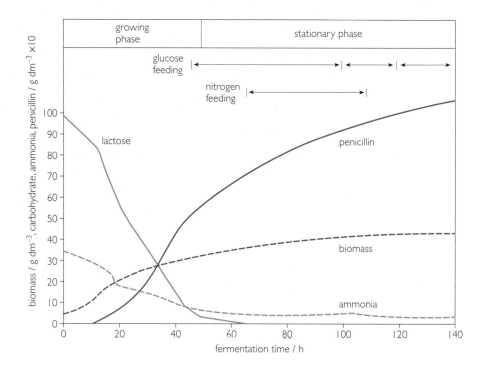

Figure 6.15 Production of penicillin by Penicillium chrysogenum. *There is little production during the growing phase but the main production occurs as the cells enter the stationary phase and can be prolonged for several days by maintaining the supply of appropriate nutrients. See page 55 for the details of penicillin production.*

Effects of antibiotics

Since penicillin was first introduced, many thousands of metabolites from fungi and from bacteria have been screened for antibiotic activity. Of these, relatively few have proved useful medically, but those which have are very successful (Table 6.2). Some antibiotics are used in food preservation and non-medically in animal feeds. Their action on other microorganisms may be described as **microbicidal** if they kill the other microbe, or **microbistatic** when they inhibit or retard growth of other microorganisms. The nature of their action may vary with concentration of the antibiotic or depend on other factors. Generally, Gram positive bacteria are more sensitive to antibiotics than Gram negative bacteria. The effectiveness of an antibiotic is described as **broad spectrum** when it acts on a wide range of Gram positive and Gram negative bacteria, whereas **narrow-spectrum antibiotics** are more specific. These can, nevertheless, be useful medically because they target a limited range of microbes, sometimes only one species. The mechanism of action

Table 6.2 *Antibiotics act differently and sometimes selectively on their target organisms. This table summarises the sites of action and mechanisms at the cellular level for some antibiotics.*

Site of action	Example of antibiotic	Mechanism of action
cell wall synthesis	penicillin, cephalosporin, vancomycin	• inhibit bonds that strengthen the bacterial cell walls, which include peptidoglycan molecules cross-linked with peptide chains. The antibiotic interferes with formation of peptide bonds. • effective only when bacteria are growing.
protein synthesis	chloramphenicol, tetracycline, erythromycin, streptomycin	• often bind to the bacterial ribosomes in preference to the mammalian ribosomes, thus interfering with and inhibiting protein synthesis. • may lead to synthesis of abnormal proteins. Streptomycin distorts the ribosome, causing an error in reading the genetic code so the wrong amino acid is inserted into the peptide chain.
nucleic acid synthesis	rifampicin, anthracyclines	• rifampicin binds selectively to RNA polymerase in bacteria in preference to that in mammals, so prevents initiation of transcription. • anthracyclines inhibit DNA synthesis in all cells, especially rapidly growing cancer cells. Effective as anti-cancer drugs, but also kill some normal cells.
cell membrane function	amphotericin B, nystatin (used against fungi) polymixin B (used against bacteria)	• damage cell membranes so interfering with function. • amphotericin has affinity for ergosterol, a sterol in fungal cell membranes, and distorts the lipid bilayer. This probably opens the channels in the membrane, allowing contents to leak to the exterior thus destroying the cell.

differs, depending on the antibiotic and microbe affected, but includes interference with cell wall synthesis (in bacteria) or with membrane function (in fungi). Antibiotics are produced as secondary metabolites (see page 56), so are not considered to be essential to the growth and metabolism of the producer organism.

Antibiotic resistance

The effectiveness of antibiotics as chemotherapeutic agents is becoming less because of the increasing resistance to antibiotics shown by different populations of microorganisms that are normally, or were formerly, sensitive to them. **Antibiotic resistance** can be defined as the acquired ability of a microorganism to resist the effects of an antibiotic to which it is normally susceptible. Some organisms are naturally resistant, whereas others may develop the characteristic through mutation. In some cases, resistance may be acquired by genetic exchange. Genetic material can be exchanged between bacteria by different processes – for example, by conjugation, transduction or transformation. When genetic material (DNA) is exchanged in this way, it can sometimes lead to the transfer of a resistance gene from a resistant bacterium to another bacterium that previously was not resistant. Spread of resistance through the population is encouraged by selection of resistant strains in the presence of antibiotics in their environment. The characteristic of resistance may have arisen in microbes as a sort of defence mechanism to neutralise or destroy their own antibiotics.

Spread of antibiotic-resistant strains is certainly linked to high use of antibiotics. Often they are used inappropriately or unnecessarily. Since the

USE OF MICROORGANISMS IN BIOTECHNOLOGY

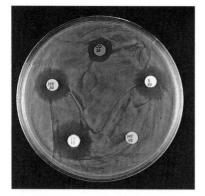

Figure 6.16 An antibiotic sensitivity test. The agar plate has been streaked with a culture of E. coli *and sensitivity discs, impregnated with antibiotics, placed on the agar. After incubation, clear inhibition zones are seen around discs that contain antibiotics to which the organism is sensitive. No inhibition zone is seen around the disc containing methicillin, showing resistance to this antibiotic.*

QUESTION

How might the practice of using antibiotics in feed for livestock affect the processing of milk into yoghurt and cheese?

1950s, which signalled the start of widespread use of antibiotics, dosages of antibiotics to combat certain diseases have been increased and in some cases treatment has become ineffective. This can be illustrated by treatment for gonorrhoea, caused by *Neisseria gonorrhoeae*, for which penicillin is no longer effective due to high incidence of resistance to it (Figure 6.17). Inevitably resistance is likely to develop, but its spread could be minimised by restricting use of antibiotics to essential cases only. They should certainly be avoided for treatment of minor infections. A further cause of the spread of antibiotic resistance has come from the use of antibiotics in agriculture, where they are used in animal feeds, both to enhance growth rate and as a prophylactic to prevent development of diseases. In Europe, there is careful regulation so that antibiotics used in animal feeds are not also used for medical treatment of humans. Modification of the chemical nature of the antibiotic molecules, say by production of semi-synthetic analogues, has in some cases given a drug which is effective against otherwise resistant strains. Such drugs can be used, at least for a short time, until resistant strains catch up with them!

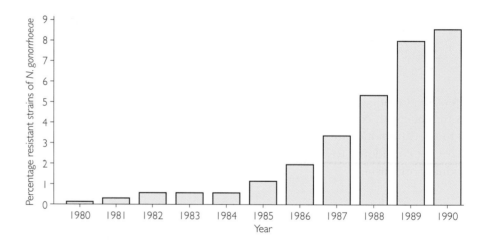

Figure 6.17 Increase of antibiotic resistance – the data show how the percentage of reported cases of gonorrhoea caused by antibiotic-resistant strains of Neisseria gonorrhoeae *has increased over a 10-year period (data from Atlanta, Georgia, USA).*

Preparation and sterilisation of media

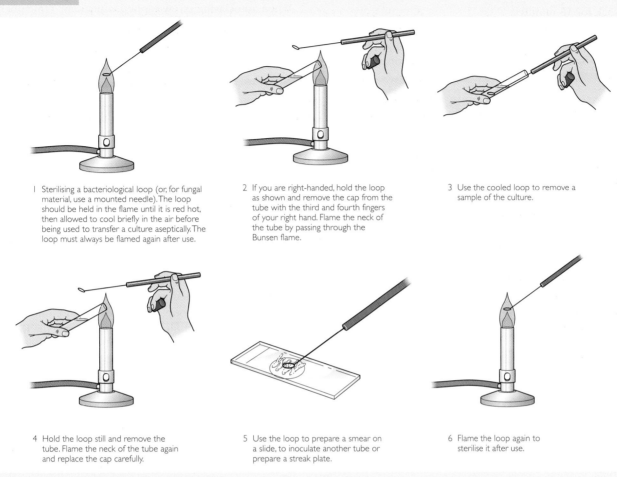

1 Sterilising a bacteriological loop (or, for fungal material, use a mounted needle). The loop should be held in the flame until it is red hot, then allowed to cool briefly in the air before being used to transfer a culture aseptically. The loop must always be flamed again after use.

2 If you are right-handed, hold the loop as shown and remove the cap from the tube with the third and fourth fingers of your right hand. Flame the neck of the tube by passing through the Bunsen flame.

3 Use the cooled loop to remove a sample of the culture.

4 Hold the loop still and remove the tube. Flame the neck of the tube again and replace the cap carefully.

5 Use the loop to prepare a smear on a slide, to inoculate another tube or prepare a streak plate.

6 Flame the loop again to sterilise it after use.

Figure P.1 Aseptic transfer of bacteria (or fungi).

Introduction

There are many different types of media that are used for the culture of microorganisms. These may be obtained in ready-formulated preparations, or can be made up using separate ingredients. In this practical, we look at the method for preparing and sterilising two different media: **nutrient broth**, which can be used for the culture of bacteria, and **malt extract agar**, which is used for the culture of fungi, such as *Penicillium*. If you are using ready-formulated media, follow the manufacturer's instructions carefully, and make up the media using distilled water.

Materials for nutrient broth

- Beef extract   1.0 g
- Yeast extract   2.0 g
- Peptone   5.0 g
- Sodium chloride   5.0 g
- Distilled water   1 dm³
  pH 7.4 (approximately).

Method

1 Add the beef extract, peptone and sodium chloride to the water, heat gently and mix continuously until the ingredients are dissolved. If a solid medium is required (nutrient agar) add 15 g of agar powder to the ingredients and stir until dissolved.

2 Dispense into suitable containers and autoclave at 121 °C for 15 minutes. If using fine agar powder be careful not to inhale any. If using prepared medium tablets, add one tablet to 5 cm³ of distilled water and soak for 15 minutes.

3 Sterilise by autoclaving at 121 °C for 15 minutes. Make sure you are familiar with safe use of the autoclave before doing this.

Materials for malt extract agar

- Malt extract   30.0 g
- Mycological peptone   5.0 g
- Agar powder   15.0 g
- Distilled water   1 dm³
  pH 5.4 (approximately).

Method

1 Add the ingredients to 1 dm^3 of distilled water and leave to soak for 15 minutes.
2 Dispense into suitable containers and sterilise by autoclaving at 115 °C for 10 minutes. If using prepared medium tablets, add one tablet to 5 cm^3 of distilled

water and sterilise by auto-claving at 115 °C for 10 minutes.

When autoclaving screw-capped containers, remember to loosen the lids slightly to allow for expansion of air inside the containers. Tighten the lids again after autoclaving, when the containers have cooled.

PRACTICAL | **Preparation of a heat-fixed smear of bacteria**

Introduction

Before staining bacteria with crystal violet, or using the Gram stain, it is necessary to prepare a heat-fixed smear. This can be stained simply with a solution of crystal violet to see the cells clearly, or stained using Gram's method to distinguish between Gram positive and Gram negative cells.

Materials

- Clean, grease-free microscope slides (Microscope slides should be kept in 70% (aqueous) Industrial Methylated Spirit (IMS) and wiped dry immediately before use. Keep away from naked flames.)
- Freshly grown broth or plate culture of a suitable bacterium such as *Bacillus subtilis*
- Inoculating loop

industrial
methylated spirit
**HIGHLY
FLAMMABLE**

- Bunsen burner
- Small bottle of sterile distilled water
- Crystal violet stain
- Discard jar containing disinfectant.

Method

1 Flame the loop, then transfer a drop of sterile distilled water to the centre of a clean microscope slide.
2 Flame the loop again, then transfer a small drop of the culture to the distilled water on the slide and mix carefully using the loop. Spread the mixture outwards to produce a thin, oval film on the slide. Flame the loop.
3 Dry the film well above, or near, a Bunsen flame. DO NOT ALLOW THE SLIDE TO STEAM.
4 When the film has dried, pass the slide quickly two or three times through the flame to heat-fix.
5 The film can now be stained.
6 After staining and examination using a microscope, the slide should be discarded into disinfectant or an autoclave.

PRACTICAL | **The Gram stain**

Introduction

On the basis of this technique, bacteria can be divided into two groups: **Gram positive** or **Gram negative**. There are major differences between the structures of the cell walls of these two groups (see page 39). Gram positive organisms retain a crystal violet-iodine complex and appear purple, whereas Gram negative organisms are decolourised by organic solvents. The cells are then counterstained using, for example, safranin. Gram negative cells appear red or pink. For reliable results, it is important to use freshly growing cultures of bacteria.

Materials

- Freshly growing broth culture or plate culture of suitable bacteria, such as *Bacillus subtilis*, *Lactobacillus*, or *Escherichia coli*
- Clean, grease-free microscope slides (Slides should be kept in 70% (aqueous) Industrial Methylated Spirit (IMS) and wiped dry immediately before use. Keep away from naked flames.)

- Inoculating loop
- Small bottle of sterile distilled water
- Crystal violet stain (Dissolve 2 g of crystal violet in 100 cm^3 of absolute alcohol. Make up a second solution containing 1 g of ammonium oxalate in 100 cm^3 of distilled water. Add 25 cm^3 of the crystal violet solution to 100 cm^3 of ammonium oxalate solution.)
- Gram's iodine solution (dissolve 1 g of iodine and 2 g of potassium iodide in 300 cm^3 of distilled water)
- Alcohol – 70% (aqueous) IMS to decolourise stained smear (Keep away from naked flames.)
- 1% (aqueous) safranin solution
- Bunsen burner
- Microscope fitted with oil-immersion objective
- Immersion oil
- Discard jar containing disinfectant.

industrial
methylated spirit
**HIGHLY
FLAMMABLE**

Method

1 Prepare a **heat-fixed smear** of bacteria on a clean, grease-free microscope slide.

2 Place the slide on staining bars over a sink and flood the slide with **crystal violet solution**. Leave for 30 seconds then rinse with tap water.

3 Cover the film with **iodine solution**. Leave for 30 seconds, then rinse off the iodine solution with tap water.

4 Rinse the slide with **alcohol**, until the washings are pale violet. Be careful not to over decolourise.

5 Rinse with tap water, then counterstain using **safranin**.

6 Finally, rinse the slide with tap water and gently blot dry.

7 Examine using oil immersion.

Results and further work

1 Compare the appearance of Gram positive and Gram negative bacterial cells

2 Find out about the importance of the Gram's stain in relation to the use of antibiotics.

PRACTICAL | # Preparation of a streak plate of bacteria

Introduction

In this practical, an agar plate will be poured using sterile nutrient agar and inoculated using a culture of a suitable bacterium, such as *Bacillus subtilis*. Streak plates are useful to isolate pure cultures, as individual colonies will have grown from a single cell. Single colonies can be used to subculture another sterile agar plate to obtain a pure isolate.

Materials

- Sterile Petri dishes
- Sterile nutrient agar
- Boiling water bath
- Bacteriological loop
- Slope culture of *Bacillus subtilis*, or other suitable bacterium
- Chinagraph pencil or spirit marker pen.

Method – pouring a sterile agar plate

1 Before starting, wipe the bench surface using a suitable disinfectant solution.

2 Melt the agar in a boiling water bath, remove carefully using tongs and allow to cool to about 45 °C. At this temperature, the agar will be cool enough to handle safely, but will remain molten. Agar starts to set below about 42 °C.

3 On the base of a sterile Petri dish, write your name, the date and the name of the organism with which the plate will be inoculated. Petri dishes should always be labelled on the base, as it is possible for lids to be transposed.

4 Working near a Bunsen burner with a blue flame, hold the bottle of molten, but cooled, nutrient agar in one hand and, using your little finger of the other hand, remove the lid of the bottle. Do not place the lid on the bench.

5 Pass the neck of the bottle through the Bunsen flame then, using the hand in which you are holding the lid of the bottle, raise the lid of the Petri dish to an angle of about 45° and carefully pour in the agar until the dish is nearly half full. Replace the Petri dish lid, flame the neck

of the bottle again and replace the lid.

6 Leave the agar plate to set.

Method – preparing a streak plate

1 Have ready your sterile agar plate and a slope culture of the bacterium to be used.

2 Sterilise the bacteriological loop by holding it in a blue Bunsen flame until red hot.

3 Allow the loop to cool and, whilst still holding the loop, remove the lid from the slope culture using the little finger of the hand in which you are holding the loop. Do not place the lid on the bench.

4 Pass the neck of the culture bottle through the Bunsen flame, then use the loop to remove a small portion of the culture. Replace the lid on the culture bottle.

5 Now lift the lid of the Petri dish and use the loop to streak out the culture as shown in Figure P.2. Be careful not to 'plough up' the surface of the agar. When you have finished, flame the loop again before placing it on the bench.

6 Fasten the lid of the Petri dish using two pieces of adhesive tape. Invert the dish, and incubate at 30 °C for 24 hours.

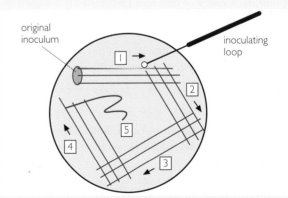

Figure P.2 Preparing a streak plate. Streak in the directions shown by the arrows. The loop should be flamed and allowed to cool between each set of three streaks. Figure 5.3 (page 53) shows a photomicrograph of a streak plate after incubation.

USE OF MICROORGANISMS IN BIOTECHNOLOGY

Results and discussion

1 Record the appearance of your streak plate after incubation. Were you successful in obtaining single colonies of the bacterium?
2 List the different methods of sterilisation which have been used in this practical.
3 Explain why is it important:
   (a) to avoid ploughing up the surface of the agar when inoculating
   (b) not to seal the dishes all the way round with adhesive tape
   (c) to invert the dishes when they are incubated.

Using pipettes and spreaders

For quantitative work, it may be necessary to inoculate an agar plate with a known volume of inoculum, for example, a culture of microorganisms growing in a broth medium, or a milk sample, to enumerate the bacteria present.

For this purpose, a sterile pipette is used to transfer, say, 0.1 cm³ of the inoculum to the surface of the agar. The inoculum is then spread evenly over the surface of the agar using a sterile glass spreader. After incubation, the number of colonies can be counted – we know that this represents the number of viable cells originally present in the volume of inoculum used.

Pasteur pipettes, previously plugged with a small piece of cotton wool and sterilised by autoclaving, can be attached to a 1.0 cm³ plastic syringe (insulin syringes, with the needle removed, are ideal for this purpose) by means of a piece of silicone rubber tubing. After use, the pipette should be placed in a discard jar containing disinfectant.

Glass spreaders can be made from glass rod. These should be sterilised immediately prior to use by dipping in a beaker containing a small volume of Industrial Methylated Spirit (IMS), then passing the spreader through a Bunsen flame and allowing the alcohol to burn off. After use, the spreader should be placed in a discard jar of disinfectant. Remember to keep the beaker of IMS well away from the Bunsen flame. If the IMS in the beaker ignites, cover with a wet cloth. An alternative, avoiding ethanol, is to use cotton wool swabs, wrapped in foil and pre-sterilised by autoclaving.

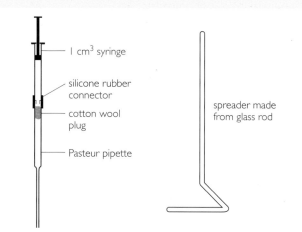

Figure P.3 A pipette and glass spreader.

Using different carbon sources for growth

Introduction

The purpose of this practical is to investigate the ability of yeast to utilise different carbon sources as substrates for respiration. A range of different carbohydrates is used as carbon sources and relative rates of respiration will be determined by measuring the production of acid by the yeast cells: the faster the rate of respiration, the faster the rate of acid production.

Materials

- 2% (aqueous) solutions of the following sugars: glucose, fructose, galactose, sucrose, lactose, maltose
- Top pan balance
- Dried yeast granules
- Seven 500 cm³ flasks, with cotton wool plugs
- Ammonium phosphate and ammonium sulphate
- Incubator, or water bath, set at 25 °C
- Burette and stand
- 0.1 mol dm⁻³ sodium hydroxide solution

- Conical flasks for titration
- 25 cm³ volumetric pipette and filler
- Phenolphthalein indicator solution.

Method

1 Add 200 cm³ of each sugar solution to separate, appropriately labelled flasks. Include one flask containing 200 cm³ of distilled water as a control.
2 Add 2 g of dried yeast and 1 g of culture nutrients to each flask. The culture nutrients are a mixture of equal masses of ammonium phosphate and ammonium sulphate. Swirl the flasks, or stir the contents thoroughly with a glass rod, to ensure that the nutrients dissolve and that the yeast is resuspended.
3 Plug each flask with cotton wool and incubate overnight at 25 °C.
4 Set up a burette containing 0.1 mol dm⁻³ sodium hydroxide solution.
5 After incubation, swirl each flask thoroughly to mix the contents and remove a 25 cm³ sample of each culture.

Place each sample in separate, labelled conical flasks. Add two or three drops of phenolphthalein indicator solution to each.

6 Titrate each sample against the sodium hydroxide solution to find the volume of alkali required to neutralise the acid produced by the yeast.

Results and discussion

1 Record your results in a table. Include class results for titrations, or duplicate your own titrations.

2 Plot a bar chart to show the volume of alkali required to neutralise the acid produced by yeast in each sugar solution.

3 From your results state which sugar produced:
   (a) the fastest rate of respiration
   (b) the slowest rate of respiration.

4 Suggest how the relative rates of respiration may be linked to the growth rate of yeast in the different sugars.

How could you extend this investigation to find the relative growth rate of yeast in the different sugars ?

Further work

This practical can be extended to investigate the effects of different nitrogen sources on the fermentation rate or growth rate of yeast. In the method above, nitrogen is provided in the form of ammonium ions, but you could investigate the effect of adding nitrogen to the medium in the form of urea or as amino acids using casein hydrolysate.

The relationship between growth and nitrogen concentration can be investigated suitably using *Chlorella* (a single-celled green alga), grown in an aerated mineral salts medium. Availability of nitrogen is then controlled by using KNO_3 in the range 1 to 10 mg dm^{-3}.

PRACTICAL ## Counting cells using a haemocytometer

Introduction

A haemocytometer consists of a special glass slide with an accurately ruled etched grid of precise dimensions (Figure P.4). Originally developed for counting blood cells, hence the name, the haemocytometer can also be used for counting microorganisms in a liquid medium. It is particularly suitable for counting yeast or *Chlorella* cells, as these are readily visible and non-motile, but is not suitable for bacteria. Unless special staining techniques are used, it is not possible to distinguish between living and dead cells, therefore this method of counting, known as a **direct count**, gives the total number of cells including both living (or viable) and dead (non-viable) cells. There are several different types of haemocytometers: one which is frequently used is known as the **Improved Neubauer**. This has two counting grids, each of which consists of a central area measuring 1 mm × 1 mm, divided into 25 large squares. Each large square is edged by triple ruled lines and consists of 16 small squares. There are therefore **25 × 16 = 400 small squares** in the counting grid.

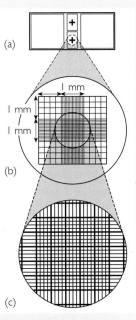

Figure P.4 The Improved Neubauer haemocytometer, viewed at increasing magnifications:
(a) × 0.4; (b) × 7; (c) × 23.

When the coverslip is correctly positioned over the counting grid, the depth of the counting chamber is 0.1 mm; the volume over one small square is therefore 1/4000 mm^3. In practice, we usually count the number of cells present in 5 large squares, that is, 80 small squares, so to calculate the total number of cells present per mm^3, the following formula is used:

$$\text{number of cells per mm}^3 = \frac{N}{80} \times 4000$$

where N is the number of cells counted in **80 small squares**. To use the haemocytometer accurately, it is essential to set it up and fill the counting chamber carefully, otherwise gross errors will be introduced.

Materials

- Improved Neubauer haemocytometer and coverslip
- IMS and tissues to clean the haemocytometer
- Broth culture of suitable organism to count
- 1 cm^3 syringe with needle
- Microscope.

industrial methylated spirit
HIGHLY FLAMMABLE

Method

1 Place the haemocytometer on a flat surface and thoroughly clean the slide and coverslip using alcohol.

2 Slide the coverslip into position using a firm, downward pressure. When correctly positioned, a rainbow pattern (Newton's rings) should be visible along the two edges of the coverslip where it is supported by the slide.

Note: if you are using an ordinary thin coverslip, do not press downwards as this can bend the coverslip downwards and decrease the volume of the counting chamber.

3 Thoroughly mix the cell culture to ensure a homogeneous suspension and, using the syringe, carefully inject a sample of the culture under the coverslip. The culture must exactly fill the silvered part of the counting chamber; it MUST NOT overflow into the grooves on either side. If it does, the counting chamber must be cleaned and refilled.

4 Leave the haemocytometer for at least 5 minutes to allow the cells to settle onto the grid, then, using a low light intensity, carefully focus under the low power of the microscope to locate the grid. When the grid is in focus, increase the magnification to $\times 400$.

5 Count the number of cells present in 5 large squares (80 small squares), using the pattern shown in Figure P.5. Some cells will lie on the boundaries between large squares, that is, touching the triple lines. To ensure a consistent counting method, count only those cells which touch the central line on the north and west sides

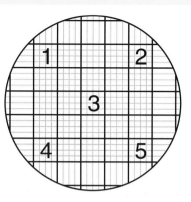

Figure P.5 Count the total number of cells in these five triple-lined squares. What are the dimensions of each triple-lined square?

of the square. Those cells touching the central line on the south and east sides should be ignored.

6 If there are too many cells to count, an accurate dilution, such as 1 in 100, should be made and your final count should then be multiplied by the dilution factor.

Counting cells using the pour plate dilution method

Introduction

Using a haemocytometer gives a direct, total count of the number of cells present in a suspension. The pour plate dilution method will count only viable cells and relies on the ability of each single viable cell to grow and produce a visible colony on an agar plate. The number of colonies will therefore correspond to the number of viable cells that were originally present in the sample. However, it is likely that the original sample will contain far too many cells to count accurately and therefore we make an accurate series of dilutions. Samples of each dilution are then plated out and the number of colonies counted in a suitable dilution. The number of viable cells originally present in the sample is then found by multiplying the number of colonies by the dilution factor.

Materials

- Six universal bottles or similar, capped containers, each containing 9 cm³ of sterile distilled water
- Six sterile Pasteur pipettes, plugged with cotton wool
- Six sterile Petri dishes
- Suitable culture for counting, such as a sample of pasteurised milk
- Supply of suitable sterile medium, molten, kept in a water bath at 45 °C (China blue lactose agar is ideal for counting the number of bacteria present in a sample of milk)
- 1 cm³ plastic syringe, fitted with silicone rubber connector, to attach to Pasteur pipettes

- Bunsen burner
- Chinagraph or spirit marker pen
- Discard jar containing disinfectant
- Incubator at 30 °C.

Method

1 Look carefully at the flow chart (Figure P.6) for this experiment and ensure that you have the necessary materials to hand. Label the containers of sterile distilled water 10^{-1}, 10^{-2}, 10^{-3}, 10^{-4}, 10^{-5} and 10^{-6}, and the six Petri dishes similarly. Remember to label the Petri dishes on their bases.

2 Shake the sample thoroughly to ensure that it is uniformly mixed then, using aseptic technique, transfer 1.0 cm³ to the container labelled 10^{-1}. Use a sterile Pasteur pipette fitted with a plastic syringe. After use, discard the pipette into a jar of disinfectant. Mix this dilution carefully, then, using a fresh sterile pipette, transfer 1.0 cm³ to the container labelled 10^{-2}. Continue in this way until you have completed the dilution series.

3 Using a fresh, sterile pipette each time, transfer a 1.0 cm³ sample of each dilution separately to the appropriately labelled Petri dishes.

4 Again using aseptic technique, carefully pour molten, but cooled, sterile agar medium into each Petri dish. Swirl very carefully to ensure that the sample and agar are thoroughly mixed. Moving the dish gently in a figure-of-eight pattern on the bench will ensure mixing, but DO NOT allow the agar to spill over the edge of the dishes.

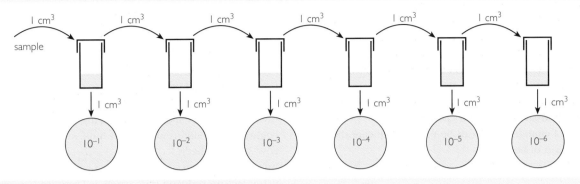

Figure P.6 Flow chart for the pour plate dilution method.

5 Allow the agar to set, then fasten each lid with two pieces of adhesive tape.
6 Invert the dishes and incubate at 30 °C.

Results and discussion

1 After incubation, count the number of colonies in a dish containing a suitable dilution.
2 Calculate the number of viable cells originally present in 1.0 cm^3 of the sample.
3 What are the possible sources of error in this method?

Optical and other methods for measuring the growth of microorganisms

Optical and other methods for measuring the growth of microorganisms

The growth of microorganisms in a broth medium can be measured using optical methods. These rely on the fact that, as the number of microorganisms increases, the medium will become more cloudy, or turbid. The turbidity of the medium is therefore related to the total number of cells in the culture. The turbidity of a cell suspension is measured using an instrument known as a nephelometer, which actually measures the light which is scattered by the cells when a beam of light is passed through the cell suspension.

A colorimeter can be used to measure the light absorbance of a cell suspension; as the number of cells increases, the light absorbance will also increase. This method provides a simple means of measuring cell growth and can be used to provide rapid results by taking samples from a broth medium while the culture is growing. If used with a rapidly growing microorganism, such as *Beneckea natriegens* (*Vibrio natriegens*), a growth curve can be obtained within about 3 hours.

A colorimeter is also suitable for monitoring the growth of *Chlorella* (a single-celled green alga) in a liquid medium. Samples can be removed on a daily basis from a culture growing in an aerated mineral salts medium, in a 500 cm^3 or 1 dm^3 flask, and the absorbance of each sample measured at either 410 nm or 665 nm. For further work, the relationship between absorbance and cell counts, using a haemocytometer, can be investigated.

To measure the **biomass** of a large-scale culture of an organism such as *Saccharomyces*, the cells should be removed by filtration and dried to constant mass, which is then recorded.

USE OF MICROORGANISMS IN BIOTECHNOLOGY

Yoghurt production

Introduction

In this practical, we investigate some of the factors that affect the production of yoghurt. Bacteria in the starter culture ferment milk sugars to produce organic acids, such as methanoic and lactic acid, and consequently the pH will fall. The rate of change in pH can be used to indicate the rate of formation of yoghurt.

Materials

- UHT milk
- Natural yoghurt to use as a starter culture
- Boiling tubes
- Pipettes or syringes
- Cling film
- Glass stirring rod
- pH meter (if unavailable, narrow range pH papers could be used as an alternative)
- Water bath at 43 °C.

Method

1 Transfer 10.0 cm^3 of UHT milk into a boiling tube, then add 1.0 cm^3 of natural yoghurt.
2 Record the pH of the mixture, cover the tube with cling film, and incubate in a water bath at 43 °C.
3 Record the pH and changes in the appearance of the yoghurt at intervals of 30 minutes for up to 5 hours.

Results and discussion

1 Record your results in a table, then plot a graph to show changes in the pH during fermentation.
2 Describe the changes which occurred in pH and in the appearance of the yoghurt during fermentation.

SAFETY NOTE: Food made in a laboratory must not be tasted

Further work

1 Investigate the effect of temperature on the rate of formation of yoghurt, by repeating the experiment at, for example, 20 °C, 30 °C, 40 °C and 50 °C.
2 Investigate the changes in pH during production of yoghurt using different types of milk, such as that from a cow, goat or sheep.
3 Investigate changes in pH during production of yoghurt using lactose-reduced milk, such as Lactolite™, or starter cultures containing *Lactobacillus acidophilus* and *Bifidobacterium bifidum*.
4 Devise a method to investigate changes in reducing sugar content during the production of yoghurt.
5 The relative viscosity of the final product can be measured by determining the time taken for a sample of the yoghurt to pass through a funnel, such as a filter funnel. This is the principle of a viscometer.
6 Devise an experiment to investigate factors affecting the rate of fermentation of sucrose solution by *Saccharomyces cerevisiae*. A simple way of measuring the rate of fermentation is to measure changes in the specific gravity of the sugar and yeast mixture, using a hydrometer. The rate of respiration can also be measured using a respirometer (see *Exchange and Transport, Energy and Ecosystems*, Chapter 1, *Practical: Using of a simple respirometer*). You could investigate the effects of factors such as:
- temperature
- pH of the medium. The pH can be adjusted by using 0.01 mol dm^{-3} citric acid monohydrate, or 0.1 mol dm^{-3} trisodium citrate dihydrate
- initial sucrose concentration (suggested range 0.25 to 2.0 mol dm^{-3})
- the effects of different substrates, such as sucrose, glucose, maltose and fructose using different strains of yeast.

Option B: Food Science

7 Food and diet

Human beings, in common with other **heterotrophic** organisms, require a supply of ready-made organic compounds in order to obtain sufficient energy and materials to sustain life. Heterotrophic organisms that obtain their food from both plant and animal sources are known as **omnivores**. Most human beings are omnivores, feeding on a mixture of products from plant and animal sources. The consumption of meat and meat products by human beings varies and is often affected by social and religious factors. Many groups, including Muslims and Jews, never eat pork or products from pigs; Hindus and Sikhs do not eat beef. **Vegetarians** eat no meat, but many include milk, milk products and eggs in their diets. **Vegans**, who only eat food from plant sources and consume no animal products at all, can be considered to be herbivores.

If we, as consumers, look closely at the origins of the food we eat, we can trace it back to a plant source in a sequence known as a **food chain**. Each organism in the chain occupies a particular trophic level. Most of these food chains are fairly short, consisting of two or three **trophic levels**, as most of our food is derived directly from plants or from animals that eat plants. Examples of food chains and more information about the interrelationships between autotrophic and heterotrophic organisms can be found in *Exchange and Transport, Energy and Ecosystems*.

Balanced diet

A healthy human diet should provide:
- sufficient energy-providing foods to enable the body to carry out internal processes and external activities
- sufficient materials for growth and for the repair and replacement of cells and tissues.

In addition, some of the nutrients we obtain from our food provide substances that are needed to maintain the internal processes of the body.

These dietary requirements are met by the inclusion of five types of nutrients: carbohydrates, lipids (fats), proteins, mineral ions and vitamins, together with water and dietary fibre (non-starch polysaccharides, or NSP).

A balanced diet is generally understood to be one which provides adequate quantities of all the nutrients required by the body and sufficient energy for optimum growth and health. Lack of a particular nutrient could cause a deficiency disease or lead to malnutrition. The quantity of nutrients and energy needed by an individual varies according to their age, gender, body size and level of physical activity.

FOOD AND DIET

QUESTION

Is your diet nutrient-dense or energy-dense? Work out a balance sheet of energy intake and energy expenditure.

Table 7.1 *Calcium and energy content of white bread, boiled potatoes and milk*

Food	Energy /kJ per 100 g	Calcium /mg per 1000 kJ
white bread	991	101
boiled potatoes	343	12
milk	272	441

QUESTION

What do you think is meant by the term 'hidden sugars'? How many of the goods you consume contain such sugars? You should check the labels.

A diet can be described in terms of its **energy density** and its **nutrient density**. The energy density of a food is determined by the quantity of dietary energy provided per unit mass. Foods that provide large quantities of dietary energy have high energy density. If we compare the amount of energy provided by 100 g of chipped potatoes (1065 kJ) with 100 g of boiled potatoes (343 kJ), we can see that, for the same mass, the chips provide the larger amount of energy. The chips have a higher energy density than the boiled potatoes.

The nutrient density is determined by the concentrations of useful nutrients in a known mass of food and it is useful to be able to compare different foods on the basis of nutrients supplied per unit of energy. Table 7.1 compares the calcium and energy content of three common foods: white bread, boiled potatoes and milk. It can be seen that the white bread supplies the greatest quantity of energy, but milk supplies the most calcium per 1000 kJ.

Similar comparisons can be made for other foods. All foods supply some energy and most will supply some nutrients. Refined or processed foods tend to have a low nutrient density, although their energy density may be high. In a healthy balanced diet, the aim should be to maintain a high nutrient density, so that all the essential nutrients are included, but to keep the energy density low. People who use up a lot of energy, due to their occupation or extra physical activity, may need to increase the proportion of energy-dense foods in their diets to satisfy their energy needs.

For the details of the chemical nature of these nutrients, reference should be made to the relevant chapter in *Molecules and Cells*. In this chapter of Option B, the emphasis is on the functions of these nutrients in the body and their sources in our food.

Carbohydrates

Carbohydrates are one of the major groups of nutrients in the human diet. The **monosaccharide** glucose is the main respiratory substrate in the body and a constant supply is required to maintain the metabolic activities of the cells and tissues. Most of the carbohydrate in our diet is in the form of **disaccharides**, such as sucrose and lactose, or **polysaccharides**, such as starch and cellulose, although some monosaccharides are present in fruits. The disaccharides and starch are digested, yielding monosaccharides, which are absorbed from the small intestine into the blood, but we do not produce enzymes that are able to digest cellulose. Some of the cellulose in the fibre in our diet may be broken down by bacteria present in the colon.

Glucose occurs naturally in grapes and other sweet fruits, onions, tomatoes and honey. **Fructose** also occurs in honey and sweet fruit juices. Monosaccharides do not have to be digested and can be absorbed into the blood from the small intestine. Both glucose and fructose are sweet-tasting, but compared with sucrose, glucose tastes less sweet and fructose tastes nearly twice as sweet. By using fructose instead of sucrose in food products, it is possible to obtain the same sweetness for half the quantity, so manufacturers can reduce the calorie content. Fructose for use in the food industry can be made commercially from glucose syrup, which is obtained by hydrolysing starch.

Naturally occurring disaccharides, such as **sucrose** and **maltose** in plants and **lactose** in milk, are also important sources of carbohydrate in the diet. Sucrose is commercially extracted from sugar cane and sugar beet, and is used extensively in the food manufacturing industry. Sucrose is also present in a large number of fruits, grasses and roots. Maltose occurs naturally in germinating seeds. It is extracted from germinating barley grains and used in the manufacture of beer. The lactose in milk provides young mammals with about 40 per cent of their energy requirements.

Disaccharides in the diet are digested by enzymes in the walls of the duodenum and the ileum. The products are monosaccharides, which are absorbed into the blood.

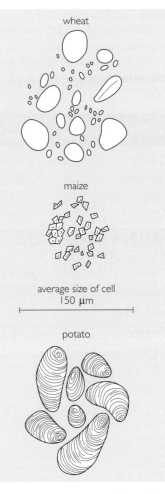

Figure 7.1 Different types of starch grains in cells.

EXTENSION MATERIAL

Oligosaccharides

Oligosaccharides are polysaccharides made up of three to ten monosaccharide units and are present in cereal grains and in vegetables, such as peas, beans, leeks, onions and garlic. These compounds pass through the gut to the large intestine, as we do not produce the enzymes necessary for their digestion. Some bacteria, particularly *Bifidobacteria* and *Lactobacillus*, present in the large intestine, are able to break down the oligosaccharides, producing short-chain fatty acids, carbon dioxide and hydrogen. The presence of the oligosaccharides in the diet promotes the growth of these beneficial bacteria at the expense of harmful bacteria, such as *Clostridium* and the coliform bacteria, which are responsible for infections in the gut.

The polysaccharide **starch** is the main carbohydrate storage compound in plants. It can be found in a variety of plant parts, including stems, roots and tubers. It is particularly abundant in the parenchyma tissue of stem tubers of the potato (*Solanum tuberosum*), the endosperm of cereal grains and the cotyledons of seeds of the Papilionaceae (legumes). The starch is found in the form of grains or granules within cells, and these grains can vary in size and shape within a tissue (Figure 7.1).

Most of the starchy food we eat is cooked. Uncooked starch is very difficult to digest, because the starch grains are contained within the cellulose cell walls of the plant tissue and thus inaccessible to our digestive enzymes. Once the tissue is cooked, the cell walls are softened, allowing water to penetrate and act on the starch grains and causing them to begin to break down and gelatinise. This starch can then be digested by amylase, either in the saliva or in the pancreatic juice. The starch is broken down to maltose, which is further digested to glucose by maltase in the walls of the ileum.

Non-starch polysaccharides (NSPs) are carbohydrates that come from the cell walls of plants. They include **cellulose**, which is insoluble in water, together with water-soluble pectins, hemicelluloses and gums. All these substances were previously referred to as 'roughage', or '**dietary fibre**',

QUESTION

What happens to rice grains as they cook? Design an experiment you could carry out to investigate the changes that occur.

QUESTION

How much fibre do you eat in a day? Check food tables and labels to make an accurate estimate.

Table 7.2 *The non-starch polysaccharide (NSP) content of some natural and processed foods. (The NSP is measured in g per 100 g of food.)*

Food	Soluble NSP	Insoluble NSP
apples	0.72	1.21
potatoes	0.54	0.5
carrots	0.92	1.02
baked beans	1.70	1.50
white bread	1.16	0.44
wholemeal bread	1.66	4.55
rolled oats	3.58	2.91
corn flakes	0.17	0.47
Kellogg's All Bran™	3.74	18.73

although neither term accurately describes their nature nor their roles in the diet. Foods which are high in NSP are usually derived from cereal grains. Wheat, maize and rice yield mostly cellulose, but oats, barley and rye contain a higher proportion of soluble NSP. Non-starch polysaccharides can also be obtained from the fruit and vegetables in the diet, but as the water content is higher, the NSP content is lower. Table 7.2 shows the NSP of some natural and processed foods. It is relevant to note the difference in NSP of white and wholemeal bread, where the use of the whole grains increases the NSP by five times.

Including significant amounts of NSP in the diet has beneficial effects on health. For a long time, it has been known that NSP speeds up the passage of food through the gut ('transit time'), thus promoting regular bowel movements. The stools are larger and softer, possibly due to the absorption of water by the NSP, and so easier to pass. In a typical British diet, the transit time is usually about 100 hours, but this can be reduced to 36 hours if the diet is high in NSP. There is a considerable amount of evidence to show that a diet high in NSP can help prevent many bowel diseases, such as constipation, diverticular disease, cancer of the colon and haemorrhoids, because of the speeding up of the transit time. High quantities of soluble NSP may help reduce the blood cholesterol level in certain people and this may contribute to lowering the incidence of coronary heart disease.

EXTENSION MATERIAL
Other effects of non-starch polysaccharides

The non-starch polysaccharides (NSP) found in cereal grains is associated with compounds which form complexes with mineral ions. The uptake and absorption of mineral ions from the small intestine is not as efficient and so people whose diet is high in NSP and low in minerals could show signs of mineral deficiency. It is recommended that a healthy diet should contain at least 18 g of NSP per day for adults and that this should come from a range of foods such as fruit, vegetables and cereals, so that it includes both soluble and insoluble NSP. An upper limit of 32 g of NSP per day is recommended, to avoid the drawback associated with too much fibre.

NSP is not digested by the digestive enzymes present in the alimentary canal, so it passes unchanged through the stomach and small intestine. When it reaches the large intestine, it is used by the bacteria there, resulting in the formation of short-chain fatty acids, carbon dioxide, hydrogen and methane. Some of the short-chain fatty acids are absorbed and can be metabolised by the body.

Lipids
The term 'lipid' is used to describe a group of naturally occurring fat-like compounds, which are insoluble in water but soluble in organic solvents such as alcohol and ether. **Oils** and **fats** are **triglycerides (triacylglycerols)**, formed from the condensation of glycerol and three fatty acid molecules.

There is no difference in the composition of oils and fats, but they are distinguished by their state at normal room temperature: usually fats are solid and oils are liquid. They form the major stores and sources of energy, having a higher available energy content ($37 \, kJ\,g^{-1}$) than either carbohydrates or proteins ($17 \, kJ\,g^{-1}$). They provide the fat-soluble vitamins A, D, E and K and, on digestion, they provide the body with **essential fatty acids (EFAs)**. EFAs are needed for synthesis and cannot be provided from other constituents of the diet. Only small amounts are needed (2 to 4 g per day) so deficiencies are unlikely to occur in normal individuals eating a balanced diet. Fat acts as a carrier of flavour and aromatic compounds and so its presence makes food more palatable.

Phospholipids have a different structure from fats. Only two of the hydroxyl groups of the glycerol are combined with fatty acids; the third is combined with a complex containing a phosphate group. Phospholipids are concerned with the transport of lipids in the blood and are also important constituents of cell membranes.

Cholesterol is a fat-like substance present in animal tissues. We do obtain a certain amount from the food we eat, but we also make it, especially in the liver. It is present in all cell membranes and is also needed for the synthesis of bile acids and some hormones.

It is of relevance here to consider the different types of fatty acids which may be present in the triglycerides which form part of our diet. There are three types, **saturated, mono-unsaturated (MUFA)** and **polyunsaturated (PUFA)**, differing in structure due to the number of double bonds in the carbon chain. The differences and examples are given in Table 7.3.

Table 7.3 *The differences in structure between saturated and unsaturated fatty acids*

Type of fatty acid	Number of double bonds in the carbon chain	Example
saturated	none	stearic acid $CH_3(CH_2)_{16}COOH$
mono-unsaturated (MUFA)	one $-CH=CH-$	oleic acid $CH_3(CH_2)_7CH=CH(CH_2)_7COOH$
polyunsaturated (PUFA)	two or more $-CH=CH-CH_2-CH=CH-$	linoleic acid $CH_3(CH_2)_4CH=CHCH_2CH$ $=CH(CH_2)_7COOH$

All naturally occurring fats contain both saturated and unsaturated fatty acids. Fats such as butter, which have a higher proportion of saturated fatty acids, are solid at room temperature, whereas those which have a higher proportion of unsaturated fatty acids, such as olive oil, are liquid at room temperature. The more double bonds present in the carbon chains of the constituent fatty acid molecules, the lower the melting point of the fat. Fats obtained from animal sources usually contain a higher proportion of saturated fatty acids than the vegetable oils, although it should be noted that fish oils are very high in PUFAs. Palm oil and coconut oil are high in saturated fatty acids.

In order to function efficiently, the body needs certain fatty acids, which it cannot synthesise. These are known as **essential fatty acids**. They are involved with cholesterol metabolism, the synthesis of some hormones and with the structure of cell membranes. These fatty acids are all PUFAs and have to be obtained from the diet. They are present in large quantities in foods such as vegetable oils, nuts and soft margarine, and it is very rare for there to be a deficiency in a normal person's diet.

EXTENSION MATERIAL

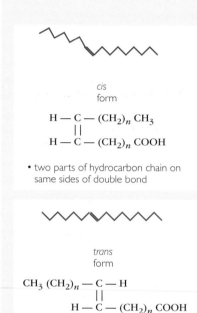

cis
form

$$H - C - (CH_2)_n\, CH_3$$
$$\|$$
$$H - C - (CH_2)_n\, COOH$$

- two parts of hydrocarbon chain on same sides of double bond

trans
form

$$CH_3\,(CH_2)_n - C - H$$
$$\|$$
$$H - C - (CH_2)_n\, COOH$$

- two parts of hydrocarbon chain on opposite sides of double bond

Figure 7.2 Cis *and* trans *forms of fatty acids.*

Cis and *trans* forms of unsaturated fatty acids

Unsaturated fatty acids exist in two forms: the *cis* form, where the two parts of the hydrocarbon chain are on the same side of the double bond and the *trans* form, where the two parts are on opposite sides of the double bond (Figure 7.2). Those naturally occurring unsaturated fatty acids which are essential fatty acids have the *cis* form, but the corresponding *trans* forms are unable to act as essential fatty acids because they are not recognised by enzymes in the body. The significance in our diet is that the process of hydrogenation of oils, used in the manufacture of margarine, brings about the conversion of some of the unsaturated fatty acids to saturated fatty acids and also converts the naturally occurring *cis* forms into *trans* forms. Similar changes can be brought about by heating. The body deals with these *trans* forms of unsaturated fatty acids in the same way as the saturated fatty acids.

The absorption of fatty acids and glycerol resulting from the digestion of fats, differs from that of the other products of digestion. As they enter the columnar epithelial cells of the villi, they recombine to form fats which pass into the lacteals. These fats then combine with proteins and other lipids, forming **lipoproteins** called **chylomicrons**, which will eventually pass from the lymphatic system into the bloodstream by means of the thoracic lymphatic duct. In the blood plasma, an enzyme hydrolyses these lipoproteins, releasing fatty acids and glycerol, which may be used in respiration or stored as fat in the liver, muscles or in the adipose tissue beneath the skin and around the body organs.

In addition to chylomicrons, there are three other types of lipoproteins found in the blood plasma, all of which are involved in the transport of lipids around the body. They are distinguished from each other by their composition and different densities, which are shown in Table 7.4. Much interest has been shown in the levels of these lipoproteins in the blood and whether they play a role in the risk of developing coronary heart disease.

Table 7.4 *The composition of the lipoproteins present in blood*

Type of lipoprotein	Percentage composition			
	Triglyceride	Phospholipid	Cholesterol	Protein
chylomicron	85	9	4	2
very low density (VLDL)	50	18	22	10
low density (LDL)	10	20	45	25
high density (HDL)	4	24	17	55

Proteins

The primary function of proteins in the diet is to supply amino acids for the synthesis of enzymes, certain hormones, and the materials required for growth and repair of the body tissues. Amino acids are not stored in the body in the same way that carbohydrates and fats are stored, and excess amino acids are broken down in a process which produces urea and some energy. So, proteins in the diet have a secondary role as a supplementary source of energy. On oxidation, they yield about the same amount of energy as carbohydrates, 17 kJ g^{-1}. For details of the structure of amino acids and of protein synthesis, reference should be made to Chapter 1 in *Molecules and Cells*.

The protein in our diet is usually supplied from both plant and animal sources. Plant proteins are obtained from cereal grains, nuts and seeds, whereas animal proteins are present in meat, fish, eggs and dairy products. Plants are able to synthesise all the amino acids they require. Animals obtain amino acids from plants and are also able to synthesise some of their own, by transamination, from those they take in. **Transamination** involves the transfer of the amino group from an amino acid to a Krebs cycle (organic) acid, forming a different amino acid (see Extension Material, Figure 7.3). Mammals, including human beings, are unable to synthesise some amino acids and these must be obtained from the diet. These are termed **essential amino acids** or **indispensable amino acids**.

The **nutritional value** of a protein depends on the variety of its constituent amino acids. Animal protein, such as is found in meat, eggs and milk, contains all the essential (indispensable) amino acids in the quantities required by an adult, so it is considered to be high-quality protein. In other foods, such as cereals and legumes, one or more of the essential amino acids may be lacking or not present in sufficient quantities. Where this is the case, the amino acid that is at its lowest level is referred to as the **limiting amino acid**. The deficiency of this amino acid will have an effect on the proteins that can be made in the body. For example, methionine is an essential amino acid, which is low in peas and beans. Low levels of methionine in a diet will limit the use of other amino acids, because as the polypeptide chains are built up, once the code for methionine is reached, protein synthesis will stop. Any amino acids coded for after methionine in that polypeptide will not be used. So, low levels, or the absence of one essential amino acid, eventually prevents the use of the others, leading to protein malnutrition. There is usually no problem in obtaining all the essential

EXTENSION MATERIAL

Transamination

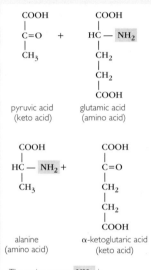

The amino group NH_2 is transferred from glutamic acid to pyruvic acid. Alanine, a different amino acid, is formed.

Figure 7.3 Transamination.

amino acids as normal diets contain a mixture of protein foods, some of plant and some of animal origin. Foods that lack one of the essential amino acids may be eaten with others that lack a different essential amino acid. A meal containing legumes (lacking methionine) eaten with bread (lacking lysine) or sweetcorn (lacking tryptophan) would supply all the essential amino acids. This is known as the complementary action of proteins.

Mineral ions

Mineral ions are needed in much smaller quantities in the diet than carbohydrates, lipids and proteins. Mineral ions are needed for growth and repair of tissues and are also involved in a range of metabolic processes in the body. Mineral ions, such as **calcium** and **phosphate**, are involved in the structure of the bones of the skeleton, **iron** is needed for the formation of haemoglobin in the blood, and **sodium** and **chloride** ions are present in blood plasma and other body fluids. Mineral ions are also important as cofactors for enzymes and enzyme activators. Information relating to some mineral ions in our diet is given in Table 7.5.

Table 7.5 *Major mineral ions needed in the human diet*

Mineral ion	Source	Role	Deficiency
*calcium (Ca^{2+})	cheese, bread, milk	needed for formation of bones and teeth, muscle contraction, nerve function, bloodclotting	poor skeletal growth; soft bones (rickets); muscular spasm
*sodium (Na^+)	all foods have some	acts with potassium in the transmission of nerve impulses; anion–cation balance in cells	muscular cramp
*iron (Fe^{2+}, Fe^{3+})	meat, liver, red wine	constituent of haemoglobin; enzyme activator	anaemia
phosphate (PO_4^{3-})	all foods have some	needed for formation of bones and teeth; component of nucleic acids and ATP	rarely deficient
potassium (K^+)	vegetables, fruit	acts with sodium in the transmission of nerve impulses; anion–cation balance in cells	rarely deficient
chloride (Cl^-)	all foods have some	solute concentration and anion–cation balance in cells; activity of nerve cells	muscular cramp
iodide (I^-) (trace)	sea foods	constituent of thyroxine	cretinism (stunted growth and mental retardation) in children; simple goitre in adults
fluoride (F^-) (trace)	drinking water	contributes to hardness of bones and teeth	dental caries especially in children

*These minerals are named in the specification.

> **QUESTION**
>
> A person has a diet deficient in iron. What symptoms would they have? Explain why these symptoms occur.

Sodium chloride, or **salt**, is an important component of the diet as it is needed for the normal functioning of the body. The sodium ions help to maintain the volume and osmotic pressure of the blood and of the tissue fluids. In addition, sodium ions are needed for the conduction of nerve impulses and help in the transport of carbon dioxide in the blood. In Britain, the average person takes in about 9 g of salt each day with their food. Excess dietary intake is lost in the urine and in the sweat. There is some evidence to show that a high dietary intake of salt is linked with hypertension (raised blood pressure). This relationship is open to debate, but reducing the salt intake in some hypertensive people has brought about a significant reduction in their blood pressure. We do eat more salt than we need to replace that which is lost each day and it has been recommended that salt intake should be restricted to 6 g per day. Babies need very little salt and will become dehydrated if too much is given in their food. Baby-food manufacturers have made significant reductions in the amount of salt added to their products, as it has been shown that, if children develop a taste for salty foods, it is difficult to cut down later in life.

Vitamins

Vitamins are complex organic compounds needed by the body in very small quantities. Most vitamins need to be provided in the diet, although vitamin D can be made in the body by the action of sunlight on the skin and vitamin B6 can be produced from the amino acid tryptophan.

Information relating to some vitamins is given in Table 7.6.

QUESTION

How much of each of the mineral ions stated do we need to remain healthy?

QUESTION

Why do humans require a source of Vitamin C in their diets but elephants do not?

Table 7.6 *Sources, roles and deficiency symptoms of the major vitamins needed in the human diet*

Vitamin	Major source	Role symptoms	Deficiency
*A retinol (fat soluble)	fish liver oil, liver, dairy products; green vegetables contain carotene which is converted to retinol in the body	needed for healthy growth and maintenance of epithelial tissues especially mucus membranes; essential for vision	night blindness
*C ascorbic acid (water soluble)	potatoes, green vegetables, fruits (particularly citrus fruits)	needed for the maintenance of healthy connective tissues	bleeding gums, failure of wounds to heal; scurvy
D calciferol (fat soluble)	fish liver oil, butter, eggs; made by action of sunlight on the skin	needed to maintain levels of calcium and phosphorus in the body; enhances calcium absorption in the intestine	leads to rickets in children in which bones fail to calcify; in adults bones may fracture easily
K phylloquinone (fat soluble)	green leafy vegetables; made by action of bacteria in the gut	needed for the normal clotting of the blood; involved in the formation of prothrombin in the liver	delay in blood clotting
B_1 thiamine (water soluble)	meat, wholemeal bread, vegetables	coenzyme in release of energy from carbohydrates	beri-beri, in which nerves degenerate
B_2 riboflavine (water soluble)	most foods, including milk	coenzyme in electron transport; needed for release of energy from food	rarely deficient
B_3 nicotinic acid [niacin] (water soluble)	meat, wholemeal bread, potatoes, yeast extract	needed for the release of energy from food	skin disease and diarrhoea, pellagra
B_{12} cobalt-containing compounds (water soluble)	liver, yeast extract	needed for nucleic acid synthesis in dividing cells	pernicious anaemia

*These vitamins are named in the specification.

Water

Water may be lost from the body in the following ways: as water vapour in exhaled breath from the lungs, in sweat, in urine, in faeces and in vomit or diarrhoea as a result of illness.

The quantity of water lost from the body varies according to the climate and the amount of physical exertion. If the climate is hot, then we produce more sweat as a way of controlling the body temperature. Evaporation of the water in sweat cools the surface of the body. Similarly, an increase in manual work or physical exercise will increase heat production in the body and cause the temperature to rise, resulting in more sweat production. Physical exercise also increases the ventilation rate, so more water vapour will be lost from the lungs. Water loss in the urine is variable. If we take in more water than we need, then the excess is removed by the kidneys. If less water is taken in, the urine becomes more concentrated and eventually dehydration could occur. As almost all the processes in the body require water, the consequences of dehydration are serious and the inclusion of fluids in the diet is essential. People can survive only for a few days without water, but will live for about 6 weeks if deprived only of food. In addition to replacing fluids lost from the body, water can be a source of mineral ions such as calcium and fluoride. In the diet, water comes mainly from the fluids we drink, but a significant quantity is present in our food, particularly in fresh fruit and vegetables.

DEFINITION

The **basal metabolic rate (BMR)** is the energy needed to maintain essential body processes when the body is completely at rest.

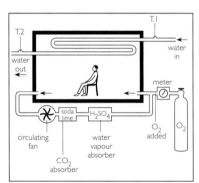

Figure 7.4 A human calorimeter.

Figure 7.5 Recording spirometer.

Energy requirements

Basal metabolic rate

The rate at which the body uses up energy is called the **metabolic rate**. This rate varies throughout the day, according to our activities, and also throughout our lives. A constant supply of energy is used to maintain the essential body processes, such as the pumping of the heart, ventilation, the maintenance of body temperature and chemical processes. These processes go on all the time, even when we are completely at rest. The energy needed for these essential processes is called the **basal metabolic rate (BMR)**, and is determined by our body mass and composition. These factors vary with age and according to gender, with males having higher basal metabolic rates than females. The basal metabolic rate is determined either directly, by measuring heat loss from the body, or indirectly as oxygen consumption per unit time. It is measured when a person is completely at rest in warm conditions and has been fasting for at least 12 hours. As heat energy loss is related to the surface area of the body, basal metabolic rate is expressed as $kJ\ m^{-2}\ h^{-1}$, but it is now considered adequate to define this in terms of the body mass. Thus, BMR can be expressed as kJ of heat energy produced per kg of body mass.

Table 7.7. gives values for the basal metabolic rate in males and females with different body masses and at different ages.

Basal metabolic rates can be measured by using a human calorimeter, such as the one illustrated in Figure 7.4, which works on the same principles as an ordinary calorimeter, measuring temperature changes over a set period of time.

Alternatively, it can be determined by measuring the uptake of oxygen using a recording spirometer, similar to the one shown in Figure 7.5.

As can be seen from Table 7.7, the BMR varies with age, with body mass and with gender. As age increases, the BMR falls and the decrease is greater for

Table 7.7 *Some basal metabolic rate (BMR) values*

Age	Male mass / kg	BMR males / MJ day^{-1}	Female mass / kg	BMR females / MJ day^{-1}
10–18	30	5.0	30	4.6
10–18	65	7.6	60	6.3
19–29	60	6.7	45	4.8
19–29	80	7.9	70	6.4
30–59	65	6.8	50	5.2
30–59	85	7.7	70	5.9

men than for women. The increase in BMR with increase in body mass is to be expected as there is a greater mass of active tissue. The gender differences have already been discussed in relation to the differences in adipose tissue. Other factors which affect the BMR are:

- pregnancy – BMR in females increases during pregnancy and remain high during lactation
- activity of the thyroid gland – overactivity of the thyroid gland (hyperthyroidism) causes an increase in the BMR as the hormone thyroxine speeds up the rate at which chemical reactions take place in the body
- disease – fever causes the BMR to increase by 13 per cent for each °C rise in temperature
- climate – very hot climates cause a reduction of about 10 per cent in the BMR.

Lean body mass

The differences between the basal metabolic rates in men and women have been attributed to the higher proportion of fatty (adipose) tissue in women. This tissue, although well supplied with blood vessels, is less metabolically active than other body tissues. At rest, when basal metabolic rate is measured, the oxygen uptake is mostly due to the activity of the non-fatty tissues, called the **lean body mass (LBM)**. If the BMR is calculated on the basis of the lean body mass, then it is similar in both sexes.

Lean body mass can be calculated from density. It is known that the density of the lean body mass is 1.10, but the density of the whole body is lower, due to the less dense fatty tissues. A thin man will have a density of about 1.075, whereas that of a plump man will be about 1.046. It is difficult to estimate lean body mass directly, as the volume of the body is not easy to measure, but measurements of skinfold thickness can give an indication of the amount of body fat. This can then be deducted from the total body mass to give the lean body mass.

Thermogenesis

As soon as food is eaten, its digestion and absorption leads to an increase in heat production by the body. This is called **diet-induced thermogenesis** and is considered to be caused by the digestive processes and the metabolism of the absorbed food. All food ingestion has this thermic effect and the increase in the BMR is proportional to the energy content of the food eaten.

Physical activity and energy requirements

Having established that the body needs a certain amount of energy to maintain essential internal processes, it is now relevant to consider the variations in energy requirements in relation to daily activities. Any physical activity involves the use of muscles and the more physical activity undertaken, the greater the amount of energy used up. This energy must be supplied by the diet. The effect of physical activity on energy requirements is variable. It will depend on:

- the intensity of the activity – some activities, such as swimming, require much more energy (1470 kJ h^{-1}) than others, such as riding a bicycle (1030 kJ h^{-1})
- the duration of the activity
- the body size – less energy is required to move a small body mass than a large one.

The energy output and hence the energy requirement of an individual depends on their occupation and their leisure activities. Different occupations are classified according to whether they are light (sedentary), moderately active or heavy. Working on the assumption that the average person spends 8 hours resting in bed, 8 hours at work and 8 hours on leisure activities, the energy requirements of people in different occupations have been estimated and are shown in Table 7.8.

Table 7.8 *Estimated energy requirements of people in different occupations*

Activity for 8 hours	Sedentary work / MJ per day	Moderately active / MJ per day	Heavy work / MJ per day
resting in bed	2.0	2.0	2.0
at work	4.0	5.5	7.5
leisure	3.0–7.0	3.0–7.0	3.0–7.0
total	9.0–13.0	10.5–14.5	12.5–16.5

Note the range of figures given for the energy needed for leisure activities: this will vary according to the activities chosen.

As already mentioned, energy requirements will vary according to age, gender and body mass. In Table 7.9, the energy requirements of a 35-year-old female clerical worker are compared with those of a 25-year-old bricklayer, both with a body mass of 60 kg. The bricklayer has moderately active, non-occupational activities, whereas the clerical worker is non-active.

Table 7.9 *Comparison of the energy requirements of a clerical worker and a bricklayer*

Feature	Clerical worker	Bricklayer
Gender	female	male
Age / years	35	25
Body mass / kg	60	60
Energy requirement / MJ per day	7.8	12.0

Unbalanced diet

If the diet contains less than the required quantities of any particular nutrient, or if it contains excessive amounts of nutrients, then it is considered to be unbalanced and thus unhealthy. Both these conditions may lead to serious nutritional disorders if they are allowed to persist.

Under-nutrition

Under-nutrition can be general, eventually resulting in starvation, or more specifically due to lack of a particular nutrient, such as a vitamin or a mineral ion, which results in a deficiency disease. In general under-nutrition, the diet is usually low in energy and protein, giving rise to the deficiency syndrome known as **protein–energy**, or **protein–calorie malnutrition**. This type of malnutrition is common in the poorer countries of the developing world, where protein foods of plant or animal origin may be too expensive or unavailable. Children are more at risk on a low-protein diet as their protein requirements are relatively higher than those of adults. Staple foods, such as cassava, may provide some energy, but they contain little protein. They can be supplemented with protein foods, such as pulses, if they are to satisfy the dietary needs. In some cases, a staple such as rice is not sufficiently energy dense and small children cannot eat enough to supply their energy requirements. Where some protein is available, one or more essential (indispensable) amino acids may be lacking. Under these circumstances, body proteins will be used as an energy source and to provide the essential amino acids.

Marasmus and **kwashiorkor** are forms of protein–energy malnutrition which occur, for example, in children in the developing world. About 20 per cent of children in some areas show mild to moderate symptoms of these diseases and a further 2 per cent are severely affected.

Marasmus is caused by early weaning of a child on to a diet which is very low in both energy and protein. It is also associated with poor hygiene, leading to gastrointestinal upsets. The sufferers are grossly underweight, with thin arms and legs, no body fat and show wasting of the muscles (Figure 7.6). The hair is usually normal, but the face appears old-looking.

Kwashiorkor appears to be linked more with a deficiency of protein in the diet, and develops at a slightly later age than marasmus. In parts of West Africa, young children are weaned on a diet of cassava or green bananas (plantains), usually on the birth of the next child in the family. The carbohydrate content of the diet appears to be adequate, but there is very little protein. This results in symptoms such as muscle wasting and swelling (oedema) in the feet and lower legs, pale thin hair and a moon face (Figure 7.7). The child appears to be miserable and apathetic, and the skin develops patches of pigmentation and becomes flaky. Fat accumulates in the liver and there is a lowering of the blood albumin levels. In severe cases of both marasmus and kwashiorkor, cells in the pancreas and the intestine die, resulting in the reduced production of digestive enzymes and a loss of area over which the absorption of nutrients can occur.

Lack of vitamin A

Vitamin deficiencies may be associated with protein–energy malnutrition and a deficiency of **vitamin A (retinol)** is common in children in developing countries. Retinol is a fat-soluble vitamin present in milk, dairy products and fish liver oils. It is not found in plants, but some carotenoids can act as precursors to vitamin A. The β-carotene present in carrots, green leafy vegetables and yellow fruits can be converted to retinol in the wall of the small intestine. This vitamin is needed for the maintenance of healthy epithelial tissues and for the formation of rhodopsin, the visual pigment required for vision at low light intensities. Deficiency of retinol in the diet results initially in night blindness, which may develop into permanent blindness and a condition known as xerophthalmia. Epithelial tissues become keratinised, leading to infections. This deficiency is linked with poverty in the developing world, where diets often lack the expensive animal products, which contain retinol, or dark green leafy vegetables, containing β-carotene which can be converted into retinol in the body.

Figure 7.6 A child suffering from marasmus.

QUESTION

Draw out a table to compare marasmus with kwashiorkor.

Figure 7.7 A child suffering from kwashiorkor.

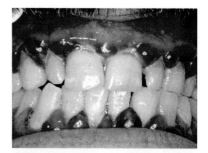

Figure 7.8 Swollen, inflamed gums in scurvy.

Lack of vitamin C

Vitamin C (ascorbic acid) is needed for the synthesis of collagen and tissue proteins, and it is one of the factors which helps in the absorption of non-haem iron. In addition, it is believed to be involved in the formation of some neurotransmitters in the brain and also with drug detoxification. It is an antioxidant and as such has a protective role in the body by preventing the accumulation of 'free radicals' formed by the spontaneous oxidation of fatty acids. It is a water-soluble vitamin which is easily absorbed, the excess being excreted in the urine. Most animals are able to synthesise their own vitamin C, but primates, including human beings, need to have it supplied in the diet. Vitamin C is essential for the formation of collagen, a fibrous protein found in connective tissues such as skin, bone, tendon and cartilage. Collagen forms insoluble fibres with a high tensile strength. It has a triple helical structure, which is maintained by hydrogen bonding between the hydroxyproline residues of the polypeptide chains. Vitamin C is a cofactor required by the hydroxylase which catalyses the synthesis of hydroxyproline from proline. If the diet lacks vitamin C, less hydroxyproline is formed, resulting in fewer hydrogen bonds holding the triple helix together. The collagen structure is therefore less stable and leads to weakness in the tissues of which it is a part. The symptoms of the deficiency disease, **scurvy**, are bleeding gums, haemorrhages under the skin, poor wound healing and painful joints, all of which can be attributed to poor formation and maintenance of the connective tissues containing collagen (Figure 7.8).

Because it aids the absorption of non-haem iron, a deficiency may also lead to iron-deficiency anaemia. Good sources of this vitamin in the diet are green vegetables, potatoes and fruit, particularly citrus fruits. Potatoes do not contain large quantities of the vitamin, but make a significant contribution due to the amounts consumed. It is an unstable vitamin, which is destroyed on exposure to high temperatures, oxidation and light. The vitamin C content of foods is reduced on cooking and significant losses take place after harvesting. A diet that does not include fresh vegetables or fruit may be deficient in this vitamin.

Lack of iron

Lack of iron in the diet can result in **iron-deficient anaemia**, which causes general debility, pale appearance and breathlessness. This deficiency is particularly common in women and may occur in infants and young children. In developing countries, the condition may be linked with the occurrence of malaria, where the parasite causes the breakdown of the red blood corpuscles. This results in the release of haemoglobin into the blood plasma: it is broken down and the iron is lost in the urine.

We obtain most of our **iron** from meat, cereals and vegetables, but it is only present in these foods in very small amounts and much of what we ingest passes through the gut without being absorbed. Most adults, eating a diverse diet, only absorb about 15 per cent of the iron present in their food. The amount of absorption is influenced by:
- the source of the iron, whether it is from meat (haem iron) or from plant material (non-haem iron)
- the presence of inhibitors or enhancers of absorption
- the amount of iron already stored in the body.

The iron in meat is organically bound and is absorbed much more readily than the non-haem iron present in plants. This has implications for vegetarians: their dietary intake of iron should be increased to compensate for the lower absorption. Events such as menstruation and pregnancy in women, or a haemorrhage, will increase the absorption of iron. Non-haem iron can combine with other components of the diet, such as phosphates and phytic acid (present in whole cereal grains), resulting in the formation of insoluble salts which cannot be absorbed. However, iron absorption is increased in the presence of vitamin C and alcohol. Vitamin C reduces ferric forms of iron to ferrous forms, which are more easily absorbed. On the other hand, tea causes the formation of insoluble tannic acid salts with iron, inhibiting uptake.

Lack of calcium

The most important sources of **calcium** and **phosphate** ions are bread, flour, milk and dairy products. The calcium in milk is absorbed readily, due to the presence of lactose which keeps it soluble. Some calcium ions are present in drinking water and significant amounts are consumed in 'hard' water areas, where there are large quantities of calcium sulphate and calcium hydrogencarbonate in the domestic water supplies. A large proportion of the calcium needed by an adult is obtained from processed cereal grains used to make flour and bread. In the process of milling cereal grains, there are significant losses of mineral ions and other nutrients and, in Britain, chalk (calcium carbonate) is added to flour to increase the calcium content, unless the flour is made from whole grains. So white bread is higher in calcium than brown bread. Calcium is absorbed through the lining of the small intestine. The ions bind with a special protein, known as a **calcium-binding protein**, which is present in the intestinal mucosa. The presence of vitamin D is necessary for the formation of the calcium–protein complex: most cases of poor calcium absorption, which may lead to rickets in children or a condition known as osteomalacia in adults, are more often due to a deficiency of vitamin D than shortage of calcium in the diet. In addition, the absorption of calcium can be inhibited by the presence of several factors, including:

- phytic acid, found in whole cereal grains
- oxalates, found in rhubarb and spinach.

These compounds react with the calcium to form insoluble compounds, which cannot be absorbed. The most readily absorbed form of iron is in the haem of haemoglobin, present in red meats, so vegetarians may be at risk of suffering from a deficiency.

Figure 7.9 Anorexia.

Anorexia nervosa and bulimia nervosa

The examples of under-nutrition so far discussed have been the result of poor diets, lacking essential nutrients because they are either unavailable or too expensive. Where the eating disorders anorexia nervosa and bulimia nervosa are concerned, the under-nutrition is self-induced.

Anorexia nervosa affects mainly adolescent girls and young women, although it does occur occasionally in young men. The condition starts with dieting to reduce weight, but the dieting may then become so obsessive that the weight loss becomes severe and the body becomes emaciated. In girls, the menstrual periods stop (amenorrhoea) and the sufferer may also have low blood pressure,

> **QUESTION**
>
> Explain how vomiting in bulimia nervosa brings about the symptoms described in the text.

cold extremities and downy hair. Anorexic people are fearful of becoming fat and will overestimate the size of their own body. They may show personality changes, a reduction in their social life and act aggressively within the family. The causes are difficult to diagnose, but psychological factors play a significant role, the sufferers often experiencing feelings of inadequacy and an inability to cope with changes taking place at puberty. Once the condition is recognised, recovery, which involves dietary help and psychotherapy, may take as long as 2 to 3 years and many sufferers never return to normal eating habits.

Bulimia nervosa involves an irresistible urge to overeat, or 'binge' on food, followed immediately by self-induced vomiting. Laxatives, diuretics or purgatives may also be used in attempts to prevent weight gain. There may be strict dieting or fasting, as well as vigorous exercising, in between the recurrent episodes of binge eating. The frequent vomiting may lead to a loss of potassium, chloride and hydrogen ions, which will upset the balance of serum electrolytes in the body. Other symptoms include dental erosion, sore throat, swollen salivary glands, fatigue and constipation. Sufferers from bulimia nervosa may not show the extreme weight loss that is characteristic of anorexia nervosa. The condition may develop in people with a history of anorexia nervosa, but bulimia is a distinct disorder and does not occur as a consequence of anorexia nervosa.

Over-nutrition

Overnourished people take in more food than they need and may become **overweight** or **obese**. It has been estimated that, in the UK, about 60 per cent of men and 40 per cent of women are overweight or **obese**. Overweight people are more susceptible to illness as they become older.

Body mass index

It is relevant here to define what is meant by 'overweight' and to distinguish between that term and obesity. An obese person has an excessive amount of body fat. In everyone, a certain proportion of the body mass is composed of fatty (adipose) tissue. There is a subcutaneous layer, necessary for insulation, and there is adipose tissue around the kidneys and other organs. In men, it is acceptable that between 12 and 17 per cent of the body weight is made up of fatty tissue. In women, this proportion rises slightly to between 20 and 25 per cent. It is useful to be able to assess whether or not a person is underweight, overweight or obese, and to do this the height and body mass are used to calculate a **body mass index (BMI)**. The body mass, in kg, is divided by the height, in metres, squared.

$$BMI = \frac{body\ mass}{(height)^2}$$

So, the BMI of a person with a body mass of 65 kg and height 1.72 m would be 21.78. Reference to Table 7.10 will indicate to which category the person belongs. For this person, the figure falls between 20 and 24.9, which is considered to be normal.

Causes and effects of overweight and obesity

It is very difficult to determine exactly what causes obesity. We know that an obese person has a greater proportion of adipose tissue than a normal person

Table 7.10 *The use of Body Mass Index (BMI) to classify body weight*

Body Mass Index (BMI)	Description of body weight
below 20	underweight
20–24.9	normal
25–29.9	overweight
30–40	moderately obese
over 40	severely obese

and we also know that weight gain occurs only if the energy content of a person's diet exceeds their energy expenditure. The excess energy intake is stored as fat. It is also known that excessive alcohol consumption can contribute to weight gain, because alcohol has a high energy content. Overweight people do not necessarily eat more than people with a normal weight – very often they eat less. As there is much interest in controlling obesity, several factors which might cause it have been considered. These include:

Figure 7.10 Obese persons.

- **metabolic factors** – do fat people have a different metabolism from thin people? The BMR of obese people may be higher than that of people of normal weight. The results of studies on metabolic rates and the thermic response to extra food in the diet suggest that there are differences in the way that food energy is used by different individuals and that overeating does not result in similar degrees of weight gain.

- **the nature of the food in the diet** – are some foods more fattening than others? There does not appear to be any evidence to suggest that any particular food can promote weight loss or weight gain. Obviously it is important to control the proportions of energy-dense and nutrient-dense foods in the diet in order to promote or prevent changes in weight.

- **levels of physical activity** – reducing physical activity in people who are overweight may contribute to weight gain, but there does not seem to be much evidence to support the idea that low levels of physical activity on their own cause obesity.

- **eating behaviour** – the more palatable the food, the more of it we are likely to eat, whether we need it or not. The reasons for eating food, apart from satisfying our daily nutritional requirements, are complex, but it has been observed that overweight people tend to underestimate the quantities of food that they consume.

- **genetic factors** – do we inherit a predisposition to obesity? It is difficult to separate out any genetic influence from all the other factors, but studies have indicated that there is some correlation between the BMIs of parents and their offspring. However, the recent rapid increase in the prevalence of obesity is unlikely to be due to a change in the gene pool, so it may be that overeating is learned by offspring from their parents.

- **hormonal factors** – these do not appear to cause obesity, but hormonal abnormalities are more likely to result from obesity. For example, overweight people are more likely to develop Type 2 (maturity onset) diabetes than people of normal weight.

- **psychological factors** – it has been suggested that overeating leading to obesity is a form of stress-induced behaviour. It has even been proposed that some people develop an addiction to carbohydrates in the same way as they might develop an addiction to drugs or alcohol.

Obese people have a higher mortality rate than people of normal weight. It has been estimated that a BMI of 35 causes the mortality rate to be twice that for people of the same age with a BMI of between 20 and 25. Obesity has been shown to be a contributory or causative factor in a number of different conditions. These include:
- coronary heart disease
- hypertension (increased blood pressure)
- mature onset diabetes

- an increased risk of osteoarthritis, especially of the knees, hips and spine
- an increased risk of complications during surgery
- infertility in women
- gall bladder disease – especially in women
- difficulties in childbirth in women
- an increased risk of developing toxaemia during pregnancy
- an increased risk of breast, cervical and uterine cancer in women
- an increased risk of cancer of the colon, rectum and prostate gland in men.

In view of these many and varied effects, the treatment of obesity is important. The main objective of any treatment is to reduce the amount of energy intake, especially from fat, whilst increasing the amount of energy expenditure by the body. Basically, this means eating less and doing more exercise. But it is not quite as simple as that, because the amount of energy expended on quite vigorous exercise is low. However, regular exercise will tone the body and help to stimulate greater diet-induced thermogenesis (heat production in response to food intake).

Ideally, weight loss should be gradual and the overweight person should recognise the benefits of making permanent dietary changes in order that, once any diet has been stopped, their weight does not increase again. Crash diets, which cut down drastically on the quantity of food consumed, are dangerous to general health, because important nutrients will be lacking. Very low-calorie diets have been popular because they lead to rapid weight loss, but they may produce unpleasant side-effects such as diarrhoea and nausea. If continued for long periods, such diets could result in deficiency symptoms. In addition, such drastic dieting does not result in a change in eating habits. The best strategy is a diet that is low in energy and fat with a high nutrient density, combined with an active lifestyle.

Diseases linked to diet

Coronary heart disease

There are a number of different factors associated with coronary heart disease, including family history of heart disease, increased plasma cholesterol, diabetes, high blood pressure, smoking and obesity, but diet is probably the most important environmental factor. The basis of coronary heart disease is the formation of arteriosclerosis, a descriptive term for hardening, thickening and loss of elasticity of blood vessel walls. The most common type of arteriosclerosis affects the large and medium-sized arteries, in which there is an underlying abnormal change in the vessel wall known as **atheroma**. This type of arteriosclerosis is, therefore, known as **atherosclerosis**. Accumulation of lipids and other changes in the structure of the vessel wall result in the formation of a raised **atheromatous plaque**, which narrows the lumen of the artery and obstructs blood flow (Figure 7.11). This type of atheroma occurs commonly in the coronary artery of cigarette-smoking males. A frequent symptom of this narrowing of the coronary artery is a condition known as angina pectoris, a pain in the chest, particularly following exertion and settling with rest. Further narrowing of the lumen of the coronary artery can abruptly reduce blood flow to the heart muscle, which becomes deprived of oxygen, resulting in tissue death. This death, or necrosis, of an area of cardiac muscle is known as **myocardial infarction**, often referred to as a **heart attack**.

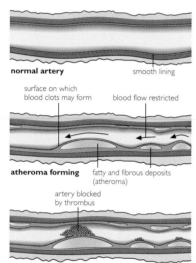

normal artery   smooth lining

surface on which blood clots may form   blood flow restricted

atheroma forming   fatty and fibrous deposits (atheroma)

artery blocked by thrombus

thrombus forming

if clot breaks free it may cause a blockage (embolism) elsewhere in the circulation

Figure 7.11 The development of atherosclerosis. Fat deposits, called atheromas, are built up under the endothelium of artery walls from low-density lipoproteins. Collagen fibres may also be laid down with the fat, forming irregular raised patches which impede the flow of blood along the artery. Eventually the endothelium breaks down and the blood comes into contact with the deposits. Blood platelets stick to the atheroma and may form a clot (thrombus), blocking the artery still further.

The factors that are likely to lead to severe atherosclerosis are now well recognised and can be divided into three main groups:
- constitutional factors, including age, sex and genetic factors
- 'hard risk' factors, including high plasma cholesterol concentration, high blood pressure and smoking
- 'soft risk' factors, such as lack of regular exercise, obesity and stressful lifestyle.

The material which accumulates in atherosclerosis is cholesterol, which is transported in the blood, associated with lipoproteins (low-density lipoproteins, LDL). The risk of coronary heart disease increases steadily with increased plasma cholesterol (Figure 7.12). Many investigations have shown that people with plasma cholesterol concentrations higher than 6.5 mmol dm^{-3} are at high risk; people with plasma cholesterol concentrations between 5.2 and 6.5 mmol dm^{-3} are at moderate risk.

The main dietary influence on plasma LDL and cholesterol is the amount and type of fat in food. Polyunsaturated fats, particularly linoleic acid, tend to lower plasma LDL and total cholesterol. Other dietary factors associated with coronary heart disease include **non-starch polysaccharides** (dietary fibre) and possibly **salt** (sodium chloride). The effect of non-starch polysaccharides depends on the type. Insoluble forms, such as cellulose, do not decrease plasma cholesterol, but soluble types, including pectins and gums, may help to reduce plasma cholesterol. Soluble non-starch polysaccharides are present in oatmeal, beans, fruit and vegetables. High salt intake probably causes high blood pressure, but the evidence supporting this is not clear. Nevertheless, it is recommended that the salt intake should not exceed 6 g per day.

Diseases of the colon

The chemical nature, sources and importance of non-starch polysaccharides (NSP) are described earlier in this chapter. The laxative effect of NSP is generally well known, but dietary NSP is important in several other aspects of health, including **constipation, cancer of the large intestine, diverticular disease** and **irritable bowel syndrome**. Diets rich in the soluble forms of NSP may help to lower blood cholesterol levels, which may, in turn, reduce the incidence of coronary heart disease. Malignant tumours of the colon and rectum are very common, particularly in Western countries, and are the second largest cause of death from cancer. It has been shown that wheat fibre, fruit and vegetables may offer some protection. Epidemiological studies have shown that stool weights below 150 g per day are associated with an increased risk of bowel cancer. NSP decreases the transit time, which reduces the time for which any potentially carcinogenic substance is in contact with the mucosa of the intestine.

Non-starch polysaccharides, which are not digested in the human stomach or small intestine, reach the colon where they are fermented by bacteria. This process produces a number of substances, including short-chain fatty acids such as butyrate. Butyrate has been shown to regulate cell growth in the large intestine and may help to prevent cells in the colon from developing into a cancer.

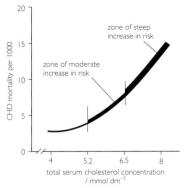

Figure 7.12 The relationship between total cholesterol and risk of coronary heart disease based on a 6-year study of over 350 000 middle-aged men in the USA.

QUESTION

What general dietary guidelines would you recommend to lower plasma cholesterol? Design a day's menu with a low fat content, which is high in NSP, antioxidant vitamins and folic acid.

FOOD AND DIET

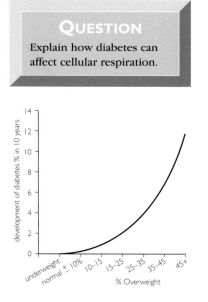

Figure 7.13 The relationship between body weight and subsequent development of Type 2 diabetes.

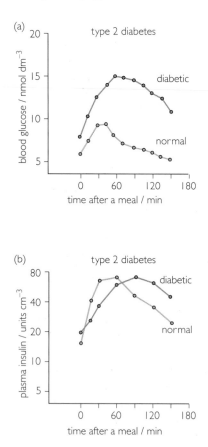

Figure 7.14 Glucose (a) and insulin (b) levels in the blood of Type 2 individuals, compared with normal levels. Levels were measured at half-hourly intervals.

Diverticular disease and constipation are both common in the elderly, although they can occur at any age and are found predominantly in the Western hemisphere. Diverticular disease arises as increased pressure within the colon results in the formation of 'pouches' of the mucosa which project through areas of the circular muscle layer. It is possible that this results from abnormally high pressure in the colon associated with low NSP diets. Irritable bowel syndrome is a condition involving the small and large intestine and is characterised by abdominal pain, constipation or diarrhoea, and nausea. There is some evidence that this is caused by sensitivity to certain foods, including dairy products, maize, some fruits, tea and coffee. It is important to ensure enough NSP in the diet to promote regular bowel habit.

Mature onset diabetes mellitus

Diabetes mellitus is one of the most common disorders of the endocrine system and, in 1996, affected about 1.4 million people in the UK. In people with diabetes, an inadequate amount of insulin may be produced. In some other affected people, decreased numbers of insulin receptors on the target cells make it impossible for glucose to be taken up by these cells even if insulin is present. Insulin, which is produced by the β cells of the pancreatic islets, increases the uptake of glucose, fatty acids and amino acids from the blood and into tissue cells. Consequently, insulin decreases the blood concentrations of these substances and promotes their metabolism by tissue cells, chiefly skeletal muscle, adipose tissue and liver. In diabetes mellitus, glucose cannot enter cells normally and the result is an increase in blood glucose concentrations, a condition known as hyperglycaemia. The normal resting levels of glucose in the blood are between 4.5 and 5.5 mmol dm^{-3}, but in hyperglycaemia the resting blood glucose concentrations may rise to 11 mmol dm^{-3}, and up to 28 mmol dm^{-3} following a meal. Glucose will be filtered out of the blood in the kidneys, but the rate of appearance of glucose in the filtrate exceeds the rate at which glucose can be reabsorbed. As a consequence, glucose appears in the urine. Glucose remaining in the filtrate has an osmotic effect, resulting in larger than normal volumes of urine being produced, with consequent dehydration and feelings of thirst. In untreated diabetes, cells are unable to use glucose as a substrate for respiration, so substances such as amino acids and fatty acids are used instead.

If glucose metabolism is severely reduced, metabolism of large quantities of fatty acids produces toxic by-products known collectively as **ketone bodies**. A build up of these substances reduces the pH of the blood from 7.4 to 7.0, resulting in a condition referred to as **diabetic ketoacidosis**. Symptoms of this include abdominal pain, nausea, a 'fruity' (pear-drops) odour of the breath, unconsciousness and coma, and, if untreated, may lead to death.

There are two main types of diabetes mellitus: **Type 1** and **Type 2**.

Type 2 diabetes, or non-insulin-dependent diabetes (Figure 7.14), is the most common form of this disorder and accounts for about 90 per cent of all cases. This type occurs most often after the age of 40 and was formerly known as **mature onset diabetes**. In this form of diabetes, insulin is still produced by the β cells, but loss of insulin receptors on the cell surface membranes of target cells may reduce the uptake of glucose from the blood. The development of Type 2 diabetes is closely associated with obesity (Figure 7.13), although hereditary factors are also important. In Type 2 diabetes, injection of insulin may not be required and hyperglycaemia can be controlled by eating a balanced diet, taking adequate exercise and maintaining body weight within normal limits.

The organisation Diabetes UK recommends that diets for people with diabetes should contain:
- at least 50 per cent of calories as carbohydrates, mostly from foods high in starch
- about 30 to 35 per cent of calories as fats, with saturated fats restricted to 10 per cent.

ADDITIONAL INFORMATION

Type 1 diabetes mellitus is also referred to as **juvenile onset diabetes**, because it usually occurs before the age of 40. In this form of diabetes, secretion of insulin is very low, or absent. People with Type 1 diabetes are required to take regular injections of insulin to control hyperglycaemia and prevent ketoacidosis. Type 1 diabetes (Figure 7.15) is therefore also known as insulin-dependent diabetes.

People with diabetes are advised to:
- eat regular meals and eat similar amounts of starchy foods from day to day
- eat foods which are high in NSP, especially beans, peas, lentils, vegetables, fruit and oats
- cut down on fried and fatty foods including butter, margarine, cheese and fatty meat
- reduce intake of sugar by replacing high-sugar foods, such as tinned fruits in syrup, for low-sugar foods
- drink alcohol in moderation only.

In Type 1 diabetes, the emphasis should be on foods which are low in fat and have a low glycaemic index, such as lentils and other legumes, pasta, All Bran™, cherries, apples, oranges and peaches. Diets which are high in non-starch polysaccharides (NSP) have also proved to be helpful to people with diabetes. In particular, the soluble forms of NSP are able to reduce the rate of uptake of glucose from the gut into the bloodstream.

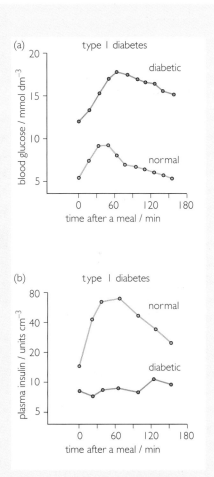

Figure 7.15 Glucose (a) and insulin (b) levels in the blood of Type 1 individuals, compared with normal levels. Levels were measured at half-hourly intervals.

8 Food additives

For centuries, humans have used a range of food additives, mainly as preservatives to increase the time for which food can be kept in a palatable condition. Foods are organic and provide a range of nutrients for microorganisms, which may cause spoilage. Unless treated in some way, numerous microorganisms, including bacteria and fungi, will grow on foods resulting in spoilage and increasing the risk of food poisoning. Cereal grains, such as wheat and barley, are an exception to this and, if kept dry, will last for years without deteriorating.

Food additives are substances that are added in small amounts to processed foods for a specific purpose. The Food Labelling Regulations (1984) define an additive as:

'any substance not commonly regarded or used as a food, which is added to or used in or on food at any stage to affect its keeping qualities, texture, consistency, appearance, taste, odour, alkalinity or acidity or to serve any other technological function in relation to food.'

Additives can be classified into two main groups: those which prevent spoilage, and those which are added to improve the flavour, texture or appearance of the food. Some examples of microorganisms that cause food spoilage are shown in Table 8.1.

Table 8.1 *Examples of microorganisms that cause spoilage of fresh foods*

Food types	Types of microorganisms	Examples that cause spoilage
fruit and vegetables	bacteria	*Erwinia, Pseudomonas*
	fungi	*Aspergillus, Rhizopus, Penicillium*
fresh meat, including poultry and seafood	bacteria	*Escherichia, Proteus, Pseudomonas, Salmonella*
	fungi	*Mucor, Penicillium, Rhizopus*
milk	bacteria	*Lactobacillus, Streptococcus*

Only substances that are known as permitted additives may be used in food. Most permitted additives have been allocated a serial number and where the use of that additive is also controlled by the European Union (EU), the number is prefixed by an E-. Some additives are permitted in the UK and some other countries, but are not covered by EU legislation. These have numbers without the E- prefix. Examples of the major types of food additives and their uses are shown in Tables 8.2 and 8.3.

Table 8.2 *Some examples of permitted food additives*

E-numbers	Category	Examples
E-100 to E-180	colouring materials	E-102 tartrazine
E-200 to E-290	preservatives	E-211 sodium benzoate
E-300 to E-322	antioxidants	E-300 ascorbic acid
E-400 to E-483	emulsifiers and stabilisers	E-412 guar gum

Table 8.3 *Examples of permitted food additives and some of their uses*

Food additives	Examples	Uses
antioxidants	ascorbic acid, propyl gallate, butylated hydroxyanisole (BHA), tocopherols	used to prevent oxidation of fats and oils by atmospheric oxygen, resulting in the development of rancid flavours
colours	natural – β-carotene, chlorophyll synthetic – tartrazine, erythrosine	mainly used to make food products look attractive to the consumer
flavour enhancers	monosodium glutamate, sodium inosinate	used to enhance the taste or smell of food without giving any flavour of their own
preservatives	sorbic acid, sulphur dioxide, sodium metabisulphite	inhibit the growth of bacteria and fungi in foods and therefore prevent microbial spoilage
sweeteners	sorbitol, mannitol, saccharin, aspartame, acesulpham-K	used to impart a sweet flavour to foods and drinks; used in low-calorie products

Sweeteners

Simple sugars, including glucose and fructose, are found in honey and various fruits. These simple sugars are often mixed with disaccharides, such as sucrose, found in sugar beet and sugar cane. The chemical nature, occurrence, digestion and absorption of sugars have been described in *Molecules and Cells*, Chapter 1, and *Exchange and Transport, Energy and Ecosystems*, Chapter 1.

The degree of sweetness varies widely and not all sugars have a sweet taste. **Sucrose** is used as the standard reference substance for sweetness. It has a threshold concentration (minimum concentration which produces a response on the tongue) of 0.01 mol dm^{-3}. The degree of sweetness of different sugars is usually compared with that of sucrose, which has been assigned a relative sweetness (RS) of 1.0. As it is not possible to say with certainty that a substance is so many times sweeter than sucrose, relative sweetness is determined by finding the concentration of the substance which can be tasted. **Relative sweetness** is then calculated from this concentration relative to the threshold for sucrose.

Fructose tastes sweeter than sucrose, but glucose, maltose and lactose are less sweet than sucrose. The relative sweetness of various sweeteners, both natural and artificial, is shown in Table 8.4. **Aspartame** is an artificial sweetener which is used in low-calorie products.

Thousands of sweet-tasting substances have been identified, including a wide range of chemical classes, but only about 20 are permitted for use in food (Table 8.5, page 104). As far as legislation is concerned, the common food sugars and glucose syrups are not considered to be sweeteners. Artificial sweeteners are classified as either bulk sweeteners or intense sweeteners. Bulk sweeteners are generally less sweet-tasting than sucrose, but intense sweeteners may be thousands of times sweeter than sucrose. Intense sweeteners are useful in the formulation of low-calorie food products, but many have the disadvantage of unpleasant aftertastes, such as bitterness or a metallic taste. Bulk sweeteners taste very similar to sucrose, but have similar calorific values. They do, however, have advantages, including stability in

Table 8.4 *Relative sweetness of various sweeteners*

Sweetener	Relative sweetness
sucrose	1.0
fructose	1.73
glucose	0.74
honey	0.97
sorbitol	0.5
aspartame	200.0
saccharin	300.0

solution, and may be used in confectionery, rendering it less harmful to teeth. Bulk and intense sweeteners are sometimes used in combinations which can create a synergistic effect, that is, the intensity of sweetness is greater than the sum of the individual parts, and the overall quality of taste may be improved.

EXTENSION MATERIAL

Table 8.5 *European permitted sweeteners from the 1994 EU directive*

Bulk sweeteners	Relative sweetness	Intense sweeteners	Relative sweetness
sorbitol	0.5	saccharin (and its Na, K and Ca salts)	300
mannitol	0.5	acesulpham-K	200
maltitol	0.9	aspartame	200
xylitol	1.0	thaumatin	3000
isomalt	0.45	cyclamate	30
lactitol	0.35	neohesperidin dihydrochalcone	1250

QUESTION

The confectionery industry produces over 2000 types of products. What are the requirements to be considered for the sweeteners they use?

Some **commercial enzymes** are used in the food-processing industry to modify carbohydrates and so alter the sweetness or other properties of the food (Table 8.6). The enzymes are often derived from microorganisms and this illustrates how the production of extracellular enzymes by microbes can be exploited (see *Molecules and Cells*, Chapter 3). Growing microorganisms on a large scale to harvest their enzymes is now big business in the food-processing industry. The microorganisms are grown in bulk in large fermenters, then the enzymes are usually separated and purified before being used for the particular process concerned. The enzymes are frequently immobilised, which allows for more efficient processing and recovery of the products.

Glucose isomerase is used in the manufacture of high fructose corn syrup (HFCS), from cheap syrups with a high glucose content (Figure 8.1). The importance of HFCS is that fructose is sweeter than glucose, but has the same

Table 8.6 *Uses of some enzymes in the food industry*

Enzyme	Product	Reason for use
glucose isomerase	soft drinks	conversion of high glucose syrup (obtained from breakdown of starch) to high fructose syrup
amyloglucosidase (glucoamylase)	sweeteners low-carbohydrate beer wine and fruit juice bread manufacture	saccharification saccharification starch removal improved crust colour
β-galactosidase (lactase)	whey syrup lactose-reduced milk and dairy products ice cream	greater sweetness removal of lactose (for those who are lactose intolerant) prevention of 'sandy' texture caused by lactose crystals

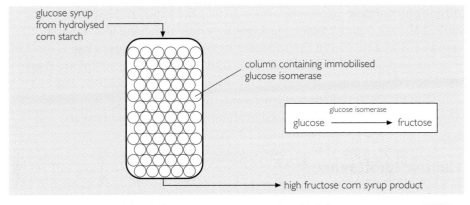

Figure 8.1 Use of immobilised glucose isomerase to produce high fructose corn syrup (HFCS) in a continuous process.

energy value. It can therefore be used in food products to give the same sweetness as glucose, but with a lower overall calorific value. Millions of tonnes of HFCS are produced each year, mainly in the USA, for use in processed foods and soft drinks. Glucose isomerase is often used commercially in an immobilised preparation such as Sweetzyme® T, in which enzyme molecules are supported in an inert substance, such as an alginate gel, or cellulose acetate. Used in this way, the enzyme can be used continuously and remains active for up to 360 days before the enzyme needs to be replaced. Sweetzyme® T has an optimum activity in the range of 55 to 60 °C, which helps to reduce contamination as many microorganisms cannot withstand this temperature.

EXTENSION MATERIAL

Sites of enzyme action on amylopectin

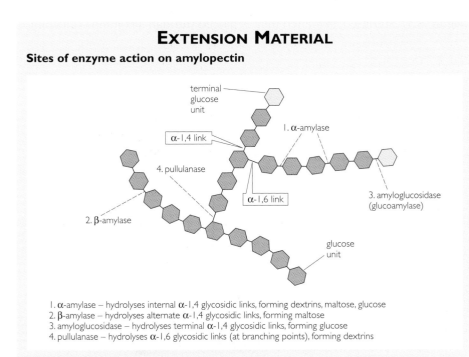

1. α-amylase – hydrolyses internal α-1,4 glycosidic links, forming dextrins, maltose, glucose
2. β-amylase – hydrolyses alternate α-1,4 glycosidic links, forming maltose
3. amyloglucosidase – hydrolyses terminal α-1,4 glycosidic links, forming glucose
4. pullulanase – hydrolyses α-1,6 glycosidic links (at branching points), forming dextrins

Figure 8.2 Activities of amylases, a group of enzymes which act on glycosidic bonds and break down complex carbohydrates, such as starch and glycogen, to simpler residues.

Amyloglucosidase (glucoamylase) is an enzyme which catalyses the hydrolysis of 1,4- and 1,6-alpha-linkages in starch, removing glucose units stepwise from one end of the substrate molecule. Amyloglucosidase is used to produce high glucose syrups from corn starch. The glucose syrups are then used directly in a range of food and drinks, including fruit sorbets, and as a substrate for the production of fructose syrups, using glucose isomerase. Amyloglucosidase can also be used in an immobilised preparation and will remain active for up to 100 hours at 60 °C.

Lactose intolerance

In adults, the global distribution of the enzyme lactase (β-galactosidase), which breaks down lactose (the sugar in milk) into glucose and galactose, shows an interesting pattern. In most ethnic groups, adults show loss of lactase after puberty, which means they cannot digest fresh milk containing lactose. Undigested lactose in the gut of these lactose-intolerant people is likely to be fermented by bacteria in the large intestine, resulting in nausea, abdominal pain and diarrhoea. Lactase is lacking in an estimated 90 per cent of Chinese and **lactose intolerance** is also found in Africans, Arabs and some people from the Indian subcontinent. However, in northern and western Europe, lactase is found in about 95 per cent of adults. Within some of areas of lactose intolerance there are pockets of people who have traditionally been pastoralists and so continued to drink milk in adulthood; these people do have the enzyme. Lactose intolerance doubtless accounts for the very low usage of fresh milk in traditional Asian foods. In fermented milk products, such as yoghurt and cheese, the lactose is reduced or eliminated, thus making them digestible and acceptable to lactose-intolerant people.

Lactase (β-galactosidase) is used in the manufacture of **lactose-reduced milk** (Figure 8.3). Sterilised, skimmed milk is passed through a column containing

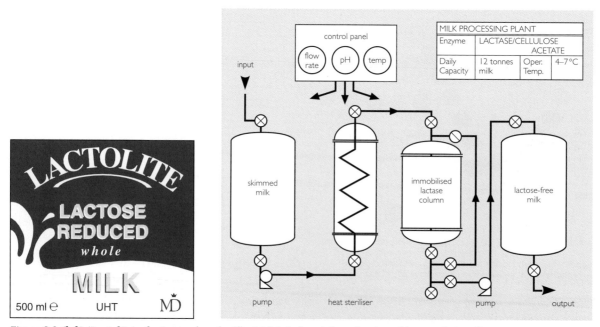

Figure 8.3 (left) 'Lactolite' – lactose reduced milk; (right) Industrial production of lactose-free milk.

beads of immobilised lactase, which breaks down the lactose present in milk to glucose and galactose. This makes milk acceptable to those with lactose intolerance.

Other additives

Colouring agents may be added to foods to return the food to its original colour if this has been changed or lost during processing. The appearance of foods can be enhanced by the addition of colouring agents – people expect foods to look appetising, and to be the appropriate colour, as well as tasting good. Many colouring agents are natural substances, such as saffron and **β-carotene**, but synthetic dyes are also used as colouring agents. Although thousands of synthetic dyes are known, most of these are too toxic to be used in foods. Those which are used include **sunset yellow** (E110), **tartrazine** (E102) and amaranth (E123). Some examples of colouring agents and their corresponding E-numbers are shown in Table 8.7.

Table 8.7 *Some examples of food colouring agents*

Colouring substance	E-number	Colour
amaranth	E-123	red
β-carotene	E-160(a)	yellow / orange
caramel	E-150	brown
erythrosine BS	E-127	red
lycopene	E-160(d)	red
tartrazine	E-102	yellow

Flavouring agents, or flavours, are added to increase the attractiveness of foods and may be used in food without restrictions. There are thousands of different flavourings available for use in food. These include natural substances, such as herbs, spices and essential oils such as pepper and **vanilla**, and a range of synthetic substances, including esters, ethers and alcohols. Many artificial fruit flavours are esters, formed by the reaction between alcohols and organic acids. These fruit-flavoured esters are the most widely used types of flavourings, some of which are shown in Table 8.8.

Table 8.8 *Some examples of esters used as flavouring agents*

Name	Uses
allyl caproate	pineapple essence
ethyl acetate	apple, pear, strawberry and peach essences
ethyl formate	rum, raspberry and peach essences
pentyl acetate	pear, pineapple and raspberry essences

Flavour enhancers (or flavour modifiers) are substances which are almost tasteless in themselves, but enhance or change the taste of food. Flavour enhancers include **salt** (sodium chloride) and **monosodium glutamate** (MSG, E621). MSG is present in soy sauce and is used in many savoury foods, including packet soups and flavoured noodles.

QUESTION

What is the difference between a flavouring and a flavour enhancer?

Rancidity is a very common form of chemical spoilage of food, resulting from the oxidation of fats and oils by atmospheric oxygen. This can be reduced by the addition of **antioxidants**. The development of rancid 'off' flavours results from the reaction of long-chain fatty acids, containing two or more double bonds, to form short-chain fatty acids. These resulting short-chain fatty acids, such as butyric acid, impart unpleasant flavours to the food.

Antioxidants include naturally occurring substances, such as vitamin E, but these are usually present in too small a quantity in foods to prevent deterioration. There are a number of antioxidants which may be added to foods (permitted antioxidants), including **L-ascorbic acid** (E300), and extracts of natural origin that are rich in **tocopherols** (vitamin E, E306).

As an example to illustrate the uses of food additives, the following list of ingredients is taken from a carton of gravy granules:

> Hydrogenated vegetable oil, starch, salt, wheat flour, dried onion, hydrolysed vegetable protein, colour (E150), sugar, flavour enhancers (E621, E635), emulsifier (lecithin, (E322)), yeast extract, herb and spice extracts.

QUESTION

Identify the colour and flavour enhancers which are present in gravy granules.

Preservatives

Preservatives are chemical substances which are added to foods to prevent the growth of microorganisms such as bacteria and moulds. Without preservatives, these microorganisms would grow rapidly and cause food spoilage or food poisoning.

Traditional preservatives include vinegar, alcohol and sodium chloride (salt), which have been used for centuries to inhibit the growth of spoilage microoorganisms. Other chemical preservatives include sodium nitrite (E250), sulphur dioxide (E220) and a range of sulphites (E221 to E227). Sodium nitrite is used as a preservative in a range of processed meat products, including sausages, bacon and ham. Products in which sulphites are used as preservatives include pickled cabbage, packet mashed potato, beer, cider and wines. Sulphites are also used to prevent the browning of raw, peeled or chipped potatoes before they are cooked. However, sulphites have an unpleasant taste and reduce the thiamin (vitamin B1) content of foods.

Concerns about additives

Concern has been expressed about possible adverse effects on consumers due to the presence of additives in foods. However, it is generally agreed that using food additives is justified if they fulfil one or more of the following functions:
- maintenance of nutritional quality
- improvement of keeping quality with less wastage
- making the food product look more attractive, without being deceptive.

Additives should never be used, for example, to disguise faulty handling or processing, or to deceive the consumer. It is essential that any risks of possible side-effects from the presence of additives in food should be negligible when compared with the corresponding benefits. Food additives approved for use in Britain have useful functions and cause no harm to the vast majority of consumers. Nevertheless, some people who are sensitive to food additives are sensitive to substances naturally present in foods, and may have adverse reactions. In a food allergy, the body's immune system responds to certain harmless substances present in food. As a result, **histamine** is released, from basophils and mast cells (leucocytes), into the bloodstream. This results in a series of symptoms, including swelling of the lips, urticaria (nettle rash), asthma, headache, vomiting and diarrhoea. The food additives commonly associated with food allergies include tartrazine and benzoates (used as preservatives in a range of products including jam, pickles and coffee essence).

Ben Finegold, a doctor working in the USA, suggested that hyperactivity in children, usually boys, would be reduced if they were fed on a diet which cut out all food and drink containing certain additives. These include synthetic colourings and flavourings, nitrates, nitrites, butylated hydroxyanisole (BHA), butylated hydroxytoluene (BHT) and benzoic acid. Foods containing natural salicylates, including almonds, apricots, plums, oranges, tomatoes and raisins, should also be avoided for 4 to 6 weeks, then reintroduced in the diet one at a time, to see whether there are any adverse effects. Although this approach has some support, there is little clinical evidence to confirm a link between additives and behavioural disorders. A study carried out at Great Ormond Street Hospital did, however, show that some children with a combination of hyperactivity and physical symptoms, including rashes and headaches, improved on an elimination diet. These children appeared to be particularly sensitive to tartrazine and benzoic acid. As a result of concern about possible adverse effects of tartrazine, manufacturers usually avoid this in their products.

Sodium nitrite (E250) is used as a preservative, particularly in processed meat products, including sausages and tinned meat. Sodium nitrite inhibits the growth of *Clostridium botulinum*, a species of bacteria that causes botulism, an often fatal type of food poisoning. However, nitrites are converted to substances called nitrosamines in the stomach. Nitrosamines have been shown to cause cancer in animals, although at concentrations far higher than those produced in humans after eating foods containing nitrites. As a precaution, the addition of nitrites (and nitrates) to foods intended for babies and small children is prohibited.

Additives that are intentionally added to foods are not harmful; they have all been thoroughly tested and are continually monitored for any adverse effects. The amounts of additives that are allowed in foods are such that the maximum intake does not exceed 1/100 of the highest concentration which has no effects in animal tests.

Table 8.9 *Foods which are likely to contain tartrazine (E-102)*

cakes
custard
fizzy drinks
fruit squashes
packet and tinned soups
pickles
salad cream
sweets
marmalade
yoghurt
ice cream
jelly
mustard
ice lollies
jam
marzipan

9 Food storage

Postharvest changes

When you pick an apple off a tree, it does not die – living metabolic processes continue for days, weeks or even months afterwards. Internal physiological changes occur which affect its chemical composition, colour, taste, texture and mass. Some of these changes contribute to qualities associated with ripeness, others lead ultimately to deterioration, spoilage and decay.

Substantial losses occur in crops after harvest. Estimates for fresh fruit and vegetables vary between 20 and 80 per cent. Mechanical damage in the form of bruising or splitting can lead to discolouration and changes in flavour. Internal changes, due to enzyme activity, contribute to deterioration and this may be exacerbated by unsuitable storage conditions. Invasion by pathogens may result in fungal or bacterial disease. Attacks by insects, slugs and snails reduce the edible portion of the produce and make it susceptible to microbial decay. On a global scale, postharvest losses reduce the food available for consumption and this can lead to a serious shortfall in regions where supplies are already inadequate. There are thus strong economic as well as social reasons for understanding postharvest biology.

In the modern food industry, considerable attention is paid to postharvest conditions for fruit and vegetables, fish and meats, which are destined to be sold fresh, without further processing. The aim of postharvest treatment is to ensure the desired freshness and nutritional value is maintained from the initial handling at harvest or slaughter, then during transport and storage until the produce is presented for sale to the consumer and finally eaten.

Fruits and vegetables

Our fruits and vegetables come from various parts of a plant and are harvested at different stages in the life cycle of the plant. Generally we can recognise three main physiological stages of development, though in the living plant, the boundary between the stages is often indistinct:

- **growth stage** – cell division and enlargement occur, resulting in rapid increase in size
- **maturity** – maximum growth of the plant organ has occurred, often associated with full ripening of a fruit
- **senescence** – catabolic processes take over from anabolic processes, leading to degradation rather than synthesis.

Even though we recognise physiological maturity as a stage within the life cycle of a plant, commercial maturity indicates the stage at which the plant organ is ready for the consumer market. This may occur at different developmental stages and does not necessarily coincide with physiological maturity (Table 9.1).

For fruits in particular, we talk about **ripeness** as the stage at which it is desirable to eat them. Ripening involves a complex series of physical and biochemical changes and effectively transforms an inedible plant organ into a

Figure 9.1 Olives and gherkins – some preserved foods which have now become speciality or gourmet foods.

> ### QUESTION
> - Why do we describe fruits and vegetables as 'perishable' commodities?
> - Name some that are virtually non-perishable.
> - List others that soon deteriorate after harvest.
> - What sort of time scale would you suggest for some of the products you have listed?

Table 9.1 *Commercial maturity – examples of parts of plants that are eaten, but not necessarily at the stage of physiological maturity*

Part of plant	Example of food that is eaten
young shoots	asparagus
stems and leaves	celery, lettuce, cabbage
inflorescences	artichoke, broccoli, cauliflower
partially developed fruits	cucumber, green bean, okra, sweetcorn
fully developed fruits	apple, pear, citrus fruits, tomato
roots / bulbs / tubers	carrot / onion / potato

food that is attractive to eat, from the point of view of its appearance, taste and texture. The flesh of an unripe 'Conference' pear, for example, is hard, gritty, white and with little flavour, but as it ripens it is transformed into a fruit with firm but soft texture, creamy white in colour and dripping with sweet and flavoursome juice. The same pear can soon become mushy and brownish inside, losing its flavour and appeal to the consumer as further changes take place. Courgettes are an example of fruits that are eaten when botanically under-ripe; 'mangetout' peas, French and runner beans, are eaten in their pods, long before the seeds (peas or beans) become mature.

The ripening process – in apples and other fruits

Once picked from the tree, apples can be stored for several months in a cool place without any special treatment. The skin colour changes from green to yellowish or red, the texture softens, the apple becomes sweeter and other subtle changes develop in the flavour. Gradually the apple shrivels, brownish patches become evident and eventually decay sets in (Figure 9.2).

In an apple, **respiration** continues after it has been harvested. This means that oxygen is taken up, and carbon dioxide, water and heat are given off. Loss of water also occurs by **transpiration**. When the apple is attached to the plant, water and respiratory substrates are replaced from other parts of the plant where active metabolic processes are taking place. Once it has been harvested, the fruit or vegetable becomes dependent upon its own food reserves and moisture. As these are lost they cannot be replaced and deterioration sets in. The rate of respiration (Figure 9.3) goes through a series of changes from the time of petal fall through the development of the fruit. The increased rate of respiration accompanying ripening is known as the **climacteric**, a feature shown in some fruits and vegetables. Linked with the climacteric peak in respiration rate is an increase in the production of **ethene (ethylene)**, a plant growth substance associated with the processes of ripening.

Figure 9.2 Home-grown apples, kept for several months. The apples were stored between layers of newspaper but otherwise had no special treatment. While some apples shrivelled, others retained their crisp texture but internal changes led to noticeable differences in taste.

After an apple has been picked, various physiological changes associated with ripening and senescence become evident:
- **pectic substances** in the middle lamella break down, giving softer texture.
- **chlorophyll** is degraded, leading to loss of the green colour. Yellows and reds of carotenoids, anthocyanins and other pigments become visible in a ripe apple.

FOOD STORAGE

QUESTION

In pears, using the Conference cultivar, measurements of the starch content can be used as an indicator of its stage of ripeness. The cut surface of a pear is dipped into a solution containing 4 per cent potassium iodide and 1 per cent iodine. Harvesting is carried out when the cut surface shows 65 to 70 per cent blue-black.

- When eating fruit, how do you judge its ripeness?
- Think about taste in relation to sugar content and acidity. How far does colour influence your perception of acceptability of the fruit?

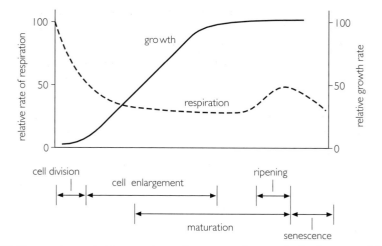

Figure 9.3 Changes in respiration rate in apples or pears from early development of the fruit through the stages of ripening and senescence.

- **organic acid** levels fall, accompanied by increased sugar content. The balance between sugars and acids makes an important contribution to taste, in terms of sweetness or sourness. In apples, malic acid is the main organic acid found and some is used as a respiratory substrate. Sugars include fructose, glucose and sucrose.
- **volatile substances** present in minute quantities contribute to the characteristic flavours. In green apples the compound 2-hexenal is an important component of the aroma, whereas in ripe apples ethyl 2-methylbutyrate is present. Other flavour and aroma compounds are synthesised during ripening.

Botanically the tomato is a fruit, even though it is classed as a vegetable for eating. Like the apple, respiration and other metabolic activities continue in the tomato up to and beyond the stage of ripeness and harvest. Starch tends to accumulate before ripeness, to be replaced by fructose and glucose as the tomato ripens, giving the characteristic sweetness of ripe tomatoes. Cherry tomatoes are notable because they contain some sucrose. These sugars account for about 65 per cent of the total 'soluble solids' in tomatoes. Malic, citric and ascorbic acids are among those which contribute to the sourness or acidity and, as the tomato ripens, the acidity decreases and sweetness increases. In addition, there are around 400 volatile compounds, present in minute concentrations, which contribute to aroma or flavour. If tomatoes are picked before they are ripe, they have not developed their full sugar content, nor do they have the full range of odour compounds. Similarly, if under-ripe tomatoes are kept and refrigerated for a week or so before being eaten, the full potential flavour is not reached. The colours in tomatoes are due to carotenoid pigments – carotenes show as orange and lycopene gives the red. These pigments are significant in that their development is associated with other metabolic changes and so are useful as indicators of the stage of ripeness.

Ethene has a very important role in ripening of fruits. It is often referred to as ethylene in the commercial world and by research workers involved with fruits and vegetables. Ethene is a gas and is synthesised from the amino acid methionine through a series of intermediates, including a compound abbreviated as ACC. An increase in ethene is associated with the rise in respiration before the onset of ripening. Ethene has an important role in the switching on and off of genes involved in the ripening programme, by activating genes controlling colour, texture and flavour. Of particular interest is the production of ethene and the relationship between polygalacturonase and firmness (see Figure 9.4). Pectinesterase (PE) and polygalacturonase (PG) are two enzymes involved in the stages of breakdown of pectic substances in the cell wall, through the pathway

$$\text{propectin} \xrightarrow{\text{PE}} \text{pectinic acid} \rightarrow \text{pectic acid} \xrightarrow{\text{PG}} \text{galacturonic acid}$$

EXTENSION MATERIAL

The ripening of tomato fruit

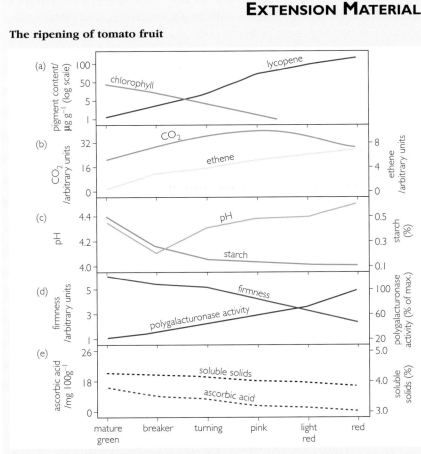

(a) **Colour changes** – as chlorophyll (green) decreases, lycopene (red) increases

(b) **Production of gases** – the increase (followed by decrease) in carbon dioxide represents changes in rate of respiration associated with ripening. This coincides with the rise in ethene, which has an important role in switching on and off genes involved in the ripening process

(c) **Sugar–acid balance** – as the tomato ripens, reserves of starch decrease and sugars (mainly glucose and fructose) increase. At the same time, the organic acids decrease, hence the rise in pH. The sugar–acid balance is reflected in the sweetness of the tomato

(d) **Firmness and softening of the tomatoes** – polygalacturonase activity (together with activity of pectic enzymes) leads to degradation of pectic substances in the cell walls and softening of the tomatoes

(e) **Ascorbic acid and soluble solids** – ascorbic acid is one of the acids referred to in (c). The soluble solids include sugar (about 65 per cent) as well as other substances in the cells of the tomato

Figure 9.4 Some changes that occur during the ripening of tomato fruit.

Use the information in Figure 9.4 to answer these questions.
- You can see how colour in tomatoes is linked to different stages of ripening. How could you detect which **pigments** are responsible for these colour changes?
- Compare the respiratory activity and the loss of stored starch. How could you measure changes in respiratory activity, or of stored starch, over time?
- How could you determine whether there is an increase in **sugars** in tomatoes and how could you measure changes in ascorbic acid content?
- How could you detect changes in **ethene** production, or monitor the effect of ethene on ripening?

Breakdown of the pectic substances is largely responsible for the changes in texture leading to mushiness in the over-ripe tomato or to the softer texture in apples when they are kept over a period of time. The enzyme PG is absent, or present in only very low quantities in unripe fruit, but is found in large quantities in ripe fruit. It acts by reducing the chain length of pectin molecules in the middle lamella and primary cell wall. Similarly, in apples the softening of the fruit is due to degradation of pectic substances in the cell wall.

Short-term and long-term storage

Fruit and vegetables

In primitive communities, the ability to store harvested crops even for short periods was an important step in the development of agriculture. In the modern food industry, the storage system used is determined by the nature of the food product and linked closely to marketing strategies. Short-term storage may just be temporary, as in the collection of harvested produce to allow enough to accumulate to send on to market. Short-term storage may also be appropriate for some crops intended for local use or for consumption in a matter of days or a few weeks after harvest – highly perishable fruits and vegetables, such as strawberries or lettuces, have a limited life. Longer term storage may extend over a period of weeks, months or even years. Produce that is stored over longer periods can then be transported and distributed over considerable distances, even globally.

Our review of postharvest changes indicates that fruits and vegetables deteriorate for a number of reasons:
- loss of water, leading to limpness or shrivelling
- loss of stored respiratory substrate (usually carbohydrate)
- loss of other nutrients, such as vitamins
- changes in taste, because of alteration of the organic acid and sugar balance
- other internal enzymatic activities, including development of different aroma compounds
- softening of tissues due to degradation of pectic substances (polygalacturonase and pectic enzymes).

QUESTION

How would you define spoilage? What do you associate with food that is spoiled, that makes it unpleasant or unfit for consumption? Think about texture, colour, taste and odour, then see how far these fit your perception of spoiled food. Then apply this to sour milk and yoghurt or other fermented milk

As well as the internal changes, there may be physical losses through **pests** or **disease** and saprophytic attack by **microorganisms**. A wide range of microorganisms is likely to be on the surface of any harvested fruits or vegetables. Others may be introduced during processing. Microorganisms are very diverse, but for growth they must have moisture, a suitable temperature together with a source of energy (usually carbohydrate), plus nitrogen and other nutrients. Many require oxygen but some are anaerobic. Their growth is likely to be sensitive to pH – bacteria are less tolerant of acid conditions than yeasts or moulds. Any food destined for humans is probably also a suitable environment for microorganisms, whose metabolic activities are then liable to alter the composition and texture of the food, often making it unfit for human consumption. Bacteria are less likely to grow on fruits because of their high sugar content, but moulds soon grow on the sugary juices, particularly if there is any damage to the skin surface.

The main emphasis of postharvest treatment of fruits and vegetables and conditions used during storage is to:

- minimise water loss
- reduce respiration
- delay ripeness until required by the consumer
- slow the onset of senescence
- avoid spoilage by microorganisms.

Humidity and water loss

Water loss, due to transpiration, can be controlled by increasing the humidity of the storage chamber. This can be achieved by spraying water as a fine mist inside the store. Though the higher humidity favours growth of microorganisms, many fresh fruits and vegetables are stored in a relative humidity between 85 and 95 per cent. Damage to the skin surface is liable to increase the rate of water loss. The natural surface of fruits and some vegetables is often waxy and can play a part in minimising water loss. To help reduce weight loss, artificial waxes have been developed which are applied as a film on the outside of fruits such as apples, citrus fruits and avocado pears. Fungicides and inhibitors of senescence can be incorporated into the wax formulation. Such coatings also affect the gas exchange, by allowing oxygen to diffuse into the apple but retaining some of the carbon dioxide produced in respiration. This effectively modifies the internal atmosphere, which also prolongs the life of the stored apple. Sometimes fruit with these coatings is polished, to increase the sales appeal. The wrapping and packaging also affect the humidity immediately around the fruit or vegetable. Leafy vegetables, such as lettuce or spinach, soon wilt unless moisture can be retained within suitable packaging.

Temperature

Most fruits and vegetables are stored at temperatures lower than their growing environment; some are pre-cooled at the time of harvest. Tomatoes are often cooled after picking by being tipped into a bath of cold water at 10 °C. Lettuces may be chilled by 'vacuum cooling'. For this, they are placed in boxes in a vacuum chamber and some moisture is boiled off. Alternatively, lettuces may be packed for transport in boxes surrounded with ice. Low temperatures reduce the rate of respiration hence the disappearance of respiratory substrate. A temperature between 1 and 4 °C is suitable for storing apples, and this also diminishes attack by fungi and bacteria. Below 0 °C, the tissues may suffer from irreversible chilling injury, since frozen tissues may fail to resume metabolic processes when thawed. The critical temperature for chilling injury varies with different cultivars and different crops. Potatoes should not be stored below a temperature of 4 °C because this favours conversion of starch to sugars. Lowering the temperature decreases the rate of ethene production and the response of tissues to the effects of ethene, thus delaying the onset of ripening. The development of the aroma in ripe fruit and the turning of the green colour to yellow are also slower at lower temperatures. The actual temperature inside the fruit or vegetable is likely to be higher than that set for the storage chamber due to the heat generated in respiration. The store should provide continual cooling, if necessary by air circulation with fans, to ensure the desired temperature is maintained. However, air circulation will encourage loss of water, so a balance must be found.

FOOD STORAGE

Storage atmosphere

Modification of the gases in the atmosphere in which apples are stored has led to considerable success in prolonging the storage life. The terms **controlled atmosphere (CA)** or **modified atmosphere (MA)**, are used to describe systems in which the atmospheric composition is different from normal air. The practice has ancient origins: burying apples or carrying them in unventilated holds of ships resulted in a much longer storage life. The effect was probably due to lower oxygen and higher carbon dioxide in the surrounding atmosphere, modified as a result of respiration in the tissue.

In modern storage systems, the atmosphere is deliberately manipulated, with levels of oxygen, carbon dioxide, nitrogen, ethene and carbon monoxide being controlled. Storage containers must be sealed and monitored closely. Respiration of the stored produce leads to a fall in oxygen concentration and rise in carbon dioxide concentration. In some cases nitrogen gas is introduced to ensure the crop rapidly reaches the required levels of oxygen and carbon dioxide. Because respiration continues, fresh air is introduced to maintain the required level of oxygen. Carbon dioxide is produced from the stored product and chemical absorbants are used to prevent the level getting too high. Controlled atmosphere storage has been applied mainly to stored apples, but it is being used increasingly with other crops, including bananas, avocados, tomatoes, cucumbers, Chinese cabbage, broccoli and potatoes (see Table 9.2).

Table 9.2 *Recommended storage conditions for a selection of fruits and vegetables*

Fruit or vegetable	Temperature / °C	Storage life	Controlled atmosphere (CA) effects
Banana	11–14	2–3 weeks	5% CO_2, 4% O_2, extends shelf life ×3
Broccoli	0	10–14 days	5–10% CO_2, 1–2% O_2
Cabbage	0–2	2–6 months	2.5–5% CO_2, 2.5–5% O_2
Cucumber	7–10	1–2 weeks	5–7% CO_2, 3–5% O_2
Marrow	10–15	2–6 months	CA has little effect
Onion	0	6–8 months	CA has variable success
Potatoes	7–10	4–8 months	CA has variable effects. Below 4 °C potatoes become sweeter
Raspberries	0	3–7 days	CA has little effect

Storage life depends on a combination of temperature, humidity and gas atmosphere. Values given here are approximate and vary with different varieties. Where CA is not recommended, decay or spoilage may increase with the controlled atmosphere. All the fruits and vegetables listed here would be kept at a relative humidity of between 85 and 95%, except for marrow and onion – these can be kept successfully in less humid conditions.

In apples stored at 5 °C, the oxygen level must be reduced to 2.5 per cent to achieve a 50 per cent reduction in respiration. Care must be taken to ensure conditions do not become anaerobic as this could lead to development of undesirable flavours. At higher temperatures with low oxygen, anaerobic respiration increases. Increased carbon dioxide levels also affect respiration: for apples, a storage atmosphere with carbon dioxide levels between 5 and 10 per cent is often used, but if higher, anaerobic respiration can occur. Low oxygen and high carbon dioxide both delay ripening and the breakdown of chlorophyll, and also reduce ethene production. This atmosphere also reduces the breakdown of pectic substances in the middle lamella, keeping the texture firm for longer. With prolonged storage in low oxygen and high carbon dioxide, undesirable flavours and odours may develop. High levels of carbon dioxide also reduce microbial activity, thus delaying the onset of decay. In practice, different products vary considerably in their tolerance to reduced oxygen and increased carbon dioxide levels. Lettuces and other salad crops can, for example, be stored for 4 weeks in containers with an atmosphere of 10 per cent carbon dioxide, 10 per cent oxygen and 80 per cent nitrogen.

Table 9.3 *Effect of storage conditions on shelf life*

Treatment (bananas)	Shelf life/days
kept in air	up to 7
sealed polythene bags	14
sealed bags, with potassium permanganate	21

Within the storage atmosphere, accumulated ethene encourages the onset of ripening so there should be adequate ventilation inside the storage chamber to remove ethene. Fruits at different stages of ripeness should not be stored together, since ethene produced from riper fruits would affect the less ripe. Chemicals, such as potassium permanganate, can be used to absorb ethene, both in the incoming air and inside the container itself. Bunches of bananas are sometimes sealed inside polyethylene bags, on or off the plant, to delay the ripening process. (See Table 9.3.) This is a relatively simple way for the subsistence farmer to create a modified atmosphere on the farm, though ethene tends to accumulate.

Pasteurised and sterilised milk

Treatment of milk by pasteurisation or sterilisation illustrates the effects of different heat treatments and the distinction between short-term and long-term storage. In the UK, about 93 per cent of milk is **pasteurised**, and the rest is either **ultra heat treated (UHT)** or **sterilised**. Only a small fraction is sold as unpasteurised milk. Pasteurised milk is popular because the flavour and nutritional content is hardly affected by the pasteurisation process. Pasteurisation aims to kill pathogenic organisms and to reduce the number of other non-pathogenic bacteria that would cause spoilage. Pasteurisation is not effective against spores. In particular, pasteurisation is expected to make the milk safe from *Mycobacterium tuberculosis*, and from *Brucella abortus*, the causative organisms of tuberculosis and brucellosis respectively. Pasteurisation extends the keeping time of the milk for a few days, provided it is kept refrigerated (between 1 and 4 °C). Sterilisation uses heat but at a higher temperature than pasteurisation and aims to destroy bacteria and other microorganisms that may not have been killed by pasteurisation, though some very resistant spores may survive the process.

QUESTION

Why can milk can go sour even after it has been pasteurised?

EXTENSION MATERIAL

The phosphatase test

The **phosphatase test** is used to check the effectiveness of pasteurisation. The enzyme phosphatase is slightly more resistant to heat than the bacterium *Mycobacterium tuberculosis*, so a test is carried out on the milk to check that the phosphatase in the milk has been inactivated. The chemical compound known as disodium *p*-nitrophenyl phosphate is added. If active phosphatase is present, this chemical breaks down, producing *p*-nitrophenol, which is detected because it gives a yellow colouration.

Pasteurisation is carried out either by heating the milk at a temperature of 62.8 to 65.6 °C for at least 30 minutes, or by heating to 71.7 °C for at least 15 seconds. This 'high-temperature short-time' (HTST) system is now widely used. The milk is passed through pipes or between plates in a heat exchanger system, surrounded by hot water kept at a temperature just above the required temperature. It is carefully controlled to ensure the milk is held at the correct temperature for the appropriate time, then rapidly cooled to about 3 °C.

Temperatures used for sterilisation are at least 100 °C, though often the milk is sealed into bottles and heated to a temperature of approximately 115 °C for 20 minutes, then cooled rapidly. The milk will then keep for several months without refrigeration, but the flavour is noticeably altered by the cooking, resulting in a caramelised taste. It has also become homogenised with loss of separated cream. There is some loss of nutrients, compared with raw fresh milk or pasteurised milk. UHT milk is prepared by heating milk to at least 132.2 °C for at least 1 second. It is sealed in cartons, aseptically packaged in sterile conditions. UHT milk has a keeping time of several months with flavour qualities close to that of pasteurised milk.

Packaging

BACKGROUND

From very early civilisations, people have used natural materials, such as baskets, pottery vessels, gourds and leather, to serve as containers for harvested or stored foods. The last few hundred years have seen the development of glass, paper and metal containers, which remain familiar materials used in packaging today. Much more recently, synthetic materials such as cellulose and polyethylene films, expanded polystyrene and other plastics have been adapted for packaging in the food industry with considerable success.

Packaging plays an increasingly important part in the retailing of foods in the modern food industry. It has a key role in **marketing**, promoting the appeal of the food to the customer, and provides a means of **identifying** the product. The packaging also contributes to the maintenance of the desired **quality** of the food. Selection and use of appropriate packaging materials is integrated closely with the postharvest biology of the different foods. The discussion here focuses mainly on the packaging of fresh fruits and vegetables. We refer mainly to the package as presented to the customer in the supermarket or other retail outlet, rather than the wider range of systems adopted at the time of harvesting, and during storage and transport of the products.

At a simple level, the packaging provides a **container** for the produce, in a discrete weight or volume. The container also acts as a **barrier** and so isolates the material from the environment outside the pack. This barrier can prevent contamination of the packed product from dirt, undesirable chemical substances or from microorganisms. Similarly, the barrier should prevent leakage of materials from the inside, say of juice from fruits or meat, or grease from fatty or oily foods. The package can provide **protection** against mechanical damage, from the time of harvest until the product reaches the home of the purchaser. To illustrate the necessity for this you need think no further than the losses incurred through broken eggs or bruised apples. The package must be strong enough to resist vibration, and damage from being compressed or even dropped, but not so heavy that it adds to costs or handling difficulties. For some foods, it is necessary for the package to protect against the effects of **light**.

A food package can be thought of as a small-scale storage system in which **humidity** and **gas atmosphere** are key features. These factors are also discussed in relation to postharvest biology and storage conditions in general (see pages 121–22). With fresh produce, such as apples and lettuce, the barrier provided by the packaging material can help to reduce water loss by transpiration, but it is equally important for the barrier to prevent uptake of water by dry foods, such as dehydrated fruits. However, if the barrier is impermeable to water, with packs of fresh fruits and vegetables, water vapour collects inside the package and would be evident as condensation or drops of water. A high relative humidity inside a pack is likely to encourage growth of moulds or other microorganisms which could lead to spoilage. If, however, the barrier is perforated so that it is *partly* permeable, it may still be possible to minimise water loss from the fruit or vegetable but, at the same time, avoid excessive build-up of water vapour inside the package.

In a similar way, with plant material, the permeability of the barrier becomes critical with respect to the levels of gases, particularly respiratory gases and **ethene**. If the barrier is impermeable, respiration leads to a depletion of **oxygen** and increase in **carbon dioxide** within the package. Whilst some reduction in oxygen or increase in carbon dioxide slows the postharvest changes associated with ripening and senescence (see pages 110–13), development of anaerobic conditions encourages deterioration of the fruits or vegetables inside the pack. If, however, the pack is *partly* permeable to gases, and perhaps differentially permeable so that the gas composition can be manipulated, we have a powerful tool that can be exploited to control the atmosphere inside the package. This is the basis of **modified atmosphere packaging (MAP)**. This technique has been made possible by the development of a range of plastic films, with different permeabilities. MAP provides a means of prolonging shelf-life of the product as well as being attractive to the consumer in the displays. MAP can be applied to meats and fish as well as to fruits and vegetables and the systems now being used are bringing about a quiet revolution in the food industry.

QUESTION
Why does it matter if apples are bruised?

QUESTION
More questions about apples:
- Why does microbial spoilage occur in a pack of apples even if the bag is completely sealed?
- What internal changes might take place in apples when the conditions become anaerobic inside the pack?

Table 9.4 *Effects of number and size of perforations in polyethylene bags on storage life of yellow globe onions. The onions were kept in 1.5 kg packs in 150 gauge polyethylene film bags, for 14 days at 24 °C. Measurements were made of the percentage relative humidity (RH) inside the bag, the number of onions which rooted and the percentage loss in weight.*

Number of perforations	Diameter of perforations /mm	RH in bag (%)	Onions rooted (%)	Loss in mass (%)
0	–	98	71	0.5
36	1.6	88	59	0.7
40	3.2	84	40	1.4
8	6.4	–	24	1.8
16	6.4	54	17	2.5
32	6.4	51	4	2.5

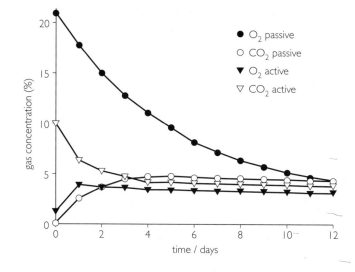

Figure 9.5 Passive compared with active modification – chilli peppers in sealed plastic film packages. Flushing the packages with gases (active modification) brought about a faster change in gas atmosphere.

DEFINITIONS

In **passive MA** the high carbon dioxide and low oxygen levels develop passively, as a result of the respiration of the product inside the package. This is relevant particularly with plant material.

In **active MA** the air originally inside the package is removed and replaced with the desired gas mixture.

In **active MA with chemicals** the desired changes in the original gas mixture are produced by chemical substances.

We can distinguish three methods of creating a modified atmosphere (MA) inside the package: **passive MA**, **active MA** and **active MA with chemicals**.

Passive MA is probably the least satisfactory, since respiratory activity of fresh produce may vary at different postharvest stages and at different temperatures (Figure 9.5). With passive MA, it also takes time for the desired gas levels to be achieved. It is more reliable to control the atmosphere by using a vacuum to remove the air from the pack, then flushing it with a gas mixture of the desired composition. Chemical substances, which either absorb or generate gases, can be placed in sachets inside the package and used to influence the composition of the atmosphere. Examples include powdered ferrous (iron(II)) compounds, metallic platinum, catechol-based compounds and ascorbic acid, which act as oxygen 'scavengers'. Ferrous carbonate can be used both to take up oxygen and release carbon dioxide. Potassium permanganate and activated carbon are two substances used to absorb ethene (Table 9.3, page 117. A further sophistication is to incorporate a colour indicator in the sachet of chemical so that the gas levels inside the packet can be judged, thus giving a measure of the degree of freshness (Figure 9.6). This is used, for example, in large catering packages but not usually in consumer packages.

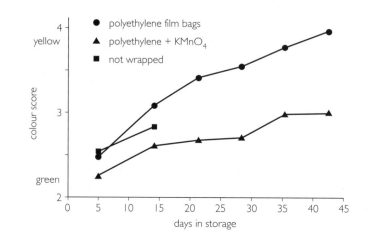

Figure 9.6 Storage of limes and the effects of packaging and of absorbing ethene. The colour score is used as an indicator of ripeness. The limes were kept at 31 to 34 °C and between 30 and 35 % RH.

Vacuum packs go a stage further in their control of the atmosphere. The package material must have low permeability to gases, particularly oxygen. This system is now used widely, for example, with beef joints packaged immediately after slaughter. The atmosphere around the meat soon becomes low in oxygen and enriched with carbon dioxide. In some cases, as the meat is enclosed in its pack, a vacuum is applied to reduce the gas remaining in the space between the meat and the package film. The oxygen-deficient environment is unsuitable for growth of aerobic microorganisms, provided the pH of the meat is low (less than 5.8). This principle has been exploited with **shrink packs**, used, for example, with frozen poultry. The chicken or meat joint is placed in the bag and a vacuum is applied before sealing. The bag is then heated in warm air or water and the bag shrinks to fit closely around the contours of the meat. A potential danger comes from survival and growth of anaerobic microorganisms inside these packs.

Plastics used for packaging

A wide range of plastics is used in packaging in different forms (Figure 9.7). Development of suitable plastic films has enabled MAP systems to become successful. Four types of film are commonly used: polyvinyl chloride (PVC), polyethylene (PE), polypropylene (PP) and polyethylene terephthalate (PET). There are variations in their properties and selection of the appropriate film requires a number of features to be taken into account:

- **degree of permeability** – to gases (particularly oxygen and carbon dioxide), and to water vapour
- **mechanical** properties – including overall strength, resistance to tearing or bursting under pressure, its ability to be handled by machines, how it can be sealed to form the package or peeled to open the package
- **stability** with respect to **environmental conditions**, particularly changes in temperature and humidity, and ability to withstand conditions during processing such as the high and low temperatures used for sterilisation and freezing
- **visibility** of the product – generally it is more appealing to the consumer to be able to see the fresh produce, though some foods deteriorate more rapidly in the light. This can be counteracted by use of appropriate opaque or dark packaging material, or large labels to cover most of the product.

Care should be taken over possible **interaction** between the packaging material and its contents – that is, that there is no attack on the material from substances in the food and that potentially toxic substances do not migrate from the package to the food.

Finally, we can see how the selection of materials for packaging is linked with the biology of the food material and that the package makes an important contribution to maintaining the freshness of a product. In addition, **labels** on packaged products offer an opportunity for communication with the purchaser, firstly to **identify** the food and then to describe the contents. Increasingly, labelling of food products has a key role in marketing strategies but the information provided must also conform with a range of legislative requirements.

Figure 9.7 Plastic films used for packaging are carefully selected and help prolong the shelf-life of fresh salads.

EXTENSION MATERIAL

Some postharvest changes in fruits and the effects of packaging or other treatments

Tables 9.5 and 9.6 show how packaging or treatment of fruits with edible coatings can be exploited to extend storage life.

Table 9.5 *Effects of different wrapping and packing materials on ripening and weight loss of plantains, stored at tropical ambient temperatures of between 26 and 34 °C and 52 to 87% relative humidity.*

Packing material	Days to ripeness	Loss in mass at ripeness (%)
not wrapped	15.8	17.0
paper	18.9	17.9
moist coir fibre	27.2	(+3.5)
perforated polyethylene	26.5	7.2
polyethylene	36.1	2.6

Table 9.6 *Changes in nutritional content of 'Satsuma' mandarins after harvest. These mandarins were treated with different edible coatings – 'Semperfresh' and 'Jonfresh' – then stored at 20 °C and 40 % RH. The control had no coating. Changes in ascorbic acid content and in citric acid content were compared over a period of 3 weeks. Coatings provide a modified atmosphere within the fruit, decrease respiration rate, reduce loss of water and can carry fungicides.*

Time / weeks	Ascorbic acid / mg 100 cm^{-3}			Citric acid (%)		
	Control	Semperfresh	Jonfresh	Control	Semperfresh	Jonfresh
0	25.2	25.2	25.2	1.57	1.57	1.57
1	17.1	18.0	21.1	1.34	1.51	1.50
2	16.6	17.1	20.7	1.06	1.21	1.42
3	14.4	17.1	18.3	0.93	1.25	1.06

QUESTION

Plantains are tropical fruits which are similar to bananas. The first table shows how different wrapping materials affected the time to ripeness and weight loss in stored plantains.

- Suggest why these different packing materials had the effects shown.
- For a small-scale farmer, do you think there is any real advantage in wrapping the plantains?
- What might be the disadvantages of using polyethylene? Think about costs, labour and the possible environmental consequences as well as the postharvest biology.

Biotechnology and food production

Biotechnology – ancient and modern

Biotechnology is a relatively modern word, but its roots lie at the very beginnings of human civilisation. The making of bread, cheese and wine are food-processing practices which are central to many human societies, traditional and modern. As humans changed from a hunter-gatherer way of life to more permanent, settled communities, the art of processing food began to develop. The origins of different discoveries were probably accidental, but the benefits were doubtless soon appreciated. Food could be kept longer, transported and stored from one season to the next. A wider range of flavours became part of the diet, and alcoholic liquor particularly assumed an importance in ceremonies and social gatherings. All this was long before people were aware of the existence of microorganisms, which are the agents responsible for many of these modifications to food.

The ancient art of modifying raw, harvested food has evolved into the modern food-processing industry. It is highly mechanised, rigorously monitored and controlled to ensure uniformity of end-products, many of which are destined for world-wide distribution. The impact of biotechnology in the modern food industry can be illustrated by the activities of microorganisms in fermentations, harvested as biomass to be consumed as food for humans or animals and in the production of extracellular enzymes.

Fermentations

The term **fermentation** is used in two senses. In the narrower, biochemical sense, fermentation is a form of **anaerobic respiration**, and is a means by which organisms, or cells within organisms, obtain energy from an organic substrate in the absence of oxygen. In the broader sense, the term is used to describe a very wide range of processes carried out by microorganisms. Many yield products of commercial importance. Some fermentations involve anaerobic respiration, but many do not.

Fermentations are a significant way of modifying raw fresh food. The fermented product has properties that are different from the original plant or animal material. The fermentation may enhance the flavour or alter the texture, palatability and digestibility of the food, and there may be changes in the nutritional content. These changes often make the food safer because it is then unsuitable for the growth of microorganisms and sometimes toxins are eliminated. Traditionally, fermentation of various foods has provided an important means of preservation, though in the modern food industry, other methods, such as freezing, have perhaps become more important.

The fermentations described in this chapter show how different microorganisms (bacteria and fungi) are involved and the changes that take place as a result of their metabolism. Often the fermentation leads to a lowering of the pH. This improves the storage properties of the foods because many microorganisms which cause spoilage do not tolerate a low pH.

BACKGROUND

It was the work of Pasteur in the mid-19th century that led to an understanding of the activities of microorganisms and their role in traditional food-processing activities. This signalled the beginnings of microbiology as a science. Today, at the beginning of the 21st century, biotechnology is concerned with exploiting the activities of living organisms, especially microorganisms. It embraces several disciplines – microbiology, biochemistry and chemistry, cell biology and genetics and engineering – to ensure the activities of the organisms can be geared to production, often in large-scale processing. Biotechnology now has medical and agricultural applications, and is involved in waste treatment, the production of fuels and in the food and beverage industries. Its future potential is considerable and is likely to increase in the 21st century. In addition, increasingly, we are seeing the application of biotechnology in the formation of products by genetically modified organisms.

BIOTECHNOLOGY AND FOOD PRODUCTION

Sauerkraut

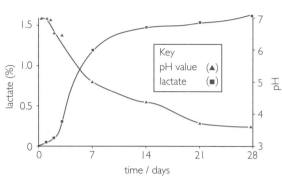

Figure 10.1 Changes in lactic acid concentration and pH during the fermentation of cabbage to sauerkraut.

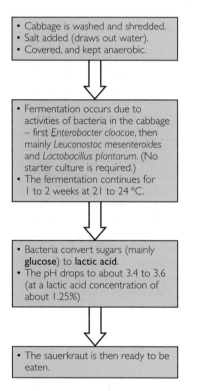

Figure 10.2 A flow diagram showing the main stages in the production of sauerkraut.

Cabbage (*Brassica oleraceae*), when fermented by bacteria under anaerobic conditions in the presence of salt, gives a product which has become acidified with lactic acid, known as **sauerkraut**. It is eaten by people particularly in central Europe and parts of the former USSR. Mature cabbage heads are used, with a sugar content in the range of about 2.9 to 6.4 per cent. The cabbage is washed in clean water and shredded, including even the central stalk. The shreds are mixed with about 2.5 per cent by weight of salt (sodium chloride), then packed into a vat, weighted down and covered closely. Plastic bags filled with water may be placed on top, acting as a weight and a seal, but still allowing gases produced during the fermentation to escape. The salt helps to draw out moisture from the cabbage, so that the shreds become immersed in brine. (See Figure 10.2.)

The natural flora of the cabbage includes bacterial populations which carry out the fermentation, so no starter culture is added. Respiration of the plant cells and of the bacteria soon removes the oxygen from the liquid in the container so that conditions become anaerobic. A number of different bacteria grow but gradually the acid fermenters become dominant. The salt helps because it favours the **lactic acid** bacteria. In the early stages *Enterobacter cloaca* produces some lactic acid, but the bacteria mainly responsible for the fermentation are *Leuconostoc mesenteroides* and later *Lactobacillus plantarum*. *Leuconostoc* ferments the sugars in the cabbage (mostly glucose and fructose) to lactic acid, to a concentration of up to 1 per cent (Figure 10.1). Carbon dioxide is given off, which helps to keep the conditions anaerobic. *Lactobacillus* is then able to utilise some of the by-products produced by *Leuconostoc*. With *Lactobacillus*, the lactic acid concentration can increase to 2.0 per cent, though the best level is about 1.7 per cent in the finished sauerkraut. This gives a pH of about 3.5. Other bacteria involved in the fermentation contribute to the flavour or lactic acid production. The temperature should be maintained above 15 °C, ideally between about 21 and 24 °C. At low temperatures, the fermentation is slow and incomplete, but if too high, undesirable fermentations by other microbes may take place. The fermentation is stopped when the desired level of acidity has been reached (usually 7 to 21 days).

Fermented milk – yoghurt

Fermentation of milk, into **yoghurt** and into cheese, is both a very ancient and a widespread practice. In Europe we are most familiar with yoghurt from cow's milk, or from sheep's milk, but milk from other mammals, including goats, buffalo and camels, is also used. Probably the first yoghurt was from the Middle East. Milk being carried under warm conditions probably became sour, developed agreeable flavours and could be kept longer than fresh milk, with obvious advantages to nomadic people. A portion of a successful ferment might have been used again to start the next batch, effectively selecting suitable strains of bacteria. See page 62 for details of the fermentation of milk to produce yoghurt.

Soya bean products – soya milk, tofu, soya sauce

The soya (soy) bean, *Glycine max*, is a legume, grown widely on a global scale. It is valued as a food because of its high protein content, as well as for its oil

QUESTION

How could you follow changes in pH during fermentation of cabbage to sauerkraut?

and vitamins. Soya bean products are particularly important in Oriental diets, and have probably been utilised in China for 4000 years or more. Mature soya beans, if eaten raw, are toxic and have an unpleasant taste, but when cooked or further processed have given rise to a whole range of different foods. Different names are given to the products, depending on the country of origin and the local method of preparation.

Soya milk and **tofu** are the simplest foods derived from soya beans. The milk is obtained by mixing the soya beans with water and grinding them to a slurry which is then boiled and filtered. The filtrate is known as soya milk. When calcium sulphate, magnesium sulphate or vinegar is added, the proteins coagulate to give the bean curd (Figure 10.3). The whey (liquid) is discarded. The bean curd is bland in taste, though it can be made into a range of foods with different uses in the diet.

Preparation of **soya sauce** uses soya beans together with a starchy crop, often wheat. There are several stages in the process. The soya beans are soaked in water, boiled and drained. The starch material is added as a flour or meal – wheat, for example, may be roasted then crushed before addition. The mixture is spread on trays and a starter culture is introduced. This culture contains a mixture of moulds and bacteria, and is either prepared freshly or carried over from a previous fermentation. The mixture ferments for about 1 week, at a temperature of 28 to 30 °C. The activity is mainly due to the mould *Aspergillus oryzae* (*soyae*) which produces amylases and proteases. The action of these enzymes results in the formation of simple sugars and amino acids which are then metabolised by other microorganisms in the later stages of the fermentation. Brine, as a solution of 17 to 22 per cent sodium chloride, is then added and the mash is transferred to large vats. Bacteria involved in this second stage of fermentation include *Bacillus*, *Lactobacillus* and *Pediococcus* species. These contribute to a lowering of the pH, partly due to lactic acid production. The yeast *Saccharomyces rouxii* is responsible for production of some alcohol and development of flavour compounds. This fermentation occurs at a temperature of between 25 and 33 °C and continues for a few months or even up to a year. When mature, the dark brown liquid soya sauce is filtered off and usually pasteurised. Variations in flavour can be achieved by altering the fermentation conditions or microorganisms present in the culture. See Figure 10.4.

Role of yeast in bread making

For a description of the role of yeast in bread making see page 67.

Improvers such as **ascorbic acid** (vitamin C), are sometimes added to bread flour to speed up the processing time. During the intense mixing, the ascorbic acid is oxidised to dehydroascorbic acid. It then interacts with the —SH groups of the gluten proteins by removing hydrogen and forming disulphide S—S bridges very rapidly. This helps the dough structure to form and tighten quickly, trapping the bubbles of carbon dioxide and giving a reduced fermentation time. Large-scale commercial bread-making processes also utilise higher levels of yeast. Other improvers have been used to bleach flour to make it whiter, though consumer preferences are now swinging in favour of unbleached flour.

Figure 10.3 Soya bean curd for sale in a market in Yunnan, southwest China.

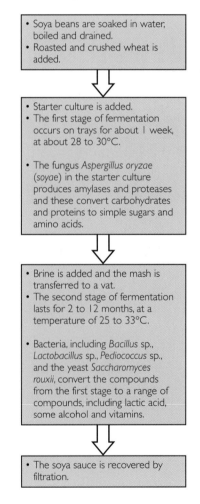

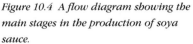

Figure 10.4 A flow diagram showing the main stages in the production of soya sauce.

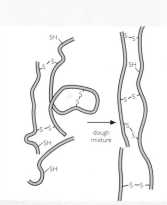

EXTENSION MATERIAL

The structure of bread

The secret to the structure of the bread lies in the properties of the proteins in wheat flour. Collectively the proteins are called glutens, made up mostly of gliadin and glutenin (Figure 10.5). A good bread flour, described as 'hard', has a protein content of 10 to 14 per cent, whereas softer flour has a protein content below 10 per cent and is more suitable for making biscuits or pastry. When the water is mixed with the flour, the proteins absorb water to form an elastic gluten complex. This allows the dough to stretch and retain the bubbles of carbon dioxide. The strength of the gluten is derived from the way the long, branched protein chains link together, to form a sort of network. This is enhanced by links between –SH (sulphydryl) groups from the amino acid cysteine, forming long, branched chains which give the dough its strength. The kneading process is important for several reasons – it mixes the ingredients allowing even dispersion of the carbon dioxide bubbles, but also plays a part in the modification of the proteins, allowing the chains to line up alongside each other and form the cross-links.

Figure 10.5 Bread dough and the kneading process. Molecular changes in the gluten proteins and the formation of cross-links between sulphydryl groups contribute to the properties of the dough which enable it to trap carbon dioxide gas.

Wine making

Making wine ranks as one of the oldest, and perhaps most pleasurable, of biotechnologies, enjoyed by countless individuals and with an important influence on successive cultures over the centuries. It is not difficult to see how a pile of surplus, discarded fruit began to ferment, and the liquor which seeped out was enjoyed for its flavour and alcoholic effects. Three thousand years ago the Greeks savoured wine which was kept in large pottery vessels. They later used barrels lined with pine resin. This increased storage time and allowed the wine to mature. The art of making wine has spread from the vineyards of Europe to world-wide production and consumption. Today, wine is generally understood to mean the alcoholic fermentation by yeast of sugars in grapes, from the vine *Vitis vinifera*, though wines are made from other fruits, vegetables or grains, such as apple, date, elderberry, parsnip and rice, as well as flowers, which contribute to the 'bouquet' of the wine. The fermentation of wine from grapes is described here, though similar principles apply to the production of other alcoholic beverages (see Figure 10.7).

The alcoholic fermentation of yeasts is represented by the following equation:

$$C_6H_{12}O_6 \rightarrow 2C_2H_5OH + 2CO_2$$
$$\text{glucose} \qquad \text{ethanol}$$

The main stages in the production of wine can be summarised as follows:
- crushing of the fruit, followed by separation of the juice
- fermentation with yeast
- drawing off the clear wine to separate it from residues
- ageing and maturation.

Grapes are harvested when they have the desired sugar content, generally between 15 and 25 per cent. The sugars are mainly glucose and fructose. Another important component is the acid content, consisting mainly of malic and tartaric acids. The sugar–acid balance is influenced by the variety of grape and the conditions under which it has grown. The grapes are removed from their stems, crushed mechanically and the juice pressed out (see Figure 10.7). Treatment with sulphur dioxide prevents further growth of wild yeasts, or of bacteria which may lead to souring of the wine by converting it to vinegar. Sometimes the juice is pasteurised by heating to 85 °C for a short time instead of using the sulphite treatment. Yeast is added to the juice in large tanks or fermenting vats. For white wine, the skins and pips are removed, but for red wine a proportion of the skins of black grapes are retained. Pigments in the skins contribute to the red colour and tannins give a characteristic taste.

Figure 10.6 Grapes growing in a Suffolk vineyard (England).

Wild yeasts naturally present on the skins of grapes can contribute to the fermentation, but in commercial production selected strains of a wine yeast are used, usually *Saccharomyces cerevisiae* var. *ellipsoideus*. Such yeasts show some tolerance to the level of alcohol produced, though this inhibits the growth of many other microorganisms. Initially respiration is aerobic, but as oxygen is depleted, the yeast switches to anaerobic respiration. There is then less growth of the yeast but the sugars are fermented to ethanol. Towards the end of the fermentation, lactic acid bacteria may ferment malic acid to lactic acid. Other bacteria may also contribute to the development of flavours in the later stages, during ageing or maturation.

For the first few days, the contents of the tank are mixed by pushing the 'cap' of floating skins and other debris into the tank of juice. This keeps the conditions aerobic and encourages growth of the yeast. The mixing is then stopped to allow anaerobic conditions to develop so that fermentation to ethanol occurs. The fermentation continues for 5 to 10 days at a temperature between 15 and 25 °C. After this, the wine is drawn off to separate it from the residues. The wine is pasteurised, or sulphite is added, to reduce the level of bacteria and then allowed to mature in barrels or bottles.

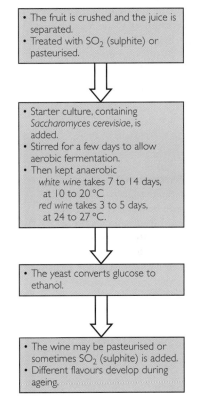

- The fruit is crushed and the juice is separated.
- Treated with SO_2 (sulphite) or pasteurised.

↓

- Starter culture, containing *Saccharomyces cerevisiae*, is added.
- Stirred for a few days to allow aerobic fermentation.
- Then kept anaerobic
  white wine takes 7 to 14 days, at 10 to 20 °C
  red wine takes 3 to 5 days, at 24 to 27 °C.

↓

- The yeast converts glucose to ethanol.

↓

- The wine may be pasteurised or sometimes SO_2 (sulphite) is added.
- Different flavours develop during ageing.

Figure 10.7 A flow diagram showing the main stages in the production of wine.

ADDITIONAL MATERIAL

Vinegar: an example of an aerobic fermentation

Vinegar is an aqueous solution (minimum 4 per cent) of ethanoic acid (acetic acid), produced by the oxidation of ethanol. Traces of other compounds, such as esters, alcohols and organic acids, give variations in the flavour. It is used world-wide for pickling or preserving foods, on salads, in cooking and to contribute to flavouring. The French word *vinaigre* means 'sour wine'. Source materials include fruit juices, such as grapes (wine vinegar), apples (cider vinegar), malted barley or other cereals (malt vinegar) and rice (rice vinegar).

There are two stages to the fermentation process:

- **anaerobic** fermentation of sugar (glucose) to ethanol by *Saccharomyces* spp. (yeast)
- **aerobic** conversion of ethanol to ethanoic acid, with ethanol (acetaldehyde) as an intermediate, by **acetic acid** bacteria, including a number of species mainly from the genera *Acetobacter* and *Gluconobacter*. Commercially a culture of mixed strains is used. These acetic acid baceria are not killed by the low pH but are sensitive to lack of oxygen.

QUESTION

Soya products are important in traditional Oriental diets. Bean curd can, for example, be fermented into a form of cheese, or dried and made into a paste. In China, cow's milk is not readily available and soya milk has been used as a substitute for human milk for feeding infants.

- Suggest why cow's milk is not part of the diet in much of China. (see page 106 for some help)
- Think of some reasons why soya milk is now being sold increasingly in European supermarkets.

QUESTION

Tempe is an Indonesian fermented food, made from soya beans. It is now being produced more widely in other parts of the world.

- Why do you think tempe is an important part of the diet for Indonesians?
- Find out which mould is responsible for the fermentation and how you could carry out this fermentation. [*You will find help in the National Centre for Biotechnology Education (NCBE) practical guides.*]

A review of these fermentations

Earlier in this chapter (page 123), you can find the statement that 'fermentations are a significant way of modifying raw fresh food' and that 'the fermented product has properties that are different from the original plant material'. To gain a better understanding of fermentations, we can now review the fermentations described in this chapter in a way that should help you become aware of some general principles that lie behind these examples of fermentations.

Aerobic or anaerobic?

Yoghurt and soya bean fermentations are aerobic; wine starts off as an aerobic process then becomes anaerobic; whereas sauerkraut becomes anaerobic at an early stage. This emphasises why it is incorrect to use the term 'fermentation' just for anaerobic respiration. The layer of carbon dioxide that forms above the surface (in wine and sauerkraut) helps keep conditions anaerobic.

Lactic acid for preservation

Fermentations for both sauerkraut and yoghurt produce lactic acid. It is the low pH that helps with preservation of the food. Lactic acid is also produced during the fermentation that makes soya sauce.

Texture and taste

In yoghurt, the low pH produced during the fermentation causes the proteins to coagulate. There is a similar coagulation of protein in soya bean curd, but here it is brought about by the addition of chemicals or vinegar rather than by the activity of microorganisms. In bread, changes in the gluten proteins, and particularly the cross-links between them, contribute to the texture of bread and enable the carbon dioxide to be held within the structure so making the bread rise. Cabbage that has been fermented to sauerkraut is quite limp and has lost the crispness of fresh cabbage. In all these fermentations, the final product tastes quite different from the material at the start.

Additives

Salt is added to cabbage mainly to help draw out water by osmosis. In bread making, sugar is added for respiration of the yeast and ascorbic acid is added to encourage rapid formation of the S—S links between the gluten proteins. Sulphite (or sulphur dioxide) is added at an early stage of wine making, and sometimes before bottling, to prevent activities of other (unwanted) microorganisms.

Bug or bugs

Under 'natural' conditions – such as alcoholic fermentation of fruit juices – a number of microorganisms may contribute to the fermentation; but in commercial production, a starter culture of one, two or more selected strains of microbe is often used. For the fermentations described here, only sauerkraut depends on its natural 'microflora' – the others all use starter cultures with selected strains of microorganisms.

Determining calorific values of foods, using a calorimeter

Introduction

A calorimeter, or heat of combustion apparatus, can be used to measure the calorific value of a sample of food. Combustion of the food in oxygen releases heat energy which will increase the temperature of the water contained in the apparatus. Measuring the rise in temperature of the water enables us to calculate the heat output of the food sample, and therefore the calorific value.

Materials

- Heat of combustion apparatus with nickel crucible
- Low-voltage power supply
- Cylinder of oxygen fitted with reducing valve and regulator
- Thermometer
- Filter pump attached to tap
- Rubber tubing to connect oxygen and filter pump
- Measuring cylinder
- Electronic balance
- Suitable food sample, such as a small potato chip or toast, previously dried and kept in a desiccator.

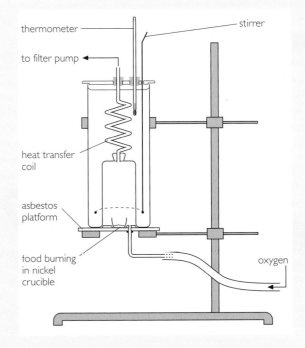

thermometer

stirrer

to filter pump

heat transfer coil

asbestos platform

food burning in nickel crucible

oxygen

Figure P.1 Calorimeter used to determine the heat of combustion of food. An electric heating coil is used to ignite the food sample.

Method

1 Fill the calorimeter jacket with water to cover the heat exchange coil, then tip the water into a measuring cylinder and record the volume. Return the water to the calorimeter.
2 Connect the apparatus to the oxygen supply, low voltage supply and filter pump, as shown in Figure P.1.
3 Weigh the nickel crucible and add a piece of suitable foodstuff.
4 Find and record the mass of food used.
5 Place the crucible centrally in the calorimeter and move the ignition coil so that it is just touching the food. Turn on the supply of oxygen and the filter pump.
6 Record the initial temperature of the water.
7 Ignite the food and then immediately move the ignition coil away from the crucible.
8 Move the stirrer steadily up and down including the doubled-walled area and the heat exchange coil. If necessary, adjust the flow rate of oxygen to keep the combustion steady.
9 Continue stirring for at least 2 minutes after the flame has gone out and record the maximum temperature reached by the water.

Results and discussion

1 Make a table to show the volume of water in the calorimeter, the mass of food used, the initial temperature and final temperature of the water, and the rise in temperature.
2 For comparative purposes, we can calculate the heat produced by the burning food by assuming that all the heat produced is transferred to the water. Naturally, this introduces an error, as it does not take into account the water equivalent of the apparatus itself. For more accurate determinations, the apparatus can be calibrated and a correction made.
3 If we assume that all the heat produced by the burning food is transferred to water and use the relationship that if 1 calorie is the heat energy required to raise 1 g of water by 1 °C, then heat produced by food (calories) = mass of water (g) × rise in temperature (°C).
4 Convert your result to joules, using the relationship: 1 calorie = 4.2 joules.
5 Compare your result with figures obtained from food tables. How closely does your result agree?
6 Consider the sources of error in this experiment.

BIOTECHNOLOGY AND FOOD PRODUCTION

Measuring percentage body fat, using skinfold calipers

Introduction

A skinfold caliper is used to measure the thickness of a fold of skin with its underlying layer of subcutaneous fat. The calipers usually have a spring which exerts a standard pressure on the skin and an accurate scale to measure the thickness in millimetres. Measurements may be made from four sites, the back of the upper arm, front of upper arm, the back below the shoulder blade and on the side of the waist, or from just one site, such as the back of the upper arm. If four readings are taken, the sum of the readings, in mm, can be converted to percentage body fat using the tables given.

It should be noted that this method may give unreliable results. More accurate data relating to body composition are obtained using the technique of bioelectric impedance analysis (BIA), which involves passing a small electric current through the body. The impedance to the flow of electric current is directly related to the level of body fat, which some meters calculate automatically.

Materials

- Skinfold caliper
- Tables to convert readings to percentage body fat.

Method

1 If possible, take skinfold measurements from all four sites of a person. A faster, but less accurate estimation can be obtained using one site. If one site is to be used, this should be the back of the upper arm
2 Using Figure P.2 to show where to take measurements, measure and record skinfold thickness from a volunteer.
3 Convert your readings to percentage body fat using Tables P.2, P.3 and P.4.

Results and discussion

1 Tabulate your results fully.
2 What is the importance of measurement of body fat?
3 What is the ideal percentage body fat?

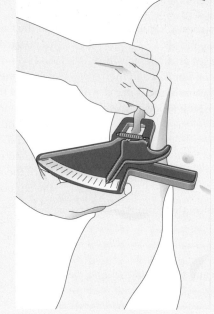

(a) At the front of the upper arm

(b) At the back of the upper arm

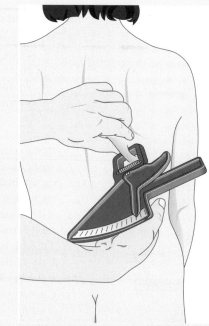

(c) On the back, below the shoulder blade

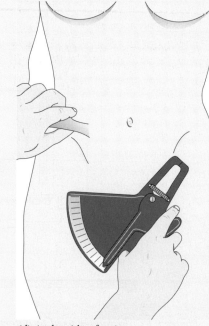

(d) At the side of waist

Figure P.2 Measuring skinfold thickness.

Table P.1 *Percentage body fat for men using sum of measurements at all four locations*

Sum of skinfold measurements / mm	Age 16–29	Age 30–49	Age 50+
20	8.1	12.1	12.5
22	9.2	13.2	13.9
24	10.2	14.2	15.1
26	11.2	15.2	16.3
28	12.1	16.1	17.4
30	12.9	16.9	18.5
35	14.7	18.7	20.8
40	16.3	20.3	22.8
45	17.7	21.8	24.7
50	19.0	23.0	26.3
55	20.2	24.2	27.8
60	21.2	25.3	29.1
65	22.2	26.3	30.4
70	23.2	27.2	31.5
75	24.0	28.0	32.6
80	24.8	28.8	33.7
85	25.6	29.6	34.6
90	26.3	30.3	35.5
95	27.0	31.0	36.5
100	27.6	31.7	37.3
110	28.8	32.9	38.8
120	29.9	34.0	40.2
130	31.0	35.0	41.5
140	31.9	36.0	42.8
150	32.8	36.8	43.9
160	33.6	37.7	45.0
170	34.4	38.5	46.0
180	35.2	39.2	47.0
190	35.9	39.9	47.9
200	36.5	40.6	48.8

Table P.2 *Percentage body fat for women using sum of measurements at all four locations*

Sum of skinfold measurements / mm	Age 16–29	Age 30–49	Age 50+
14	9.4	14.1	17.0
16	11.2	15.7	18.6
18	12.7	17.1	20.1
20	14.1	18.4	21.4
22	15.4	19.5	22.6
24	16.5	20.6	23.7
26	17.6	21.5	24.8
28	18.6	22.4	25.7
30	19.5	23.3	26.6
35	21.6	25.2	28.6
40	23.4	26.8	30.3
45	25.0	28.3	31.9
50	26.5	29.6	33.2
55	27.8	30.8	34.6
60	29.1	31.9	35.7
65	30.2	32.9	36.7
70	31.2	33.9	37.7
75	32.2	34.7	38.6
80	33.1	35.6	39.5
85	34.0	36.3	40.4
90	34.8	37.1	41.1
95	35.6	37.8	41.9
100	36.3	38.5	42.6
110	37.7	39.7	43.9
120	39.0	40.8	45.1
130	40.2	41.9	46.2
140	41.3	42.9	47.3
150	42.3	43.8	48.2
160	43.2	44.7	49.1
170	44.6	45.5	50.0
180	45.0	46.2	50.8
190	45.8	46.9	51.6
200	46.6	47.6	52.3

Table P.3 *Percentage body fat for men using measurement on back of upper arm*

Skinfold thickness / mm	Age 16–29	Age 30–49	Age 50+
3			12.1
4		14.4	15.7
5		16.6	18.6
6	10.8	18.6	20.6
7	12.5	20.2	22.9
8	13.9	21.5	24.6
9	15.2	22.6	26.2
10	16.4	23.6	27.6
11	17.4	24.5	28.8
12	18.4	25.3	30.0
13	19.3	26.1	31.1
14	20.1	26.8	32.1
15	20.9	27.5	33.0
16	21.6	28.1	33.9
17	22.3	28.7	34.7
18	22.9	29.2	35.5
19	23.5	29.8	36.2
20	24.1	30.3	36.9
22	25.2	31.2	38.2
24	26.2	32.1	39.5
26	27.1	32.9	40.6
28	28.0	33.6	41.6
30	28.8	34.3	42.6
32	29.5	34.9	43.5
34	30.3	35.5	44.3
36	30.9	36.1	45.2
38	31.6	36.7	45.9
40	32.2	37.2	46.7
45	33.6	38.4	48.4
50	34.8	39.4	49.9
55	35.9	40.4	51.3
60	37.0	41.3	52.5
65	37.9	42.1	53.7
70	38.8	42.9	54.8
75	39.7	43.6	55.8
80	40.5	44.3	56.8

Table P.4 *Percentage body fat for women using measurement on back of upper arm*

Skinfold thickness / mm	Age 16–29	Age 30–49	Age 50+
4		11.2	12.6
5	10.8	14.0	15.8
6	13.3	16.4	18.4
7	15.3	18.5	20.7
8	17.2	20.2	22.7
9	18.8	21.8	24.5
10	20.2	23.2	26.1
11	21.5	24.5	27.5
12	22.8	25.7	28.8
13	23.9	26.8	30.1
14	24.9	27.8	31.2
15	25.9	28.8	32.3
16	26.8	29.7	33.3
17	27.7	30.5	34.2
18	28.5	31.3	35.1
19	29.3	32.1	36.0
20	30.0	32.8	36.8
22	31.4	34.1	38.3
24	32.6	35.4	39.7
26	33.8	36.5	41.0
28	34.9	37.9	42.2
30	35.9	38.6	43.3
32	36.9	39.5	44.4
34	37.8	40.4	45.3
36	38.6	41.2	46.3
38	39.4	42.0	47.2
40	40.2	42.8	48.0
45	42.0	44.5	50.0
50	43.6	46.1	51.8
55	45.0	47.5	53.4
60	46.3	48.8	54.8
65	47.6	50.0	56.2
70	48.7	51.1	57.5
75	49.8	52.2	58.7
80	50.8	53.1	59.8

Quantitative estimation of sugars

Introduction

Concentrations of reducing sugars can be determined semi-quantitatively using Benedict's reagent and a range of colour standards. Quantitative estimations of glucose concentrations may be determined conveniently using suitable test strips, such as Diabur 5000. The concentration of sucrose can be estimated by first adding a drop of 10% invertase (sucrase) concentrate to 2 cm^3 of the solution to be tested and leaving for 30 minutes at room temperature. After enzyme treatment, the solution is tested for the presence of a reducing sugar. This method is preferable to acid hydrolysis.

Materials

- Range of food samples to be tested
- Mortar and pestle
- Beaker to use as boiling water bath
- Test tubes
- Diabur 5000 reagent strips
- Benedict's reagent
- Pipettes or syringes
- 10% invertase (sucrase) concentrate
- Standard glucose solutions: 2.0, 1.0, 0.5, 0.1, 0.05, 0.02 and 0.01%.

WEAR EYE PROTECTION

Method

1 To produce a range of colour standards, use a series of glucose solutions of known concentration. Add 3.0 cm^3 of each of these solutions to a series of appropriately labelled test tubes, each containing 5.0 cm^3 of Benedict's reagent. These test tubes should then be placed in a boiling water bath for 8 minutes, then left to cool in air.

2 To estimate the concentration of reducing sugars in the food samples, pipette 5.0 cm^3 of Benedict's reagent into a test tube and add 3.0 cm^3 of the solution to be tested. Heat in a boiling water bath for 8 minutes, leave to cool, then compare the colour produced with the colour standards.

3 If using Diabur 5000 test strips, a strip should be dipped into the solution to be tested, removed, and the colours produced compared with the colour chart after 2 minutes. This method is specific for glucose, and will give quantitative results.

Results and discussion

1 Tabulate all your results suitably.
2 Present the results in a suitable graphical form.
3 What are the sources of error in this experiment? How could it be improved?

Further work

1 Estimate the reducing sugar content of a range of fruit juices, both fresh and packaged.
2 Investigate the changes in reducing sugar content during, for example, the ripening of fruit.
3 Find out about other quantitative methods for the determination of reducing sugar content.

Quantitative estimation of ascorbic acid

Introduction

Ascorbic acid (vitamin C) is a reducing agent and can be detected using a dye, DCPIP (phenol-indo-2,6-dichlorophenol). DCPIP is blue in the oxidised form (which turns red in acidic solutions) and turns pale yellowish-brown when reduced. During the test, the tubes should not be shaken as atmospheric oxygen can reoxidise the DCPIP, giving inaccurate results.

Materials

- 0.1% ascorbic acid solution (1 mg ascorbic acid per cm^3)
- 0.1% aqueous DCPIP solution (this should be made up fresh each time)
- Samples of fruit juice, such as lemon, grapefruit, lime, grape and apple
- Test tubes
- 1 cm^3 syringes fitted with needles.

Safety note: Take care when handling syringes fitted with needles.

Method

1 Use a syringe or pipette to transfer exactly 1.0 cm^3 of DCPIP solution into a test tube.
2 Fill another 1 cm^3 syringe with the standard 0.1 % ascorbic acid solution and, keeping the end of the needle below the surface of the DCPIP, carefully add the ascorbic acid solution until the DCPIP is decolourised. Do not shake the mixture, it may be gently stirred using the needle.
3 Record the volume of ascorbic acid solution required to decolourise the DCPIP.
4 Repeat this test with 1.0 cm^3 of fresh DCPIP solution and fruit juice, such as lemon juice.
5 Record the volume of fruit juice required to decolourise the DCPIP.
6 Repeat the procedure with samples of different fruit juices.

Results and discussion

1 Record your results in a table.
2 Calculate the concentration of ascorbic acid in the fruit

juice sample, using the following relationship. Suppose that the volume of standard ascorbic acid solution required to decolourise 1.0 cm^3 of DCPIP was x cm^3, and the volume of fruit juice required to decolourise the same volume of DCPIP solution was y cm^3, then the concentration of ascorbic acid in the fruit juice sample will be $x \div y$ mg of ascorbic acid per cm^3. Note that 1 mg cm^{-3} of ascorbic acid is equivalent to a concentration of 0.1%. To convert your values from mg cm^{-3} to a percentage, multiply by 0.1. For example, 0.8 mg cm^{-3} is equivalent to $0.8 \times 0.1 = 0.08\%$.

3 Present your results in a suitable graphical form so that the ascorbic acid content of the different fruits can be compared.

Further work

1 Investigate differences in the ascorbic acid content between fresh fruit juice and bottled fruit juice, or juice from a carton.

2 Investigate changes in the ascorbic acid content of fruit during storage.

3 Investigate the effect of boiling on ascorbic acid content of fruit juice.

PRACTICAL

The resazurin test, methylene blue test and turbidity test

Introduction

The tests in this practical investigate the freshness of milk, by using methods which indicate the activity of bacteria, and also the effectiveness of pasteurisation and sterilisation.

Resazurin is an indicator which shows metabolic activity of bacteria. The indicator is blue in the oxidised state but changes, when reduced, through pink to white. Although this test does not show the types of bacteria present, it can be used as a means of comparing the bacterial content of milk samples. Tubes containing milk which changes colour to white, pink or white mottling have failed the test.

Methylene blue is a sensitive redox indicator which, like resazurin, shows bacterial activity in the milk sample. Methylene blue is decolourised when reduced, so recording the time taken for the blue colour to disappear gives an indication of bacterial activity in the milk sample.

The turbidity test is used to check for the efficiency of sterilisation. The procedure depends on changes in the properties of milk proteins after treatment at different temperatures and after the addition of ammonium sulphate. After addition of ammonium sulphate and filtration, the filtrate should remain clear on boiling if the sterilisation procedure has been effective.

(a) The resazurin test

Materials

- Milk samples
- Resazurin tablets
- Distilled water
- Pipettes or syringes
- Sterile screw-capped containers, such as universal bottles
- Water bath at 37 °C.

Method

1 Dissolve one resazurin tablet in 50 cm^3 of distilled water.

2 Add 1.0 cm^3 of this solution to 10.0 cm^3 of milk to be tested in a sterile container. Replace the lid, label the container and invert once to mix the contents.

3 Incubate in a water bath at 37 °C, filled so that the level of water is just over the level of milk in the container.

4 Set up a control tube containing 10.0 cm^3 of boiled milk plus 1.0 cm^3 resazurin solution.

5 Examine the samples after 10 minutes and note any colour changes.

6 Replace in the water bath and examine again after 1 hour.

7 Compare the colour of each sample with that of the control tube, which should remain blue.

(b) The methylene blue test

Materials

- Milk samples
- 5.0% acetaldehyde (ethanal) solution (Add a few drops of phenolphthalein indicator, followed by a dilute solution of sodium carbonate until the mixture just turns pink.)
- 0.01% methylene blue solution.
- Distilled water
- Pipettes or syringes
- Test tubes
- Aluminium foil
- Water bath at 40 °C.

Method

1 Measure 5.0 cm^3 of pasteurised milk into a test tube, add 1.0 cm^3 of the acetaldehyde solution and 1.0 cm^3 of methylene blue. Mix the contents by shaking the tube gently, then cover the top of the tube with a small piece of aluminium foil.

2 Stand the tube in a water bath at 40 °C and note the time taken for the methylene blue to become decolourised. A blue ring may remain at the top of the sample.

3 Repeat this procedure with other samples of milk.

BIOTECHNOLOGY AND FOOD PRODUCTION

(c) The turbidity test

Materials

- Milk samples: sterilised, pasteurised, pasteurised and boiled for 5 minutes
- Ammonium sulphate
- Electronic balance
- Conical flasks, 50 cm^3
- Measuring cylinder, 100 cm^3
- Filter funnels and filter paper
- Test tubes
- Beaker to use as a boiling water bath
- Pipettes or syringes
- Bench lamp.

WEAR EYE PROTECTION

Method

1 Weigh 4 g of ammonium sulphate and transfer to a conical flask.

2 Add 20 cm^3 of the milk sample to be tested to the ammonium sulphate.

3 Shake the flask for at least 1 minute to dissolve the ammonium sulphate.

4 Leave the flask to stand for 5 minutes.

5 Filter the contents of the flask and transfer 5.0 cm^3 of the filtrate to a test tube.

6 Place the test tube in a boiling water bath and leave for 5 minutes.

7 Cool the tube in a beaker of cold water, then examine the contents by holding the tube in front of a bench lamp.

Results and discussion

1 Record all your results in a suitable table.

2 Compare the results of each test for the different samples of milk used and comment on their significance.

3 Find out about the possible health risks associated with untreated (raw) milk. What steps are taken to minimise these risks?

PRACTICAL   ## Investigating weight loss in packaged foods

Introduction

Various packaging materials, such as paper, PVC films and cling wrap, are used for fruit and vegetables. These can help to reduce water loss, and also modify the atmosphere surrounding the produce and thereby increase the shelf-life. If fruits are enclosed in a plastic film, they continue to respire, using up oxygen and producing carbon dioxide and water. The increase in carbon dioxide reduces the metabolic rate of many fruits and increases their shelf-life. However, if a covering film is impermeable to water vapour, the increase in humidity surrounding the produce encourages the growth of fungal or bacterial spores, resulting in food spoilage.

The purpose of this practical is to investigate the effect of different packaging materials on weight loss, and changes in the appearance of fruit and vegetables.

Materials

- Containers, such as small plastic boxes or punnets
- Packaging materials, such as thin PVC film, cling wrap, paper
- Selection of fruit and vegetables – apples, mushrooms, small lettuces and carrots are suitable
- Electronic balance.

Method

1 Weigh the containers and packaging materials separately, introduce the produce, wrap suitably and weigh again. Record the mass of produce. Remember to include one uncovered container as a control.

2 Reweigh at suitable intervals. This will depend on the nature of the produce; it may be necessary to carry out a

preliminary experiment. Record the mass of each container of produce.

3 If you have access to a refrigerator, place one set of containers in the salad compartment and leave one set at room temperature. Record mass as before.

4 Record changes in the appearance of the produce.

Results and discussion

1 Record all your results in a suitable table.

2 Calculate the percentage change in mass of the produce.

3 Plot graphs to show percentage change in mass against time.

4 Compare the results for each type of packaging material.

5 What effect did temperature have on the rate of loss in mass?

6 Consider which factors are important in the choice of packaging materials.

Further work

This experiment lends itself to a number of investigations into ways of increasing the shelf-life of fruit and vegetables by slowing deterioration. It is possible to modify the composition of the atmosphere in the container by, for example, including a small beaker of soda water to increase the concentration of carbon dioxide. Alternatively, you could try including a small amount of potassium permanganate, which will remove ethene (ethylene) from the atmosphere in the container. Remember to include suitable controls in your experiments.

1 Investigate the effect of raising the concentration of carbon dioxide on the shelf-life of lettuce.

2 Investigate the effect of removing ethene (ethylene) from the atmosphere on the keeping qualities of bananas.

Changes in food during fermentations

Introduction

In Chapter 10, we have described some of the chemical changes which occur in foods during the process of fermentation. In this practical, we look at the changes in pH which occur in milk during the formation of yoghurt. Bacteria in the starter culture ferment milk sugars to produce organic acids, such as methanoic and lactic acid, and consequently the pH will fall.

Materials

- UHT milk
- Natural yoghurt to use as a starter culture
- Boiling tubes
- Pipettes or syringes
- Cling wrap
- Glass stirring rod
- pH meter (if unavailable, narrow range pH papers could be used as an alternative)
- Water bath at 43 °C.

Method

1 Transfer 10.0 cm^3 of UHT into a boiling tube then add 1.0 cm^3 of natural yoghurt.
2 Record the pH of the mixture, cover the tube with cling wrap, and incubate in a water bath at 43 °C.

3 Record the pH and changes in the appearance of the yoghurt at intervals of 30 minutes for up to 5 hours.
4 Dispose of incubated milk carefully after completing the practical. Equipment should be sterilised after use.

Results and discussion

1 Record your results in a table, then plot a graph to show changes in the pH during fermentation.
2 Describe the changes which occurred in pH and in the appearance of the yoghurt during fermentation.

Further work

1 Investigate the changes in pH during production of yoghurt using different types of milk, such as cow's, ewe's or goat's.
2 Investigate changes in pH during production of yoghurt using lactose-reduced milk, such as Lactolite™, or starter cultures containing *Lactobacillus acidophilus* and *Bifidobacterium bifidum*.
3 Devise a method to investigate changes in reducing sugar content during the production of yoghurt.
4 The principle of this experiment could be extended to, for example, measurement of changes in pH during fermentation of cabbage to make sauerkraut.

Perception of sweetness in drinks or food

Introduction

The degree of sweetness of sugars varies, and some sugars therefore taste sweeter than others. Sucrose is used as the standard reference substance for sweetness and the degrees of sweetness of other sugars are usually compared with that of sucrose. The aim of this practical is to compare the taste of different sugars and to arrange them in order of apparent sweetness.

Safety note: If this activity is to take place in the laboratory ensure that lab benches have been thoroughly cleaned, and that sugars are not contaminated. The sugars should not be stored with other chemicals.

Materials

- Disposable plastic cups
- Supply of drinking water
- 4% solutions of sucrose, lactose, maltose, glucose and fructose, made up in drinking water. Label the solutions A, B, C, etc.

Method

1 Taste each of the solutions in turn, rinsing your mouth out

with water between each solution. Decide which solution tastes:
(a) the most sweet
(b) the least sweet.
2 Arrange the solutions in order of sweetness, from the most sweet to the least.

Results and discussion

1 Record your results in a suitable table, including the identity of each solution.
2 Refer to Table 8.4 on page 97. To what extent do your results agree with these values for relative sweetness? Suggest reasons for any differences.

Further work

1 Investigate the threshold concentrations, by tasting a range of concentrations of each sugar, for example, 0.001, 0.01, 0.05, 0.1 and 0.2 mol dm^{-3}.
2 Compare the relative sweetness and note any 'aftertaste' of artificial sweeteners such as aspartame and saccharin.
3 Consider how you might develop this practical to include statistical treatment of the results.

Option C: Human Health and Fitness

11 Body systems

Normal functioning of all the body systems is necessary to maintain health. When considering the physiology of exercise and, in particular, training to achieve improvement in a sport, it is necessary to understand the way in which the healthy organs function. It is also important to appreciate the interrelationships between organ systems: the effect of increased exercise on one system may affect other systems. In addition, a sound understanding of the body systems can help some of the common disorders which affect human beings in modern society.

In this chapter, we consider four of the major body systems:
- the **cardiovascular** system – concerned with the heart and the circulation
- the **pulmonary** system – concerned with the lungs and breathing
- the **musculo-skeletal** system – concerned with the structure and functioning of muscles and bones
- the **lymphatic** system – concerned with transport and also with the immune response of the body.

These systems are not treated in isolation, as there are interrelationships evident. A greater understanding of the cellular components of blood, particularly with respect to the functions of lymphocytes, links with the lymphatic system, and there are obvious links between the cardiovascular system and both the pulmonary and musculoskeletal systems.

Some aspects of the cardiovascular and pulmonary systems are already covered in *Exchange and Transport, Energy and Ecosystems* and you should refer to the relevant chapters of this text for details. The extra detail given here extends the knowledge of these systems and emphasises the way in which the systems are controlled.

> ### DEFINITION
>
> The **cardiovascular system** consists of:
> - the **heart** – a pump
> - the **blood** – the transport medium for nutrients and other solutes
> - the **blood vessels** – linking the heart with the body organs.

The cardiovascular system

The cardiovascular system consists of:
- the **heart**, which is the pump supplying the force to propel the blood around the body
- the **blood vessels** (**arteries, veins** and **capillaries**), in which the blood is transported
- the **blood**, which is the transport medium for nutrients and other substances to and from the body organs and systems.

All the cells in the organs of the body must receive nutrients (such as glucose for respiration) and have waste products removed, so it is essential that the blood is kept in a state of continuous circulation. The force generated by the heart propels the blood into thick-walled arteries which deliver blood to the organs. The blood is returned to the heart through thinner-walled veins. In the tissues of the organs, the blood passes through a network of capillaries, where exchange of materials occurs between the blood and the tissue fluid. The circulatory system is a double one, consisting of the **systemic circulation**, in which oxygenated blood is pumped from the left side of the heart to the organs of the body, and the **pulmonary circulation**, in which deoxygenated blood is pumped from the right side of the heart to the lungs for oxygenation.

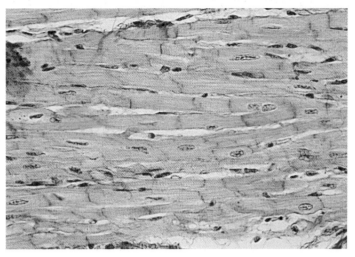

The heart – histology of cardiac muscle and myogenic stimulation

It is important to understand the external appearance of the human heart, the location of the major blood vessels, and the location of the different chambers and systems of valves which control the passage of blood during the cardiac cycle. These details can be found in *Exchange and Transport, Energy and Ecosystems*. The emphasis in this chapter is on the structure and function of the cardiac muscle, its stimulation and control.

The wall of the heart is made up of three distinct layers:
- the outer **epicardium** of flattened epithelial cells and connective tissue
- a thick muscular **myocardium** composed of **cardiac muscle**
- the inner **endocardium** of flattened epithelial cells supported by a delicate layer of connective tissue.

Cardiac muscle (Figure 11.1) contains actin and myosin filaments and cross-striations similar to those found in striated (skeletal) muscle. In cardiac muscle, there is a three-dimensional network of columns of short fibres. Each cardiac muscle fibre is surrounded by a **sarcolemma**, similar in structure to a cell surface membrane, and may contain one or more centrally placed nuclei. Adjacent fibres are connected by **intercalated discs** At intervals along these discs are **gap junctions**, where the membranes of adjacent fibres are closer together. These junctions form areas of low electrical resistance permitting the rapid spread of excitation along the fibres when the muscle is stimulated. Within each fibre are large numbers of fairly conspicuous myofibrils, showing cross-striations similar to those observed in striated muscle fibres. There is a **sarcoplasmic reticulum**, consisting of a network of membranes, and a well-developed system of transverse tubules (the **T system**) extending across each fibre. The **myofibrils** in the sarcoplasm of each fibre are 0.08 mm or less in length and have a diameter of about 15 μm. Between the fibres, there is connective tissue, with collagen and elastic fibres, and a very rich blood capillary network supplied with blood from the coronary arteries. Large numbers of mitochondria are present.

Cardiac muscle is said to be **myogenic**, which means that it is self-exciting and does not depend on nervous stimulation for the initiation of contraction.

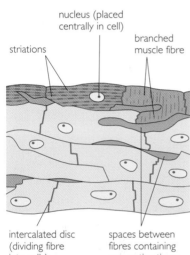

Figure 11.1 (top) Photograph of cardiac muscle tissue as seen using a light microscope; (bottom) cardiac muscle structure.

DEFINITION

Cardiac muscle is **myogenic**, that is, it is self-stimulating and does not rely on nervous stimulation to initiate contractions.

Within the heart there are groups of muscle fibres which are atypical. These are known as the **Purkinje (Purkyne) system**. The fibres of this system differ from the normal cardiac muscle fibres in having fewer myofibrils and a clear area around the central region in which the nuclei are located. The stimulus for the contraction of the heart muscle originates in a region known as the **sinoatrial** or **sinuatrial node (SAN)** (also known as the 'pacemaker'), which is close to where the vena cavae open into the right atrium. At this point, the fibres of the Purkinje system are spindle shaped and branched. The SAN initiates the heartbeat, but the rate at which contraction occurs can be varied by nervous or hormonal stimulation.

The modified muscle cells of the SAN maintain a differential ionic concentration of –90 mV across their membranes. Sodium ions continually diffuse in, giving the cells a high sodium conductance. The influx of sodium ions produces a depolarisation which then leads to the generation of an action potential in the cardiac fibres next to the SAN. Once the contraction has been initiated, it spreads rapidly due to the areas of low electrical resistance provided by the gap junctions in the intercalated discs. A contraction is immediately followed by a refractory period, during which the muscle cannot be stimulated to contract again. In this way the muscle does not become easily fatigued. The refractory period for cardiac muscle is longer than that for other types of muscle tissue, enabling vigorous, rapid contractions without fatigue. Cardiac muscle cannot develop tetanus (a state of sustained contraction) or build up an oxygen debt.

In addition to the SAN, the conducting system of the heart (Figure 11.2) comprises:

- the **atrioventricular node (AVN)**, consisting of modified cardiac muscle cells similar to those of the SAN, located in the wall of the right atrium near the opening of the coronary sinus
- the **bundle of His** and its branches, consisting of specialised muscle cells called **Purkinje** (or **Purkyne**) **fibres**, which extend into the ventricular myocardium.

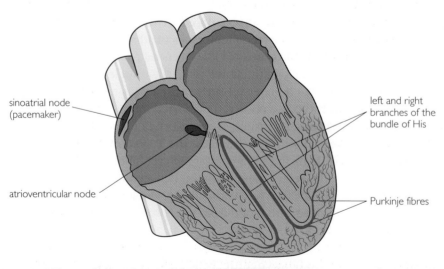

sinoatrial node (pacemaker)

atrioventricular node

left and right branches of the bundle of His

Purkinje fibres

Figure 11.2 The conducting system of the human heart.

As the SAN generates an action potential, the wave of excitation spreads over the atria, causing the muscle fibres to contract. When the excitation reaches the AVN, it is conducted by means of the Purkinje fibres in the bundle of His to the ventricular myocardium at the base of the heart. Contraction of the cardiac muscle fibres of the ventricles begins here and forces the blood out of the ventricles into the arteries.

Because the muscle fibres in the atria are completely separate from those of the ventricles, due to the presence of the atrioventricular septum, which is composed of non-conducting connective tissue, the AVN is the only means by which the wave of excitation can pass from the atria to the ventricles. There is a delay of about 0.15 seconds between the initiation of the impulse in the SAN leading to the contraction of the atria and the conduction of the impulse to the AVN, which leads to the contraction of the ventricles. This arrangement of the conducting tissue in the heart ensures that contraction of the atria (atrial systole) is completed before contraction of the ventricles (ventricular systole) and that the electrical excitation reaches most of the cardiac muscle fibres in the ventricles at the same time so that there is a single, coordinated contraction.

> **QUESTION**
>
> Explain how the atria contract from the top of the heart downwards and the ventricles from the apex of the heart upwards.

Control of the cardiac cycle

A description of the structure of the mammalian heart and its associated coronary circulation is given in *Exchange and Transport, Energy and Ecosystems*, Chapter 2. Reference should also be made to this chapter for a description of the cardiac cycle.

Although the SAN normally initiates the heartbeat, the rate can be influenced by a number of factors, due to the changing needs and activities of the body. Control of the heart rate is achieved by a combination of nervous and hormonal mechanisms.

The SAN is supplied with nerve endings from the **autonomic nervous system**. This system is part of the peripheral nervous system and controls internal activities, such as heart rate and sweating, which are normally involuntary (not under our conscious, voluntary control). It consists of motor neurones which penetrate the muscle of internal organs and is divided into two parts :
- the **sympathetic** system
- the **parasympathetic** system.

It is not necessary to have a detailed understanding of the autonomic nervous system, but it is helpful to understand some of the differences between the sympathetic and the parasympathetic systems in order to appreciate the control of the cardiac cycle. The major features of the two systems, as they relate to the control of the cardiac cycle, are summarised in Table 11.1.

The effects of the stimulation of the two systems are generally antagonistic: stimulation of the heart by the sympathetic system increases the heart rate, but stimulation by the parasympathetic system decreases the rate. The inhibitory effect of the parasympathetic system prevents the heart rate from becoming excessive. Eventually, the heart rate will be restored to its normal

Table 11.1 *Major differences between the sympathetic and parasympathetic nervous systems*

Sympathetic nervous system	Parasympathetic nervous system
noradrenaline secreted as transmitter substance	acetylcholine secreted as transmitter substance
increases amplitude of heart beat	decreases amplitude of heart beat
increases rate of heartbeat	decreases rate of heartbeat
activated during periods of activity and stress	controls routine activities when body at rest
diffuse effect	localised effect

level when a balance between the secretion of noradrenaline and the secretion of acetylcholine is reached.

The activity of the nerves of both systems is controlled by the **cardiovascular control centres** in the **medulla oblongata** of the brain. There is a cardioacceleratory centre and a cardioinhibitory centre, both of which receive sensory information from small stretch receptors in blood vessel walls. These stretch receptors are called **baroreceptors**. Changes in the pressure of the blood flowing through the vessels is detected and impulses are transmitted to the control centres in the brain. The responses involve either the parasympathetic system or the sympathetic system, depending on the information received. Baroreceptors are present in the walls of the carotid sinuses, the aortic arch and the venae cavae.

If the blood pressure in the venae cavae rises, as a result of vigorous muscular activity increasing the volume of blood returning to the heart, there is an increase in the number of impulses from the baroreceptors. These impulses are transmitted by sensory neurones to the cardioacceleratory centre, which is stimulated to transmit impulses via the sympathetic nerves to the SAN, AVN and cardiac muscle, with the result that noradrenaline is released at the neuromuscular junctions. The SAN is stimulated, and the delay at the AVN is reduced so that the rate of the heartbeat is increased. The force of each muscle contraction is also increased. This is a reflex pathway, known as the **Bainbridge reflex**, which regulates the venous pressure in the heart.

The carotid sinus reflex maintains the correct supply of blood to the brain (Figure 11.3). The carotid arteries supply blood to the brain and each artery has a swelling at its base, called a carotid sinus, in which there are baroreceptors. If the blood pressure rises, the sinus wall is stretched and impulses are transmitted from the baroreceptors to the cardioinhibitory centre in the medulla oblongata. From this centre, impulses are transmitted, via the vagus nerve of the parasympathetic system, to the SAN and AVN in the heart. Acetylcholine is released and the heartbeat is slowed, because the SAN is suppressed and the delay at the AVN is increased. The blood pressure falls, so the stimulation of the baroreceptors is decreased as the walls of the sinuses are less stretched.

The aortic reflex, which controls the general systemic blood pressure, works in a similar way. It is initiated by the stimulation of the baroreceptors in the walls of the aortic arch and the effect is to reduce the rate of the heartbeat.

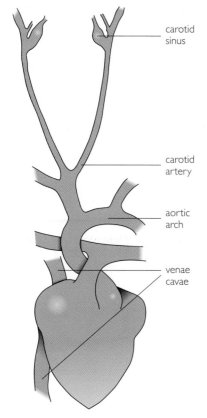

carotid sinus

carotid artery

aortic arch

venae cavae

Figure 11.3. Diagram of heart and associated blood vessels to show location of baroreceptors.

QUESTION

Compare the response to a rise in blood pressure in the venae cavae with a rise in blood pressure in the carotid sinus or the aortic arch.

The cardiac cycle can also be affected by changes in the composition of the blood. During periods of vigorous activity, there are changes in the oxygen and carbon dioxide tensions in the blood and these changes affect the pH of the blood. As exercise continues, the oxygen tension decreases as more oxygen is required by the respiring cells. More carbon dioxide is produced and its tension increases, causing the pH of the blood to be lower. Such changes are detected in the cardiovascular control centres in the medulla and impulses are transmitted to the heart via the sympathetic system, so that the heart rate is increased.

The hormone adrenaline, which is released at times of stress or excitement, can affect the heart rate. It mimics the sympathetic system in its effects: it increases the amplitude (stroke volume) and the rate of the heart beat, and increases blood pressure.

Artificial pacemakers and the treatment of heart disease

Artificial pacemakers can be used to correct slow heart rates caused by disease or ageing of the heart (Figure 11.4). These are electronic devices which generate an impulse and they are usually surgically implanted into the muscle of the chest. Some types have a fixed rate at which the impulses are delivered and this rate is not affected by the person's heartbeat. Other types are sensitive to the heartbeat and only deliver an impulse when the heart misses a beat. The devices are fairly small and powered by lithium batteries.

Phagocytosis and the immune response

The roles of the cellular components of the blood are vital in the transport of respiratory gases and in defence against disease. The role of the red blood corpuscles (erythrocytes) in the transport of respiratory gases described in *Exchange and Transport, Energy and Ecosystems*. The roles of the white cells (leucocytes) are concerned with the defence of the body against disease and it is relevant to consider both phagocytosis and the immune response in this section.

White blood cells (leucocytes) are nucleated cells present in the blood. They arc less numerous than the red blood corpuscles: there are about 7000 per mm^3 of blood compared with about 5 000 000 red cells. Most white cells have a lifespan of only a few days, but red cells can be in the circulation for a period of 3 months.

Details of the different types of leucocytes, both granulocytes and agranulocytes, are given in *Exchange and Transport, Energy and Ecosystems*, Chapter 2. In this chapter, the roles of three different types of leucocytes are considered. **Neutrophils** and **monocytes** carry out **phagocytosis**, which involves engulfing and destroying bacteria and foreign particles that enter the body. **Lymphocytes** secrete antibodies and form part of the body's immune response.

Neutrophils are granulocytes, with lobed nuclei and granular cytoplasm. They originate from stem cells in the bone marrow and are the most numerous of

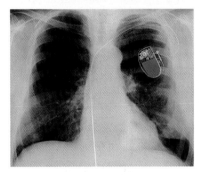

Figure 11.4 (top) Artificial pacemakers; (bottom) coloured X-ray of a pacemaker in situ.

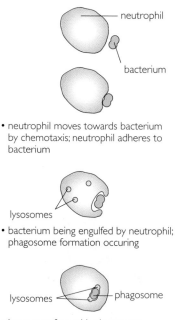

• neutrophil moves towards bacterium by chemotaxis; neutrophil adheres to bacterium

• bacterium being engulfed by neutrophil; phagosome formation occuring

• lysosomes fuse with phagosome membrane; hydrolytic enzymes released into phagosome

• digestion of bacterium; soluble products of digestion diffuse into cytoplasm of neutrophil

Figure 11.5. Phagocytosis by a neutrophil.

the white cells. They are capable of amoeboid movement and can squeeze between the cells of capillary walls, a process known as **diapedesis**. Monocytes also show diapedesis, but they are agranulocytes, each with a bean-shaped nucleus and clear cytoplasm. Both the neutrophils and monocytes migrate to infected and damaged tissues, where they ingest bacteria and foreign matter by endocytosis.

Neutrophils are attracted to damaged tissues, possibly due to the release of chemicals from the ruptured cells. Bacteria and foreign matter are identified by the plasma proteins, called **opsonins**, which become attached to them. The neutrophils recognise the bacteria, stick to them and then engulf them. The resulting vacuole, known as a phagosome, is enclosed in the cytoplasm of the neutrophil. Lysosomes, containing hydrolytic enzymes and acid, empty their contents into the **phagosomes**. The bacteria are digested and eventually the soluble products are absorbed into the surrounding cytoplasm (Figure 11.5).

Monocytes behave in a similar way. In addition, it is worth mentioning the **macrophages**, which are similar to the monocytes and also derived from the stem cells in the bone marrow. These cells are present in the liver, spleen and lungs. The lung alveolar macrophages move around but the macrophages in the liver, called Kupffer cells, are fixed. All these white cells confer **non-specific** or **natural immunity** and are the first cells to be active during an infection of the body.

The **complement system** is another non-specific defence system present in humans. It consists of about 20 blood serum proteins which can be activated when bacteria and foreign matter enter the body. The complement proteins can assist the humoral response and we have already referred to the attachment of opsonins to invading bacteria. The presence of the opsonins enables the bacteria to be more easily recognised by the white cells and then makes phagocytosis easier. Other complement proteins cause swelling and reddening of the tissues around an infection, referred to as the inflammatory response, increase in permeability of blood capillaries and the chemotactic migration of the white cells to the invading bacteria.

Lymphocytes are small white cells with little cytoplasm and spherical nuclei, which originate from stem cells in the bone marrow. There are two types of lymphocytes:
• **B cells** which mature in the bone marrow and then migrate to the lymph nodes
• **T cells** which migrate to the thymus gland for a period of maturation before migrating to the lymph nodes.

Once the lymphocytes are mature, they circulate in the spleen, lymph nodes, adenoids and tonsils, as well as in the lymphatic system and the general circulation of the blood. Both types are activated by the presence of specific foreign molecules: each B cell and T cell can only be activated by one particular **antigen**.

An antigen is a foreign molecule which provokes the production of an **antibody**, highly specific to the particular antigen. The antibody may neutralise the antigen or destroy the organism producing the antigen. Antigens are organic molecules, such as proteins, glycoproteins or polysaccharides. They may be free or may be present on the surface of cells or organisms, such as bacteria. All human cells have antigens on their surfaces: they are recognition factors and only provoke an immune response if they are foreign, or non-self. An example of this is seen in the ABO system of human blood groups, which is determined by the presence of certain molecules on the membranes of the red blood cells.

Antibodies are proteins known as **immunoglobulins (Ig)** (Figure 11.6). They are synthesised in response to the presence of foreign substances. Each antibody molecule has:
- two identical heavy chains of amino acids (H) of 50 000 to 60 000 relative molecular mass
- two identical light chains of amino acids (L) of 23 000 relative molecular mass.

In each antibody, there are constant regions where the amino acid sequence is the same or very similar and variable regions where the amino acid sequence varies and is unique to different molecules. The variable regions form a specific three-dimensional structure, called the **antigen-binding site**. The antigen-binding site is specific to one type of antigen.

B cells have Ig molecules on their surfaces, which act as receptors. When a B cell detects complementary antigens, it is activated and undergoes a large number of mitotic divisions, producing **plasma cells** and **memory cells**. The plasma cells synthesise large quantities of antibodies, specific to the particular antigen which triggered the response. These antibodies are released into the blood plasma and tissue fluid, where they neutralise toxins or speed up phagocytosis by adhering to the surfaces of the invading organisms. The memory cells produced have Ig receptor molecules identical to the original activated B cell and they will recognise the antigen which stimulated their production. If there is exposure to the same antigen at a later date, these memory B cells are activated and there is a rapid production of the specific antibodies, referred to as the **secondary response**. Memory cells may remain in the body for many years. The production of antibodies by B cells is referred to as the **humoral immune response**.

As already discussed, the T cells undergo maturation in the thymus gland and then pass to the lymph nodes and the spleen. T cells can also recognise antigens by means of specific receptors and, once activated by a specific antigen, they undergo mitotic divisions to produce a clone of T cells, with different functions:
- **killer T cells** – can attach themselves to invading cells and destroy them; they also attract macrophages and help to activate phagocytosis
- **helper T cells** – help the humoral response by involvement in the maturation of B cells and by triggering the production of antibodies by the B cells
- **memory T cells** – work in the same way as the memory B cells, ensuring a rapid response on subsequent exposure to the same non-self antigens
- **suppressor T cells** – regulate the immune response by suppressing the activity of the killer T cells and the B cells.

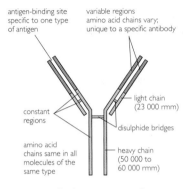

Figure 11.6. The structure of an immunoglobulin antibody molecule.

BODY SYSTEMS

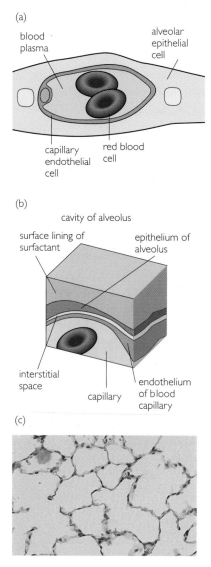

(a)

blood plasma

alveolar epithelial cell

capillary endothelial cell

red blood cell

(b)

cavity of alveolus

surface lining of surfactant

epithelium of alveolus

interstitial space

capillary

endothelium of blood capillary

(c)

Figure 11.7 (a) The relationship between the lung capillary and the alveolar epithelium; (b) the alveolar – capillary membrane which separates the alveolar air from the blood; (c) photomicrograph of lung tissue.

The response made by the T cells is referred to as the **cell-mediated immune response**. Killer T cells cause cells infected with virus particles to lyse. T cells in the thymus gland, sometimes referred to as thymocytes, manufacture and release molecules called **lymphokines**, which include **interferon**. Interferon prevents the replication of viruses.

Active and passive immunity

Active immunity is acquired naturally as a result of exposure to an antigen. The antigen triggers the production of antibodies, which react against the antigen, and also results in the presence of memory cells, which are capable of producing specific antibodies should there be a subsequent invasion by the same antigen.

Passive immunity is acquired naturally by a child from its mother. Before birth, antibodies pass across the placenta from the mother's blood to the developing fetus. After birth, the child obtains antibodies from the colostrum and the mother's milk during breast-feeding.

Immunity may be artificially induced, either by giving an individual antibodies, as in the case of immunisation against diphtheria or tetanus, or by introducing small quantities of the antigen into the body and stimulating the production of the specific antibodies by the individual. In the latter case, the antigens are administered in the form of a vaccine.

The pulmonary system

The structure of the pulmonary system is described in *Exchange and Transport, Energy and Ecosystems* and you should familiarise yourself with the details of the structure of the thorax and the mechanism of ventilation as outlined in Chapter 1. In this chapter, the emphasis is on the histology of the lung tissue and the ways in which the ventilation mechanism is controlled.

Lung tissue

Most of the lung tissue (Figure 11.7) consists of tiny air-filled sacs called **alveoli**. The branching of the bronchi results in a fine network of bronchioles ending in the alveolar air sacs, which lead into the alveoli. The clusters of alveoli are separated from each other by elastic connective tissue. Each alveolus has a diameter of about 200 μm and is surrounded by a capillary network. For further details of the structure of the lung tissue, see *Exchange and Transport, Energy and Ecosystems*, Chapter 1.

In order to appreciate the efficiency of the exchange of respiratory gases, it should be noted that the gases need to pass through:
• the endothelium of the blood capillary (0.04 to 0.2 μm)
• an interstitial space (0.02 to 0.2 μm)
• the alveolar epithelium (0.05 to 0.3 μm)
• a surface lining of surfactant (0.01 μm)
making a total blood-to-gas distance of between 0.2 and 0.6 μm.

Gas exchange occurs through this very thin respiratory membrane by diffusion down gradients of partial pressure. The partial pressures of oxygen and carbon dioxide in the blood going to the lungs are around 7 kPa and 6.3 kPa respectively. In the alveoli, the partial pressure of oxygen is 13.3 kPa and that of carbon dioxide 5.3 kPa. The alveolar membrane offers little resistance to the diffusion of the gases so that, by the time the blood leaves the alveolar capillaries, it is in complete equilibrium with the alveolar gas.

Control of the ventilation mechanism

The ventilation rate is controlled by a **respiratory centre** (Figure 11.8) situated in the hindbrain. In this centre, there are three separate areas:

- the **medullary rhythmicity centre**, controlling the basic rhythm of ventilation and made up of an **inspiratory centre** (C) and an **expiratory centre** (D), located in the **medulla oblongata**
- the **apneustic area** (B), located in the pons, capable of activating the inspiratory centre and prolonging its action
- the **pneumotaxic area** (A), also located in the pons, acting on the inspiratory centre to turn it off when the lungs become overstretched or full of air.

During normal breathing, nerve impulses from the inspiratory centre stimulate the contraction of the external intercostal muscles and the diaphragm muscles. These impulses are maintained for about 2 seconds, during which time impulses are also sent to the expiratory centre to switch it off. The inspiratory centre then becomes inactive and the expiratory centre fires impulses which stimulate the internal intercostal muscles and abdominal muscles to contract, causing air to be expelled in expiration. Impulses also go to the inspiratory centre and inhibit it. This lasts about 3 seconds, after which the inspiratory centre becomes active again. The two centres in the pons act antagonistically on the inspiratory centre.

The respiratory centre responds to a change in the hydrogen ion concentration (pH) of the blood. If there is an increase in tissue respiration as a result of exercise, the concentration of **carbon dioxide** in the blood will rise, resulting in an increase in the hydrogen ion concentration, which is detected by chemoreceptors as the blood flows through the medulla oblongata in the brain. The respiratory centre responds to this increase by causing an increase in the rate and the depth of ventilation. This is achieved by reducing the time that the inspiratory centre is active, which in turn reduces the duration of the activity of the expiratory centre, thus increasing the ventilation rate. The extra carbon dioxide is eliminated and more oxygen is available to supply the muscle cells during the increased exercise. When the carbon dioxide levels return to normal, the resting rhythm is re-established. A decrease in the level of carbon dioxide in the blood has the opposite effect and decreases the rate and depth of ventilation.

The response to differing concentrations of **oxygen** in the blood is more difficult to interpret. First of all, whereas slight changes in the concentration of carbon dioxide in the blood cause an alteration in ventilation rate, it takes a relatively large drop in oxygen concentration to effect a change. Chemoreceptors in the walls of the aortic arch and the carotid bodies detect decreases in oxygen concentration and cause reflex stimulation of the inspiratory centre. It appears that an increase in the oxygen concentration has little effect on the ventilation rate.

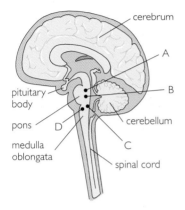

Figure 11.8 Diagram of the brain, showing the respiratory centre (A=pneumotaxic area, B=apneustic area – both located in the pons; C=inspiratory centre, D=expiratory centre – both located in the medullary rhythmicity centre).

QUESTION

How are the changes in the concentration of carbon dioxide and oxygen in the blood detected?

QUESTION

Compare the effect on the ventilation rate of changes in the concentrations of carbon dioxide and oxygen in the blood.

There are large numbers of **stretch receptors** present in the walls of the bronchi and bronchioles. If these receptors are stimulated during excessive inspiration, sensory impulses are transmitted via the vagus nerve to the respiratory centre, and the inspiratory and apneustic areas are inhibited so that expiration occurs and the lungs deflate. As deflation occurs, the stretch receptors are no longer stimulated and the inspiratory centre becomes active again. This reflex is referred to as the **inflation reflex**, or **Hering-Breuer reflex**.

Other factors which may influence the rate of ventilation include:
- changes in **blood pressure**, detected by baroreceptors in the aortic arch and the carotid bodies; a sudden increase in blood pressure may decrease the ventilation rate and, conversely, a decrease may increase it
- a rise in body **temperature**, such as may occur during vigorous exercise or during illness, can cause an increase in ventilation rate.

The musculo-skeletal system

In this section, we consider the structure of muscle and bone tissues and the relationships between muscles and bones in bringing about movement. It is important to have a sound understanding of the nature of striated (skeletal) muscle and the structure of bones and joints. The relationship between stimulation of the nervous system and muscle contraction is also described.

Compact bone

Compact bone is a calcified connective tissue composed of bone cells, called **osteocytes**, embedded in a matrix of collagen fibres and inorganic salts. The **matrix** of the tissue consists of:
- 30 per cent organic material – the **collagen fibres**
- 70 per cent inorganic material – mostly a complex salt called **hydroxyapatite**, containing calcium, phosphate, magnesium and hydroxyl ions.

The matrix is organised into **Haversian systems**, consisting of concentric cylinders of lamellae surrounding a central canal, called the Haversian canal (Figure 11.9). The canal contains blood vessels, nerves and lymphatic vessels. The osteocytes lie in cavities in the matrix, called **lacunae**, from which fine channels, the **canaliculi**, radiate. The canaliculi contain cytoplasm and form links with other bone cells and with the central Haversian canal.

A long bone, such as the humerus in the upper arm or the femur in the upper leg, consists of a hollow shaft, called the **diaphysis**, with a head, or **epiphysis**, at each end (Figure 11.10). The bone is surrounded by a tough, fibrous membrane called the **periosteum**. The hollow shaft is called the bone marrow cavity and produces many different types of blood cells. The rounded epiphyses articulate with other bones and are the sites of attachment of tendons and ligaments, which hold the muscles in place and the bones of a joint together respectively. The diaphysis is made of compact bone tissue, such as has been described, but the epiphyses are composed of spongy bone tissue with a thin layer of compact bone tissue on the outside. This arrangement of tissues within the bone gives it strength and enables it to withstand compression forces.

The blood vessels in the Haversian canals supply the living bone cells with nutrients and oxygen and remove waste substances. Transverse Volkmann's

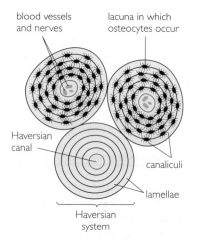

blood vessels and nerves

lacuna in which osteocytes occur

Haversian canal

canaliculi

lamellae

Haversian system

Figure 11.9 Compact bone tissue.

canals connect the bone marrow cavity with the longitudinal canals. The periosteum contains bundles of collagen fibres, referred to as Sharpey-Schafer fibres, which project into the bone and make a firm connection between the periosteum and the bone.

Synovial joints

Joints are formed where bones meet and they make movement possible A variety of joints exists in the human skeleton.

Hinge and ball-and-socket joints, such as are found at the elbows and hips respectively, are **synovial joints** (Figure 11.11). The features of synovial joints are:

- a thin covering of **cartilage** over the articulating surfaces of the bones involved
- the presence of **ligaments** forming a tough capsule of collagen fibres holding the bones together
- a **synovial membrane** lining the capsule
- the presence of **synovial fluid** secreted by the synovial membrane into the cavity of the capsule.

The cartilage provides a smooth surface to the articulating bones, reduces friction during movement and acts as a shock absorber. The synovial fluid, formed from the blood plasma, is a solution of nutrients and includes mucin and phagocytic cells. This fluid provides nutrients for the cartilage and lubricates the joint, also reducing the friction between the bones. The synovial fluid is kept around the joint because the synovial membrane is waterproof and provides an effective seal.

The structure and histology of striated muscle

Striated muscle, such as the biceps muscle in the arm, is made up of parallel, multinucleate cells, called muscle fibres, which may be several centimetres in length and between 0.1 and 0.01 mm in diameter. Each muscle fibre is surrounded by a membrane, the **sarcolemma**, which is very similar in structure to a cell surface membrane. Within each muscle fibre are large numbers of **myofibrils**, with characteristic cross-striations, the **Z lines** or **Z bands**. These Z lines occur at regular intervals along each myofibril and the region between two Z lines, about 2.5 μm in length in a relaxed muscle, is called a **sarcomere**.

In the myofibrils, thin filaments of the protein **actin** extend from the Z lines into the sarcomeres on either side. In the centre of each sarcomere, the actin filaments are interspersed with thick filaments of another protein, **myosin**. The cytoplasm of the myofibrils is referred to as the **sarcoplasm** and consists of a network of membranes forming the **sarcoplasmic reticulum**. A system of transverse tubules, known as the **T system**, extends across the muscle fibre and is in contact with the sarcolemma. The actin and myosin filaments are cross-linked, and when contraction of the muscle occurs, the thin actin filaments slide between the thick myosin filaments, shortening the length of each sarcomere. These structures are shown in Figure 11.12.

In the sarcomeres of each myofibril, the alternating light and dark bands, termed **I bands** and **A bands** respectively, correspond to areas of actin only

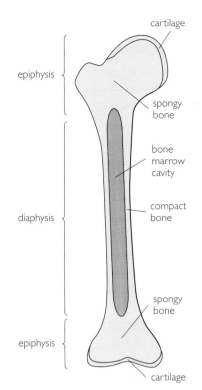

Figure 11.10 The structure of a long bone.

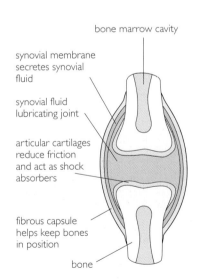

Figure 11.11 Section through synovial joint. The bones would also be held together by ligaments which are not shown in the diagram.

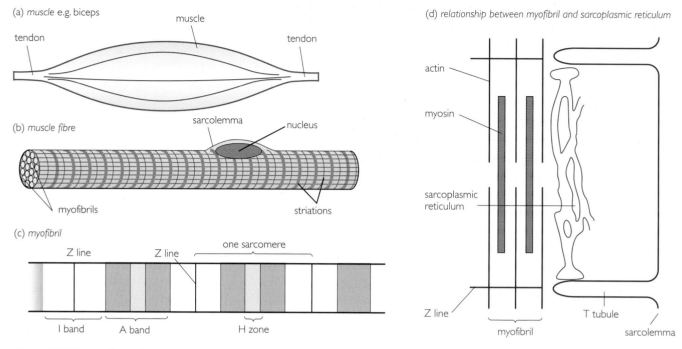

(a) *muscle e.g. biceps*

(b) *muscle fibre*

(c) *myofibril*

(d) *relationship between myofibril and sarcoplasmic reticulum*

Figure 11.12 Striated muscle structure.

(I bands) and actin and myosin together (A bands) (Figure 11.13). Within the A band, a central zone, the **H zone**, appears lighter than the regions on either side. In this zone, there are only myosin filaments, but in the darker regions either side there is overlap of the actin and myosin filaments. Transverse sections through the myofibrils indicate that the myosin filaments are regularly arranged in a lattice formation and, where overlap with the actin filaments occurs, six actin filaments surround each myosin filament.

When contraction occurs, the I bands shorten and the H zones become narrower because the actin filaments are pulled in between the myosin

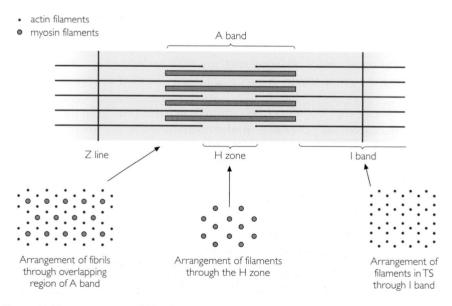

Figure 11.13 Arrangement of filaments in a sarcomere.

filaments and there is a greater overlap between the two sets (Figure 11.15). As a result, the Z lines are drawn closer together and the length of each sarcomere shortens. Note that the A bands always stay the same length.

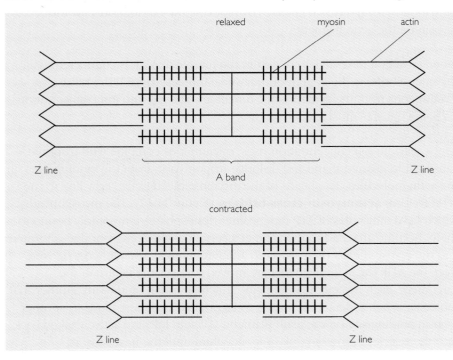

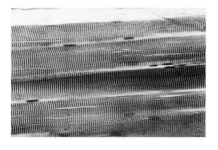

Figure 11.14 Striated muscle fibres (longitudinal section) as seen using a light microscope. The cross striations are clearly visible.

Figure 11.15 Arrangement of the thick (myosin) and thin (actin) filaments before and after contraction.

A motor end plate, or neuromuscular junction, is the place where the terminal branch of a motor nerve fibre comes into close proximity to the sarcolemma of a muscle fibre (Figure 11.16). This junction is similar to that of a synapse. When an action potential reaches the terminal branch of the nerve fibre, acetylcholine is released and diffuses across the cleft that separates the presynaptic membrane and the postsynaptic membrane (the sarcolemma of the nerve fibre). Depolarisation occurs and an action potential is generated in the muscle fibre.

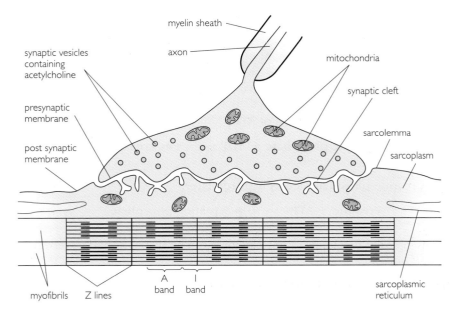

Figure 11.16 Motor end plate.

The contraction of the muscle fibres involves troponin and tropomyosin, two proteins present in the thin (actin) filaments, and the calcium ion concentration. In the absence of calcium ions, these proteins inhibit the formation of actin–myosin linkages by blocking the binding sites for the myosin on the actin filaments.

When an action potential is created in the muscle fibre, it is conducted to all the microfibrils via the system of transverse tubules, causing the release of calcium ions from the sarcoplasmic reticulum. The calcium ion concentration rises and initiates muscle contraction.

As the calcium ion concentration rises, calcium ions combine with troponin, causing it to change shape and dislodge tropomyosin from the binding sites on the actin molecules. The heads of the myosin molecules can now link to the actin to form **actomyosin cross-bridges** (Figure 11.17). The myosin heads, which have molecules of ATP (adenosine triphosphate) temporarily bound to them, become attached to the actin at a certain angle. A cross-bridge is formed and the myosin heads then swivel to a different angle, using energy derived from the ATP. The actin filaments are moved towards the centre of the sarcomere. Each myosin head remains attached until it binds with another ATP molecule, when it detaches, reverts to its original angle and binds to another myosin-binding site on the actin filament. Calcium ions are actively taken back into the vesicles of the sarcoplasmic reticulum until the next wave of depolarisation arrives.

ATP is the immediate source of energy for muscle contraction as it is the only substance that the muscle proteins can use directly. In a resting muscle, only small quantities of ATP are present, probably only enough for eight to ten rapid muscle twitches. In an active muscle, ATP needs to be restored rapidly. This process involves **creatine phosphate**, which is present in the muscle in larger amounts (see below). The adenosine diphosphate (ADP) released as ATP is used, is reconverted to ATP using phosphate from the creatine phosphate. Restoration of the creatine phosphate occurs by the oxidation of fatty acids or glycogen yielding ATP, which is then used to phosphorylate the creatine.

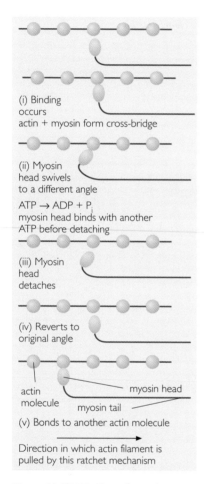

(i) Binding occurs
actin + myosin form cross-bridge

(ii) Myosin head swivels to a different angle
$ATP \rightarrow ADP + P_i$
myosin head binds with another ATP before detaching

(iii) Myosin head detaches

(iv) Reverts to original angle

actin molecule — myosin head
myosin tail —
(v) Bonds to another actin molecule

Direction in which actin filament is pulled by this ratchet mechanism

Figure 11.17 Binding of myosin to actin, forming cross-bridges.

During muscle contraction:

$$ATP \longrightarrow ADP + P_i + \text{energy for contraction}$$

In order to restore levels of ATP:

$$\text{creatine phosphate} + ADP \longrightarrow \text{creatine} + ATP$$

Creatine phosphate levels restored later:

$$\text{creatine} + ATP \longrightarrow \text{creatine phosphate.}$$

Microscopically, two kinds of muscle fibres can be distinguished in vertebrate striated muscle:
- **fast** or **twitch**, sometimes referred to as white fibres
- **slow** or **tonic**, sometimes referred to as red fibres.

Table 11.2 *Differences between fast and slow muscle fibres.*

Fast (twitch) fibres	Slow (tonic) fibres
lower myoglobin content so look pale or white; poor in sarcoplasm; small, regular fibrils; nuclei irregular; nuclei peripheral	higher myoglobin content, so look red; much granular sarcoplasm; longitudinal striations are marked; transverse striation central in position
associated with large nerve fibres (10 to 20 mm in diameter)	associated with small nerve fibres (about 5 mm in diameter)
conduction velocity of nerve fibres is between 8 and 40 m per second	conduction velocity of nerve fibres is between 2 and 8 m per second
quick contractile response: used in jumping	slower, graded muscular contraction: used to maintain the posture of the body; abundant in muscles in constant action
limited blood supply; fewer mitochondria; use glycogen stores in muscle; fatigue more rapidly; fewer motor end plates; contain myosin ATP-ase	well supplied with blood vessels; more mitochondria; use glucose from blood; can contract vigorously for long periods; more motor end plates

The two types of fibres differ both in their structure and their function. The differences are summarised in Table 11.2.

Twitch fibres are used for rapid movements and tonic fibres are used to maintain low-force, prolonged contractions. Some muscles are composed entirely of twitch fibres, some of only tonic fibres and some are a mixture of both. The twitch fibres, when stimulated to contract, respond to the 'all-or-nothing' rule, that is, complete contraction when the stimulus exceeds a certain threshold value. Any further increase in the intensity of the stimulus gives no further increase in response. However, with the tonic muscle fibres, where the terminal contacts of the nerve fibres are distributed along the muscle fibres, there is a summation on repetitive stimulation and no all-or-nothing response. In other words, there is a small response to a single stimulus and repeated stimulation is required to achieve a significant increase in contraction of the tonic fibres.

The lymphatic system

The lymphatic system consists of a series of vessels and glands, which connect with the cardiovascular system (Figure 11.18). The fluid contained within the vessels is known as **lymph** and is similar in composition to the tissue fluid.

When blood reaches the arterial end of the capillary beds in the body tissues, fluid from the plasma is forced out of the capillaries by the blood pressure. This fluid, called **tissue fluid**, is an aqueous solution containing glucose, amino acids, fatty acids, inorganic ions, oxygen and hormones, and bathes the cells of the tissues. The cellular components of the blood and large plasma proteins remain within the capillaries. The tissue fluid provides a source of nutrients and oxygen for the metabolic activities of the tissue cells, so these substances diffuse into the cells, and the waste products of metabolism diffuse out.

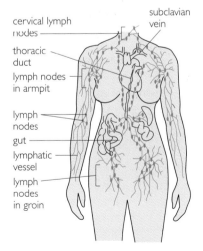

Figure 11.18 Diagram to show the main lymphatic vessels of the human body.

cervical lymph nodes

subclavian vein

thoracic duct

lymph nodes in armpit

lymph nodes

gut

lymphatic vessel

lymph nodes in groin

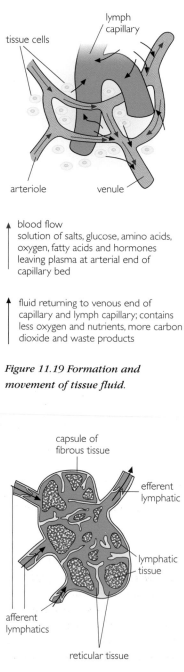

blood flow
solution of salts, glucose, amino acids, oxygen, fatty acids and hormones leaving plasma at arterial end of capillary bed

fluid returning to venous end of capillary and lymph capillary; contains less oxygen and nutrients, more carbon dioxide and waste products

Figure 11.19 Formation and movement of tissue fluid.

Figure 11.20 Structure of a lymph node.

Most of the tissue fluid, now containing fewer nutrients and less oxygen but more carbon dioxide and metabolic waste products, passes back into the venous end of the capillary network and then back to the heart (Figure 11.19). The remainder passes into blind-ending **lymph capillaries** which also permeate the tissues. These capillaries join to form larger vessels, called **lymphatics**. Once the tissue fluid is in the lymph capillaries it is known as **lymph**. The lymphatics resemble veins in their structure, having:

- an outer coat of fibrous tissue
- a middle coat of muscular and elastic tissue
- an inner lining made up of a single layer of endothelial cells
  but there are more valves present.

Movement of the lymph is aided by the movement of the skeletal muscles pressing on the tissues in which the lymphatics are present as there is no pump present in this system.

During its passage back into the cardiovascular system, the lymph passes through **lymph nodes**, where any pathogenic organisms, toxins or cell debris are removed by the resident monocytes or macrophages by phagocytosis. Antibodies and lymphocytes are released into the lymph.

The lymph enters the blood circulation by means of two **thoracic ducts**. Most of the lymphatic vessels drain into the main lymphatic duct, which opens into the left subclavian vein. Lymphatic vessels from the right side of the head, the right side of the thorax and the right arm drain into the right lymphatic duct, which opens into the right subclavian vein.

It is worth noting here that the products of the digestion of the lipids in the diet, fatty acids, glycerol and tiny lipid droplets, are absorbed into the lacteals of the villi of the small intestine. These lacteals drain into the lymphatic system, so the composition of the lymph has a higher lipid content than the blood plasma.

A lymph node has a capsule of fibrous tissue surrounding reticular and lymphatic tissue which contains large numbers of lymphocytes (Figure 11.20). Lymph enters a node through afferent lymphatics which penetrate the capsule and is carried away by a single efferent vessel. Within the node, large numbers of lymphocytes are formed from activated lymphocytes. There are also macrophages lining the sinuses.

The role of the lymph nodes in the immune response has already been described earlier in this chapter.

Exercise physiology

12

Exercise and the cardiovascular system

During exercise, there is an increased demand by muscles for oxygen, which may exceed the resting requirement by a factor of 15 to 25. The main purpose of the cardiovascular and pulmonary systems is to supply sufficient oxygen and to remove wastes from body tissues. The circulatory system also transports nutrients and has an important role in temperature regulation. The circulatory system and the respiratory system work together as a functional unit: the circulatory system supplies oxygenated blood and nutrients to tissues, and the respiratory system adds oxygen and removes carbon dioxide from the blood. In other words, these two body systems work together to maintain oxygen and carbon dioxide homeostasis in the body tissues.

The transport of oxygen by the blood is described in *Exchange and Transport, Energy and Ecosystems*. You should remember that **erythrocytes** (red blood cells) have an essential role in the transport of both oxygen and carbon dioxide in the body. In humans, erythrocytes are small, non-nucleated biconcave discs, measuring $7.5 \ \mu m \times 2 \ \mu m$. Each erythrocyte contains an estimated 200 million to 300 million molecules of **haemoglobin** and each molecule of haemoglobin can combine reversibly with four oxygen molecules to form oxyhaemoglobin. One gram of haemoglobin can combine with $1.34 \ cm^3$ of oxygen, so $100 \ cm^3$ of blood, which normally contain 15 g of haemoglobin, can carry approximately $20 \ cm^3$ of oxygen when saturated, for example, in the alveolar capillaries. At increased partial pressures of carbon dioxide, oxyhaemoglobin readily dissociates to release oxygen, which is then available for aerobic respiration.

Myoglobin is a pigment similar to haemoglobin and is found in the sarcoplasm of muscle fibres, particularly slow twitch (Type I) fibres. Each molecule of myoglobin consists of a single polypeptide chain, surrounding a haem group, which binds to a single molecule of oxygen. Myoglobin has a higher affinity for oxygen than does haemoglobin and functions as a store of oxygen within muscle fibres, which can be used quickly at the beginning of exercise (Figure 12.1).

To meet the increased demand for oxygen during exercise, two major adjustments must be made to blood flow:
- there is an increased **cardiac output**
- there is a **redistribution of blood flow** away from relatively inactive organs to the active striated muscles.

However, it is important that blood supply to other tissues, particularly the brain, is maintained during exercise. To illustrate changes in blood flow during exercise, Table 12.1 shows the blood flow to a number of organs, at rest and during severe exercise.

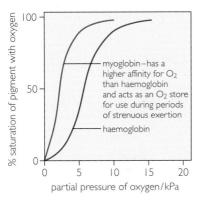

Figure 12.1 Oxygen dissociation curves for haemoglobin and myoglobin. The curve for myoglobin is situated to the left of the dissociation curve for haemoglobin. This indicates that myoglobin has a higher affinity for oxygen, at a given partial pressure, than haemoglobin.

Table 12.1 *Changes in blood flow in a 70 kg man, measured at rest and during severe exercise*

Organs	Typical blood flow/cm³ min⁻¹	
	Rest	**Severe exercise**
Brain	750	750
Kidneys	1100	600
Muscles	1200	12 500
Skin	500	1900
Spleen and gastrointestinal tract	1400	600

Cardiac output is defined as the volume of blood pumped by each ventricle in 1 minute, as shown by the formula:

$$\dot{Q} = SV \times HR$$

where $\dot{Q}$ is the cardiac output, SV is the stroke volume (the volume of blood pumped out of each ventricle each time it contracts), HR is the heart rate (beats per minute). The dot placed over Q is a convention to indicate that the measurement is taken per unit time (usually 1 minute).

Cardiac output can therefore be increased as a result of a rise in either heart rate or stroke volume and, during exercise, the increase in cardiac output is due to an increase in both the heart rate and the stroke volume, as shown in Table 12.2.

Table 12.2 *Typical resting and maximum exercise values for heart rate, stroke volume and cardiac output for college-age untrained individuals and trained endurance athletes. The gender differences in heart rate and stroke volumes are due mainly to differences in body size.*

	Subject	Heart rate /bpm	Stroke volume /cm³	Cardiac output /dm³ min⁻¹
Rest	Untrained male	72	70	5.04
	Untrained female	75	60	4.50
	Trained male	50	100	5.00
	Trained female	55	80	4.40
Maximum exercise	Untrained male	200	110	22.00
	Untrained female	200	90	18.00
	Trained male	190	180	34.20
	Trained female	190	125	23.75

Venous return during exercise

The heart can pump only the volume of blood it receives. This means that cardiac output depends on the volume of blood returning to the right side of the heart. As an example, a cardiac output of 22 dm³ per minute needs a matching venous return of 22 dm³ per minute. There are three main mechanisms for increasing venous return during exercise:

- contraction of the veins (venoconstriction)
- the pumping action of contracting striated muscle (muscle pump)
- the pumping action of the respiratory system (respiratory pump).

QUESTION

Explain why people who have to stand still for long periods, such as at wedding ceremonies, often faint.

Venoconstriction increases venous return because it reduces the volume of blood in the veins. This results in the increased movement of blood back towards the heart. Venoconstriction occurs by a reflex action controlled by the sympathetic nervous system. The muscle pump is a result of the action of rhythmic contraction of striated muscles. As muscles contract, they compress veins and this pushes blood towards the heart. During muscle relaxation, the veins refill with blood and the process is repeated. Blood flow towards the heart is assisted by one-way valves in the larger veins, which prevent blood flowing away from the heart when muscles relax. The rhythmic pattern of breathing also helps to increase venous return. During inspiration (breathing in), the pressure within the thorax decreases and the pressure within the abdomen rises. This encourages venous blood flow into the thorax, towards the heart. The effect is enhanced during exercise because of the greater rate and depth of breathing.

Exercise and the pulmonary system

The structure of the breathing system and the mechanism of ventilation are described in *Exchange and Transport, Energy and Ecosystems* and you may find it helpful to review the topic at this stage. The main function of the pulmonary system is to provide a means of gas exchange between the body and the external environment. The exchange of oxygen and carbon dioxide occurs as a result of the processes of **ventilation** and **diffusion**. The term ventilation refers to the movement of air into and out of the lungs. This is brought about by changes in the volume of the thorax. Inspiration at rest, involves contraction of the diaphragm and the external intercostal muscles, and is therefore an active process. Expiration (breathing out), is largely a passive process, involving relaxation of muscles and the elastic recoil of the lungs. As the rate and depth of breathing increase with exercise, this requires increased muscular efforts and expiration also becomes an active process. The muscles involved with ventilation, including the diaphragm and intercostal muscles, use glucose as a respiratory substrate, and oxygen. During severe exercise the oxygen used by the muscles of ventilation can account for 10 per cent of the total oxygen uptake.

Diffusion of oxygen from the alveoli into the blood occurs because the partial pressure of oxygen in the lungs is higher than that in the blood. Carbon dioxide diffuses out of the blood because the partial pressure of carbon dioxide is higher in the blood than in the lungs. Diffusion occurs rapidly because there is a large surface area within the lungs and a very short diffusion distance between the air in the alveoli and the blood. The system for gas exchange is so efficient that blood leaving the lungs has an oxygen concentration almost at equilibrium with that in the alveoli.

Quantitative recordings of lung volumes can be made using the technique of **spirometry**. A spirometer (Figure 12.2) is an instrument used to measure the volumes of air exchanged during breathing. The person breathes into and out of a closed system in which air is trapped in a container floating in water.

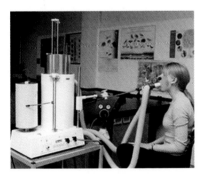

Figure 12.2 A recording spirometer. The drum near the centre of the picture contains oxygen and is floating in a container filled with water. As the person breathes into and out of the spirometer, the drum moves up and down; this is recorded on the chart on the left of the picture.

EXERCISE PHYSIOLOGY

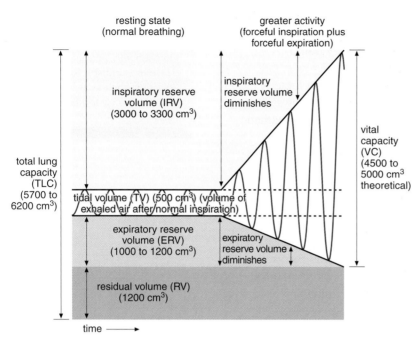

resting state
(normal breathing)

greater activity
(forceful inspiration plus
forceful expiration)

inspiratory
reserve volume
diminishes

inspiratory reserve
volume (IRV)
(3000 to 3300 cm³)

vital
capacity
(VC)
(4500 to
5000 cm³
theoretical)

total lung
capacity
(TLC)
(5700 to
6200 cm³)

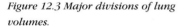

tidal volume (TV) (500 cm³) (volume of
exhaled air after normal inspiration)

expiratory reserve
volume (ERV)
(1000 to 1200 cm³)

expiratory
reserve volume
diminishes

residual volume (RV)
(1200 cm³)

time ⟶

Figure 12.3 Major divisions of lung volumes.

Up-and-down movements of this container are recorded on a chart; the resulting record is referred to as a **spirogram**.

A spirogram shows a number of lung volumes and capacities, including tidal volume and vital capacity (Figure 12.3). The volume of air breathed out after a typical inspiration is referred to as the **tidal volume (TV)**, which is about 500 cm³. **Vital capacity (VC)** is the maximum volume of air that can be expired after a maximum inspiration. This depends on a number of factors, including the body size, age and gender of a person. Vital capacity is the sum of the inspiratory reserve volume (IRV), the tidal volume (TV) and the expiratory reserve volume (ERV), that is:

$$VC = IRV + TV + ERV$$

The term *volume* is used for one individual component of lung capacity, lung *capacities* are the sum of two or more lung volumes.

After the deepest possible expiration, the lungs and airways still contain about 1200 cm³ (1.2 dm³) of air, this is referred to as the **residual volume (RV)**. No matter how forcefully a person exhales, this volume always remains in the lungs and airways. The **respiratory minute volume**, or pulmonary ventilation, is the volume of air inspired, or expired, in 1 minute. Minute volumes can be expressed as $\overset{\bullet}{V}_E$, the volume of air expired in 1 minute, or $\overset{\bullet}{V}_I$, the volume of air inspired in 1 minute. At rest, the breathing rate is about 12 breaths per minute and the tidal volume is 500 cm³, so the minute volume is about 6 dm³. After exercise, this may increase to a maximum of 100 to 150 dm³.

This rise in ventilation can be brought about by an increase in the tidal volume and in the breathing rate. In exercise involving repeated movements, such as running and cycling, the breathing rate is often adjusted so that is in time with the movements. In moderate exercise, ventilation increases mainly by an increase in the tidal volume, with only a small increase in the breathing rate. Later, the rate of breathing increases. As the level of exercise increases, ventilation increases proportionally until ventilation begins to rise exponentially. This point is referred to as the **anaerobic threshold**. The reasons for the increase in ventilation during exercise are complex and involve a number of interacting factors, including:

- nerve impulses from higher centres in the brain and from receptors in joints and muscles, which increase ventilation at the start of exercise and during moderate exercise.
- an increase in the production of carbon dioxide. An increase in the partial pressure of carbon dioxide in the blood stimulates breathing via both peripheral chemoreceptors and central chemoreceptors situated in the medulla oblongata. The peripheral chemoreceptors are situated in the aortic and carotid bodies. Chemoreceptors are very sensitive to changes in the partial pressure of carbon dioxide.
- production of lactate, which also stimulates breathing.

Training has the effect of increasing the alveolar capillary network and slightly increasing lung volumes, which increases the efficiency of gas exchange. The respiratory muscles become stronger, which results in an increase in both the volume of air breathed and in the rate at which air can be exhaled, so the efficiency of ventilation also increases. Overall, however, the effects of training on the pulmonary system are less significant than the effects on the cardiovascular system

Exercise and the musculo-skeletal system

Aerobic and anaerobic respiration are described in Chapter 1, but it will be helpful to summarise these processes, and to look in more detail at the role of anaerobic respiration in muscle tissue. Muscle contraction requires ATP as an energy source, but muscles have limited supplies of ATP, which can be depleted in about 2 seconds in a sprint. During muscle contraction, ATP is broken down into ADP and inorganic phosphate (Pi). The ATP is reformed by three main **energy systems**, referred to as the alactic anaerobic system, the lactic acid system and the aerobic system.

The alactic anaerobic system

Muscles contain a substance called phosphocreatine (abbreviated to PCr), which acts as an energy reserve. Phosphocreatine is used to convert ADP to ATP:

$$PCr + ADP \rightleftharpoons ATP + creatine$$

This reaction is catalysed by the enzyme creatine kinase. During vigorous exercise, such as a 100 m sprint, ATP supplies are rapidly regenerated by this mechanism. No oxygen is used and no lactic acid is formed, so this is referred to as the **alactic anaerobic system** (ATP-PC system). The importance of this system is that it provides an immediate source of energy for muscle contraction.

The lactic acid system

This system is important in events such as a 400 m race, when the demand of muscles for oxygen exceeds the supply. Glucose is broken down, via glycolysis, to pyruvate, which is then reduced to lactic acid. Glycolysis yields a net gain of two molecules of ATP per molecule of glucose (Figure 12.4).

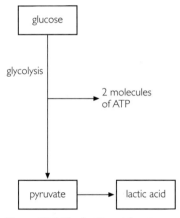

Figure 12.4 The lactic acid system.

Accumulation of lactic acid results in muscle fatigue and deterioration of physical performance. After the exercise has stopped, more oxygen is needed to remove the lactic acid. This extra volume of oxygen is referred to as the **oxygen debt** (or **excess postexercise oxygen consumption**, **EPOC**). Much of the lactic acid produced is fully oxidised to carbon dioxide and water; the remainder is transported in the bloodstream to the liver and converted back into glucose. This is a process which requires ATP and is known as **gluconeogenesis**. Some of this recycled glucose returns to muscle tissue where it is converted to glycogen for storage.

Lactic acid, in solution, dissociates to form lactate and hydrogen ions. At rest, the normal concentration of lactate in the blood is about 1 mmol per dm^{-3}. In aerobic exercise, this concentration remains constant, but in medium intensity exercise, such as a 30 minute run, the concentration increases to about 4 mmol dm^{-3}. This concentration is referred to as the **lactate threshold**, or the **onset of blood lactate accumulation (OBLA)**.

EXERCISE PHYSIOLOGY

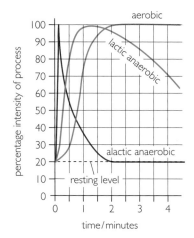

Figure 12.5 The percentage contribution of the alactic anaerobic system, the lactic anaerobic system and aerobic respiration as a function of time during a 1 mile race.

During the late 1960s and early 1970s, conditioning programmes for endurance athletes were designed. Since the maximum blood lactate concentration for steady-state swimming or running on a flat track is about 4 mmol dm^{-3}, the swimming or running speed which maintains this concentration could be used to maximise endurance performance. Speeds greater than this lead to accumulation of lactate and the onset of muscle fatigue.

The aerobic system

Provided that sufficient oxygen is available to muscle tissue, substrates such as glucose and fatty acids can be completely metabolised to produce carbon dioxide, water and ATP. Aerobic respiration is described in detail in Chapter 1, but we can summarise the process into three main stages:

- glycolysis
- the Krebs cycle
- oxidative phosphorylation.

In muscle tissue, glycolysis occurs in the sarcoplasm; the Krebs cycle and oxidative phosphorylation occur within mitochondria. The importance of aerobic respiration is that the complete oxidation of glucose yields much more ATP than anaerobic respiration. The total yield of ATP in aerobic respiration is between 36 and 38 molecules of ATP per molecule of glucose; the actual yield depends on the exact biochemical pathway of the substrate.

All three energy systems, that is, the alactic anaerobic system, the lactic anaerobic system, and the aerobic system are involved from the start of any exercise involving continuous movement. Figure 12.5 shows the contributions made by each energy system over a 1 mile race in a top-class performance.

Notice that the alactic anaerobic system is used first, to produce ATP using stored phosphocreatine. This is followed by an increase in the lactic anaerobic system, as demand for oxygen by the working muscles exceeds supply. Then, as adjustments are made in the cardiovascular and pulmonary systems, aerobic respiration increases.

Muscle spindles

Striated muscles contain complex sensory structures termed **muscle spindles** (Figure 12.6). A muscle spindle is up to 6 mm long and less than 1 mm in diameter. As the name suggests, muscle spindles are wider in the middle and taper towards each end. Muscle spindles are arranged in parallel with the surrounding muscle fibres, and are enclosed in connective tissue. Each spindle contains between about 2 and 12 modified muscle fibres, referred to as **intrafusal fibres**. These differ from normal muscle fibres (or extrafusal fibres) in several ways. Intrafusal fibres are much smaller than extrafusal fibres, and are associated with **sensory receptors**, such as annulospiral endings. The sensory receptors are stimulated by stretching of the intrafusal fibres and, via a reflex arc, stimulate contraction of the surrounding extrafusal fibres. This forms the basis of a muscle stretch reflex, such as the knee jerk reflex in which contraction of the quadriceps muscle in the thigh results from stimulation of stretch receptors in the same muscle. Extrafusal muscle fibres are supplied by large effector neurones, referred to as alpha (α) motor neurones. Intrafusal

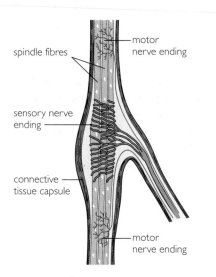

Figure 12.6 Diagrammatic structure of a muscle spindle. The muscle spindle consists of a number of specialised muscle fibres (intrafusal fibres) which lie parallel to 'normal' muscle (extrafusal) fibres within the muscle. A connective tissue capsule encloses the spindle fibres. The diagram shows sensory nerve endings and motor nerve endings on the spindle fibres, from small efferent neurones.

fibres, within the muscle spindles, are supplied by their own effector neurones, known as gamma (γ) motor neurones. The gamma motor neurones control the contraction of the intrafusal fibres to maintain the sensitivity of the stretch receptors as the surrounding muscle tissue changes in length. Muscle spindles provide important sensory feedback on the state of muscle contraction, length, position and rate of change of the length of muscle, which is essential for coordinated movement.

Muscles, strength and fatigue

Striated muscles contract in response to nerve impulses, sent to the muscles by their motor neurones. This results in the release of acetylcholine at the neuromuscular junction, which depolarises the muscle membrane, or sarcolemma. This sets off an action potential in the muscle fibre, followed by a wave of contraction. Each motor neurone and the muscle fibres it supplies together constitute a **motor unit**. When a nerve impulse reaches the muscle fibres of a motor unit, all the fibres contract simultaneously, giving a **muscle twitch** which lasts for a fraction of a second. The number of muscle fibres in a motor unit varies from a few to many hundreds. This fact is important in the relationship to the function of the muscle as a whole. As a rule, the fewer the number of muscle fibres in a motor unit, the more precise the movements that muscle can produce. For example, motor units in the muscles that move the eyes contain fewer than five muscle fibres, whereas in the large muscles in the legs, there may be more than a thousand muscle fibres in each motor unit.

Movement is not, however, brought about by a series of uncoordinated muscle twitches, but by smooth and sustained contractions of muscles. These are produced by a series of nerve impulses in rapid succession, so that the muscle does not have time to relax completely before the next contraction begins. This effect is referred to as **multiple wave summation**, because many muscle twitches have been added together to produce a sustained contraction, known as a **tetanus** (see Figure 12.7).

We recognise two types of muscle contraction, known as **isotonic** and **isometric**. In an isotonic contraction, the tension developed in the muscle remains the same, but the length of the muscle decreases. In an isometric contraction, the muscle length remains the same, but the tension developed in the muscle increases. For example, if you support a heavy weight in your hand, muscles will be in a state of sustained contraction to support the weight. Isometric contraction is also important for the maintenance of balance and posture, for example, when standing still or sitting upright. In an isometric contraction, individual myofilaments do shorten and, in doing so, stretch the elastic components of the muscle, such as the connective tissue within the muscle.

The isometric tension developed by a muscle depends on its length. The tension is at a maximum when the length of the muscle is approximately the same as its resting length in the body. The tension drops to zero when the muscle is either shorter or longer than this.

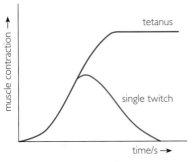

Figure 12.7 Contraction of a muscle following a single stimulus (single twitch) and repeated stimulation to produce a sustained contraction, or tetanus.

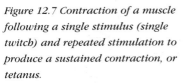

QUESTION

What is the difference between isotonic and isometric contraction?

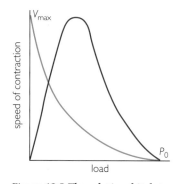

Figure 12.8 The relationship between muscle force and speed of contraction. The red line shows how the power produced by the muscle (force × contraction speed) varies with the load applied.

In an isotonic contraction, the smaller the load, the faster the muscle contracts. This is illustrated in Figure 12.8, which shows the relationship between the muscle-shortening speed, the power produced and the load applied to the muscle.

The graph shows that, when the load is minimal, the muscle contracts at maximum speed (V_{max}). When the load is such that no external shortening can occur, the maximum tension is termed P_0.

The maximum force that can be generated by a muscle is directly related to its cross-sectional area, rather than its length. All striated muscles generate about the same force, 20 to 30 N per cm^2. Exercise may cause an increase in muscle size, referred to as **hypertrophy**. This can be enhanced by strength training, such as weight lifting. This type of training increases the number of myofilaments, but the number of muscle fibres remains the same. Endurance training, often referred to as aerobic training, does not usually result in muscle hypertrophy. Instead, this increases the ability of a muscle to sustain moderate exercise over a long period. Activities such as running and cycling increase the number of capillaries in muscles without significantly affecting their size. The increased blood flow allows a more efficient delivery of oxygen and glucose to muscle fibres during exercise. Endurance training also increases the number of mitochondria in muscle fibres and therefore increases their ability to produce ATP.

Fatigue

Muscle fatigue is a state of exhaustion, produced by strenuous muscular activity. Physiological muscle fatigue may be caused by a relative lack of ATP, depletion of glycogen stores and high levels of lactic acid or other metabolic waste products. Fast twitch fibres, although capable of generating large forces, fatigue rapidly, probably as a result of their low aerobic capacity and anaerobic metabolism producing lactic acid.

Training

The overall aim of a sports-conditioning programme is to improve performance by increasing the energy output during a particular activity. We have already described the different metabolic pathways which produce ATP and most sporting activities use a combination of these pathways. A well-designed conditioning programme allocates the appropriate time for aerobic and anaerobic conditioning to match the energy demand of the sport.

It must be emphasised that training is a long-term process, and even light exercise, taken regularly over a period of time, has a beneficial effect on health and fitness. One of the general principles of training is referred to as **overload**, that is, activities that are harder or more intense than the normal exercise taken by a person. This places the body systems under stress and the systems respond by adapting to the stress. Every training session should consist of three components:
- warm-up
- workout
- cool-down.

The warm-up has several important objectives, for example, warm-up exercises increase cardiac output and blood flow to muscles. It also results in an increase in muscle temperature, which increases muscle enzyme activity. A proper warm-up may also reduce the risk of muscle injury due to strains. Immediately after a training session, a period of light cool-down exercises should be carried out. This helps to return pooled blood from the exercise muscles back to the general circulation, and flushes the capillaries with oxygenated blood to allow full recovery from the oxygen debt.

Training programmes also need to deal with both the specific muscle groups used in the activity and the energy system providing the ATP. As examples, specific training for a 100 m sprinter would involved repeated high-intensity dashes, whereas specific training for a marathon runner would involve long, slow-paced runs in which almost all of the ATP needed by the working muscles would be derived from aerobic metabolism.

Training to improve aerobic power

Three principal aerobic training methods are used by athletes:
- interval training
- long, slow, distance (low-intensity) training
- high-intensity, continuous exercise.

Interval training involves repeated bouts of exercise, with brief recovery periods between each. Long, slow, distance training became a popular means of training for endurance events during the 1970s. This method involves performing exercises at low intensity which generally involve greater distances than the competition distance. The objective of high-intensity continuous training is to exercise at a heart rate near the lactate threshold (page 157) for about 25 to 50 minutes, the actual time depending on the fitness of the athlete.

Training to improve anaerobic power

Athletic events that last for less than 60 seconds depend mainly on the anaerobic production of ATP. Sports such as weight lifting and 100 m sprinting rely on the ATP-PC system (alactic anaerobic system, see page 157) to provide most of the energy. Therefore, a training programme is required that will maximise the production of ATP by the ATP-PC pathway. This involves a special type of interval training to stress the ATP-PC pathway, for example, such a training programme might involve repeated 30 m dashes, with a rest of 30 seconds between each. Because of the short interval of this exercise (5 to 10 seconds), little lactic acid is produced and recovery is rapid. Many athletes take creatine as a dietary supplement. This results in an increase in phosphocreatine in muscle, which helps to improve athletic performance by stimulating the production of more ATP.

The effects of exercise on various body systems have already been described, but we can summarise the main effects of training as follows:
- there is an increase in the maximal cardiac output and an increase in the maximal blood supply to muscles
- the ability of muscles to use oxygen increases, partly due to an increased blood flow

> **QUESTION**
>
> List the effects of training on:
> - the cardiovascular system
> - the pulmonary system
> - the musculo-skeletal system.

- athletes trained for endurance events obtain more of their energy from fat and less from carbohydrates
- training leads to less fatigue.

Training and diet

In order to maintain good health, the diet should contain the following:
- **carbohydrates** and **fats** to provide energy
- **proteins** as a source of amino acids for protein synthesis
- **vitamins** and **minerals**
- **water**.

These compounds should be in sufficient quantities and in the correct proportions to give an adequate, balanced diet. A balanced diet for one individual person depends on a number of factors, such as age, gender, body size and activity. Carbohydrates, fats and proteins are needed in larger quantities than the other components of the diet, as these compounds supply the energy for metabolism and the materials for growth and maintenance of the body. Only small quantities of vitamins and minerals are needed and the volume of water will vary according to the activity of the person and the prevailing climatic conditions.

Both carbohydrates and fats are used to provide energy for all types of physical activity, but the proportions of each actually used depend on the type of muscular activity, as shown in Table 12.3.

Table 12.3 *Exercise and fuels used*

Intensity of exercise	Duration of exercise	Fuel used
maximal sprint	short	carbohydrate
low to moderate	moderate, up to 2 hours, e.g. jogging	carbohydrate and fat equally
severe	prolonged, e.g. cycling	more fat than carbohydrate

Most muscles depend on fatty acids for their resting metabolism. Fatty acids, such as palmitic acid, are oxidised to form carbon dioxide, water and ATP. Carbohydrate is stored in muscle tissue in the form of **glycogen** and the store of glycogen depends on the availability of carbohydrates in the diet. Resting muscle contains about 345 g of glycogen, but the size of this store depends on the diet and activity of the muscle. During exercise, glycogen is rapidly broken down to provide glucose as a substrate for respiration and the glycogen stores are depleted within a few hours, resulting in fatigue. After a short-distance, high-intensity activity, such as an 800 m race, muscle glycogen stores are replenished within about 2 hours. Glycogen stores can be increased by special dietary and exercise regimes. This process, known as **glycogen loading** (or supercompensation), can help to increase the period of exercise before fatigue sets is. Glycogen loading is based on the principle that, if glycogen stores are used up and maintained at a low level for a few days, by eating mainly fats and proteins, then when carbohydrates are available in the diet, the body overcompensates and increases its stores of glycogen above the normal level. The overall effect is to improve endurance capacity significantly. In one study, the benefits of glycogen loading were shown by comparing the performance of ten runners, timed over two 30 km cross-country races. The first race was run after the runners had eaten a normal, mixed diet in the days before the race. The other race was run after a glycogen-loading regime. The performance times of the runners improved by an average of 8 minutes after glycogen loading.

13 Human disorders

So far we have described the structure and function of several body systems and considered the effects of exercise on each system. To conclude this Option, we outline the causes and treatment of a number of specific disorders affecting the cardiovascular system the pulmonary system and the musculo-skeletal system.

Coronary heart disease and hypertension

Coronary heart disease (CHD) is a general term for any disease which restricts the coronary artery blood supply to the heart muscle. The main cause of this is coronary artery atherosclerosis, a condition in which lipids and other substances, including collagen-like fibres, build up on the inside of blood vessels. This restricts blood flow by blocking the vessel, and therefore reduces blood supply so that sufficient oxygen cannot reach the heart muscle cells supplied by that vessel. A frequent symptom of this is a condition known as angina pectoris, a pain in the chest particularly following exertion and settling with rest. Further narrowing of the lumen of the coronary arteries can suddenly reduce blood flow to the heart muscle, which becomes deprived of oxygen, resulting in tissue death. This death, or necrosis, of an area of cardiac muscle is known as **myocardial infarction**, often referred to as a **heart attack** (more details of this can be found on page 98). There are a number of risk factors which are likely to lead to atherosclerosis and these include:

- age and gender – an increasing incidence occurs with age and is higher in men up to the age of 75
- cigarette smoking
- high plasma lipoprotein levels, particularly the high-density types
- genetic factors – some families have an increased risk which is independent of other factors.

The symptoms of angina can be reduced by stopping smoking, avoiding strenuous exercise and slimming if overweight. Treatment with drugs, including glyceryl trinitrate, can provide rapid relief from angina. Coronary by-pass surgery is a frequently used treatment for those with severely restricted coronary artery blood flow. This procedure involves the removal of veins from other parts of the body, for example, the legs, which are then used to provide detours around the blocked coronary arteries.

High blood pressure, or **hypertension**, occurs when the diastolic pressure exceeds 95 mm Hg and the systolic pressure exceeds 160 mm Hg (World Health Organisation classification). Many risk factors have been identified in the development of hypertension and these include:

- genetic factors
- gender – hypertension is more common in young men than in young women
- age
- high stress levels
- obesity
- smoking.

There are numerous complications of untreated hypertension, including atherosclerosis, heart failure, kidney failure, and stroke. Hypertension can be treated by reducing weight if obese, and reducing alcohol and salt intake if these are contributory factors. Drugs used in the treatment of hypertension include diuretics, beta-adrenoceptor blocking drugs ('beta-blockers'), calcium-channel blockers and angiotensin-converting enzyme inhibitors (ACE inhibitors). (See *Practical: Measuring percentage body fat, using skinfold calipers,* page 130).

Disorders of the pulmonary system

These include **bronchitis, tuberculosis (TB), pneumoconiosis,** and **lung cancer**. Bronchitis is a condition which is characterised by inflammation of the airways and excessive mucus secretion. This obstructs air flow and is one cause of chronic obstructive airway disease, resulting in coughing, wheezing and breathlessness. Cigarette smoking is the most important factor in the development of bronchitis, so avoiding smoking is usually the most effective treatment. Air pollution is also an important contributory factor and city-dwellers have a higher incidence than those who live in the country.

Tuberculosis is one of the most serious infectious diseases of the developing world. It is caused by the bacterium *Mycobacterium tuberculosis* (Figure 13.1) and infection is acquired by inhalation of *M. tuberculosis* in dust or droplets. Infection from droplets is efficient because infected people cough up enormous numbers of the bacteria, which are able to withstand drying and can survive in the air or household dust for long periods of time.

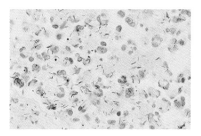

Figure 13.1 Mycobacterium tuberculosis *(stained red) in lung tissue.*

Following infection with *M. tuberculosis*, small lesions, called tubercles, form in the lungs around colonies of bacteria. This produces symptoms of cough, weight loss, chest pain and fever. Tuberculosis can invade other tissues and organs in the body, including the lymphatic system and bone tissue. Mycobacteria are resistant to many antibiotics, so treatment involves the use of specific antituberculous drugs. These are used in combination therapy, given in two phases. The initial phase involves using at least three different drugs for 2 months, followed by a continuation phase using two drugs for a further 4 months. Drugs used in the treatment of tuberculosis include isoniazid, rifampin and ethambutol.

Pneumoconiosis is a term given to a group of disorders, all of which arise from the inhalation of dust particles. The particles are deposited in the lungs and give rise to a condition termed fibrosis. This increases the amount of collagen fibres in the walls of the alveoli, resulting in thickening of the alveolar wall and reduced efficiency of gas exchange. The most common forms of pneumoconiosis follow inhalation of mineral dusts, such as silica and asbestos, usually over a long period of exposure. Silicosis is the form of pneumoconiosis associated with exposure to silica dust and tends to occur in miners. Inhalation of silica particles results in the development of collagenous tissue in the lungs, a condition referred to as **fibrosis**. Progressive fibrosis may cause pulmonary hypertension (an increase in pulmonary blood pressure) and respiratory failure. When asbestos fibres are inhaled they become coated with a protein

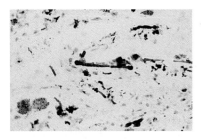

Figure 13.2 Asbestos bodies (stained blue) in lung tissue, magnification × 400.

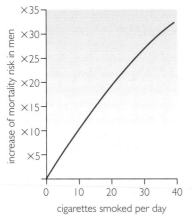

Figure 13.3 Cigarette smoking and lung cancer mortality.

material in the lungs to form asbestos bodies, which typically have a 'beaded' appearance (Figure 13.2)

Apart from its adverse effect on gas exchange, exposure to asbestos leads to complications such as increased likelihood of the development of certain types of cancers, especially in cigarette smokers.

Cancer develops when a cell undergoes a change and begins to divide out of control, forming a mass of cells referred to as a tumour. Malignant cancers are able to spread and invade other body tissues, forming secondary tumours. Lung cancer is the major cause of death in the western hemisphere and approximately 40 per cent of all male cancer deaths in England and Wales are from lung cancer. The risk of developing lung cancer is directly related to the number of cigarettes smoked per day (Figure 13.3).

Treatment of cancer includes surgical removal of the tumour, radiotherapy using gamma rays to kill the tumour cells, or chemotherapy using anticancer drugs.

Disorders of the musculo-skeletal system

Osteoarthritis is a degenerative disorder in which a weight-bearing joint is damaged by wear and tear and other factors. The protective layers of cartilage are worn away and the joint becomes swollen and painful, making movement difficult. Treatment to alleviate the pain and reduce inflammation with paracetamol or non-steroidal anti-inflammatory drugs (such as ibuprofen) may give some relief. Often the joint is so damaged that replacement is required. Replacement of damaged hip joints is now routine and replacement of other joints, including knees and fingers, can also be done. The artificial hip consists of a metal and plastic structure which totally replaces the damaged parts. The femur shaft and ball are usually made of a titanium alloy and the socket has a polyethylene liner. These materials are used for their durability and for their similar properties to the tissues being replaced.

Rheumatoid arthritis is a chronic inflammatory disease of connective tissue, of unknown cause. It is characterised by destruction of the synovial membrane, which results in joint deformity, particularly in the hands and knees. Initially, joint mobility is limited by pain and swelling, then later by destruction of cartilage and bone. Certain drugs, including gold (in the form of sodium aurothiomalate), penicillamine and immunosuppressants, are used in the treatment of rheumatoid arthritis.

Osteoporosis is an example of a metabolic disorder of bone in which the bones become porous, brittle, and fracture easily under stress. Osteoporosis is common in postmenopausal women, but other risk factors include low body weight, cigarette smoking, excess alcohol intake, lack of physical activity and family history of osteoporosis. Those at risk should maintain an adequate dietary intake of calcium and vitamin D. For postmenopausal osteoporosis, hormone replacement therapy (HRT) is often recommended, but needs to be continued for 5 to 10 years to be beneficial.

Histology of striated muscle, cardiac muscle and lung tissue

Introduction

The aim of this practical is to familiarise you with the histology of striated muscle, cardiac muscle and lung tissue, as seen using a light microscope. Before looking at the preparations of these tissues, it will be helpful to refer to your theory notes and to use these, and any other pictures of the tissues, to help you identify the important features. Make annotated drawings of each type of tissue to show the main histological features.

Materials

- Prepared microscope slides of
    striated muscle (longitudinal section)
    cardiac muscle (longitudinal section)
    lung (tranverse section)
- Microscope.

Method

Examine preparations of each tissue in turn, first using low magnification (× 40), before turning to high magnification (× 100 and × 400). Use the notes and photomicrographs below to help you to interpret each tissue.

Striated muscle

Using a light microscope, striated muscle can be seen to consist of long, unbranched **fibres**, with many flattened nuclei, situated beneath the muscle membrane, or sarcolemma (Figure P.1). The regular pattern of cross-striations is a prominent feature. Each

Figure P.1 Striated muscle fibres, longitudinal section, magnification × 400.

muscle fibre consists of many **myofibrils**, lying parallel to one another. The arrangement of the contractile proteins, actin and myosin, within each myofibril gives rise to the striated appearance of the muscle fibre.

Cardiac muscle

In longitudinal section, cardiac muscle cells can be seen to contain one or two nuclei and a branched cytoplasm which gives rise to a three-dimensional network (Figure P.2). Cardiac muscle cells have cross-striations, similar to those in striated muscle, due to the

Figure P.2 Cardiac muscle, longitudinal section, magnification ×400.

arrangement of contractile proteins. The cross-striations in cardiac muscle may, however, appear less distinct than those

in striated muscle. Cardiac muscle has unique junctions between adjacent cells, known as **intercalated discs**, which appear as transverse, dark bands. Intercalated discs have areas of low electrical resistance to allow the rapid spread of electrical excitation throughout the heart muscle.

Lung

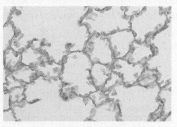

A section of lung tissue will show numerous thin-walled **alveoli**; airways of varying diameters and blood vessels with also be present (Figure P.3). Alveoli are the sites of gas exchange; the walls of the alveoli consist of surface epithelium, with supporting connective

Figure P.3 Lung tissue, transverse section, magnification ×400.

tissue including elastic fibres, and a network of capillaries which surround each alveolus. Air enters each lung via the **principal bronchus**, which divides repeatedly to form airways of progressively smaller diameter. The smallest diameter airways are known as **terminal bronchioles** (bronchioles are airways less than 1 mm in diameter); these branch further to form **respiratory bronchioles** and **alveolar ducts** which lead into the alveoli. Each type of airway has characteristic structural features, but there is a gradual change from one type of airway to the next. The airways are lined with epithelium and contain variable amounts of cartilage in their walls. Features of some of the airways are shown in Table P.1.

Table P.1 *Features of some of the major airways*

Airway	Type of epithelium	Goblet cells	Cartilage
Principal bronchus	pseudostratified, ciliated columnar	present	present
Small bronchus	pseudostratified, ciliated columnar	a few present	a little present
Terminal bronchiole	simple ciliated columnar	absent	absent
Respiratory bronchiole	simple ciliated cuboidal	absent	absent
Alveolar duct	simple cuboidal	absent	absent

Conventional microscopic preparations of lung tissue are about 5 μm thick. Sections which are embedded in plastic resins (thin sections, about 1 μm thick) give much better resolution and show more structural detail. If you have them available, examine a plastic-embedded section of lung, and an injected preparation, to show the network of capillaries surrounding the alveoli.

HUMAN DISORDERS

PRACTICAL · The effect of ATP on muscle contraction

Introduction

This experiment was first described by Szent-Györgyi in 1942 and provides an example of a simple investigation into one aspect of muscle physiology. Fresh meat, such as pork, obtained from a butcher, is used to provide the muscle fibres, which can be kept in 50% glycerol in a refrigerator before the practical.

Materials

- Microscope slide
- Strand of muscle tissue
- Glass rod with flame-polished ends
- Rule
- ATP solution in a 1 cm^3 syringe
- Ringer's solution (one quarter strength Ringer's solution tablet dissolved in 125 cm^3 of warm water).

Method

1 Prepare thin strands of muscle fibres by removing tissue from fresh, lean pork or shin beef, using blunt forceps.
2 Place the strands in warm Ringer's solution.
3 Place on strand on a microscope slide and carefully straighten using a glass rod. Blot off the excess Ringer's solution and measure accurately the length of the muscle strand.
4 Add **one drop** of ATP solution to the muscle and measure the length again.
5 Collect class results.

Results and discussion

1 Tabulate the results suitably and calculate the percentage change in length for each muscle strand.
2 Describe the role of ATP in muscle contraction.

PRACTICAL · The effects of physical activity on heart rate

Introduction

The aim of this practical is to investigate the effect of exercise on heart rate. A number of digital pulse monitors are available, but as an alternative, the pulse rate can be found by placing the index and third fingers firmly over a pulse point, such as the radial artery in the wrist. The pulse rate is used to determine the heart rate and the timing should start with the first pulse, which should be counted as 0. The next is counted as 1, then 2, and so on. The pulse can be recorded for 10 seconds and multiplied by 6 to give the heart rate in beats per minute (bpm). In this practical, it may be helpful for a partner to record your pulse rate at each stage in the investigation.

Materials

- Digital pulse monitor (if available)
- Stopwatch.

Method

1 Record your pulse rate before the investigation begins.
2 Start the period of exercise by stepping on and off a bench at a regular rate, for a period of 3 minutes.

A metronome could be used to indicate a fixed rate of stepping.
3 Record your pulse rate as follows:
   1 minute after the start of the exercise
   2 minutes after the start of the exercise
   at the end of the exercise period.
4 Continue to record your pulse rate every minute during the recovery period until your heart rate returns to its value before the exercise began.
5 Repeat the investigation, but using an increased workload, by increasing the rate of stepping.

Results and discussion

1 Tabulate your results in the table below.
2 Plot a graph of your results, with heart rate in beats per minute on the y-axis and time on the x-axis.
3 Discuss your results, giving physiological explanations for the changes in heart rate during this investigation.
4 A low heart rate during exercise and a small increase in heart rate in response to an increased intensity of work generally indicate a high level of **cardiovascular fitness**. If possible, compare your results with those of other students.

Table P.2 *The effect of physical activity on heart rate*

Intensity of exercise	Heart rate before exercise / bpm	Heart rate 1 min after start of exercise / bpm	Heart rate 2 min after start of exercise / bpm	Heart rate at end of exercise (after 3 min / bpm)	Heart rate during recovery period / bpm
Low					
High					

PRACTICAL

The effects of physical activity on blood pressure

Introduction

A **sphygmomanometer** is an instrument used for the measuring blood pressure. This instrument consists of an inflatable cuff which is attached to a pressure- recording device, such as a mercury manometer or an aneroid pressure gauge. The cuff is wrapped around the upper arm and rapidly inflated until the pressure within the cuff is higher than in the artery and the cuff compresses the artery. **Do not inflate the cuff to a pressure of more than 180 mm Hg**. At this time, no pulse can be felt at the wrist. A stethoscope is placed over the brachial artery on the inside of the elbow and the pressure within the cuff allowed to fall steadily. When the pressure in the cuff is approximately the same as the maximum pressure in the artery, the artery opens slightly to allow a small spurt of blood through. This produces a distinct tapping sound, heard using the stethoscope. As the pressure in the cuff continues to fall, the tapping sounds become louder and more frequent, then suddenly become muffled and disappear. These sounds are known as the Korotkov sounds. When the sounds first appear, the pressure in the cuff is approximately the same as the **systolic pressure** in the artery; the point at which the sounds become muffled indicates the **diastolic pressure**. The sphygmomanometer therefore gives two readings: the systolic pressure and the diastolic pressure. Blood pressure is usually quoted in millimetres of mercury (mm Hg), although this is not an SI unit. One kilopascal equals 7.5 mm Hg, so to convert mm Hg to kPa, divide by 7.5.

Typical values for blood pressure in an adult are about 120 mm Hg during systole and 80 mm Hg during diastole. This is usually written as 120/80, where the first figure represents the systolic pressure and the second represents the diastolic pressure. The difference between the systolic and diastolic pressure is referred to as the **pulse pressure**.

There are a number of digital sphygmomanometers available, some of which have a built-in air pump and automatically inflate and deflate the cuff (Figure P.4). Digital sphygmomanometers display the systolic and diastolic pressures on a screen and may also show the heart rate. When using a sphygmomanometer, follow the instructions carefully. The subject should be seated comfortably, with the lower arm resting on a table. The pressure cuff is wrapped around the upper arm and should be level with the subject's heart. **Values for blood pressure should be interpreted with caution as there are many factors that influence pressure**.

Method

1 Measure and record your resting systolic and diastolic blood pressures.
2 Perform some vigorous physical activity for 1 minute, then measure and record your blood pressure.
3 Collect class results.

Figure P.4 A digital blood pressure monitor with printer. This monitor includes a built-in printer for permanent records of blood pressure and pulse rate.

Results and discussion

1 Tabulate the results and plot suitable graphs to show the change in blood pressure following exercise.
2 Account for the results as fully as you can.
3 List the factors which influence blood pressure.

Further work

You could include readings for heart rate in your results and discussion. If you have a liquid crystal strip thermometer, you could also investigate changes in skin temperature.

PRACTICAL

Measuring vital capacity

Introduction

The vital capacity (maximum volume of air which can be expired following maximal inspiration) of a person can be measured simply by using a suitably calibrated glass bell jar, supported in a sink of water (Figure P.5).

Materials

- Large (5 dm³) calibrated bell jar
- Wide diameter rubber or PVC tubing
- Suitable supports for the bell jar.

Method

1 First calibrate the bell jar by inverting it and pouring in known volumes of water. Use a marker pen to graduate the jar.
2 Fill the jar and invert into a large sink filled with water. Support the jar on suitable blocks.
3 If available, use a standing waste so that the sink is about two-thirds full.
4 Each student then uses the tubing and, following maximal inspiration, exhales as far as possible into the jar.
5 The vital capacity can then be recorded.

HUMAN DISORDERS

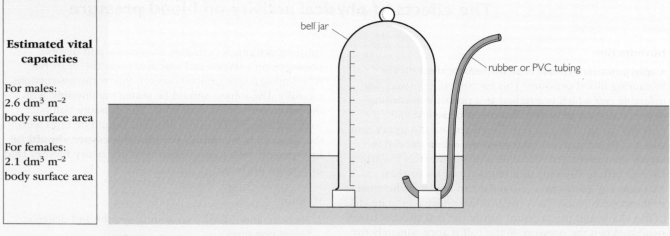

Estimated vital capacities

For males:
2.6 dm³ m⁻² body surface area

For females:
2.1 dm³ m⁻² body surface area

Figure P.5 Method for determining the vital capacity.

Results and discussion

NB: When investigating physiological parameters, it should be noted that there is always variation from person to person. The data should therefore be interpreted with care as there are many factors which can influence the results obtained.

1 Record class results in a suitable table.

2 Is there a consistent difference between the vital capacity of males and females ? If so, can this be quantified?
3 Investigate the effect of posture on vital capacity and suggest reasons for the results.
4 If available, use a surface area nomogram to determine your body surface area and, using the relationship in the margin above, calculate your estimated vital capacity. Suggest reasons for any differences there may be.

The effect of a training programme

Introduction

This is a relatively long-term investigation – a training programme cannot be carried out in one practical class! The activity should be spread out over a minimum of 2 weeks and it is recommended that jogging should be done with a partner so that a conversation can be held during the exercise. The purpose of this is to avoid breathlessness and to stress your aerobic energy systems.

Method

1 Measure and record your resting breathing rate and pulse rate.
2 Carry out an initial jog of 1600 m, aiming to finish in 10 minutes. Measure and record your pulse rate after finishing, then after a rest of 1 minute.
3 These measurements are taken for three further sessions as shown in Table P.3 below, spread over a minimum of 2 weeks.

Results and discussion

1 Record your results in the table below.
2 Work out the recovery rate for each session. Recovery rate can be expressed as shown below:

$$\text{recovery rate} = \frac{\text{pulse rate at}}{\text{end of run}} - \frac{\text{pulse rate}}{\text{after 1 minute rest}}$$

3 Discuss your results fully, making comparisons between the first and last sessions.

Further work

Devise and carry out a specific training programme relevant to your own sporting interest. Examples of training programmes are included in: *Physical Education and the Study of Sport*, 3rd edition, B Davis, R Bull, J Roscoe and D Roscoe, Mosby, ISBN 0 7234 26422.

Table P.3 *The effect of a training programme*

Approximate length of run / m	Time to aim for / min	Breathing rate before activity / breaths per min	Pulse rate before activity / bpm	Pulse rate finish / bpm	Pulse rate 1 min after finishing / bpm	Recovery rate / bpm
1600	10					
2400	15					
3200	20					
1600	10					

The effect of exercise on ventilation

Introduction

The aim of this practical activity is to investigate the effect of incremental exercise on ventilation (Figure P.6). You could, for example, investigate the effect of cycling at progressively faster speeds, such as 5, 10, 15 and 20 km per hour for a fixed period of time, using an exercise cycle. Alternatively you could do progressively more sit-ups in, say, 30 seconds. Tidal volume may be measured using a spirometer or a pocket spirometer. If these are unavailable, breath volume kits (supplied by Philip Harris) are a suitable alternative.

Materials

- Exercise cycle or bicycle ergometer
- Stopwatch
- Spirometer or breath volume kits.

Method

1 Measure and record your resting breathing rate and tidal volume.
2 Perform some mild exercise, such as cycling at 5 km per hour for 2 minutes.
3 Again, measure and record your breathing rate and tidal volume.
4 Rest for 5 minutes, then repeat the investigation at progressively higher levels of activity. Immediately after each period of activity, measure and record your breathing rate and tidal volume. Rest for 5 minutes between each bout of exercise.

Figure P.6 The effect of exercise on ventilation.

Results and discussion

1 Record all your results in a suitable table.
2 Calculate your respiratory minute volume ($\dot{V}_E$), by multiplying breathing rate by tidal volume.
3 Plot graphs to show changes in breathing rate, tidal volume, and respiratory minute volume against activity level.
4 Discuss your results as fully as you can.

Further work

You could combine this practical with investigations into the effect of incremental activity on the cardiovascular system, by also measuring changes in heart rate and blood pressure. Compare results from students who exercise regularly and students who do not.

Assessment questions

Unit 4

The following questions have been chosen from written assessment tests and selected to introduce you to the range of styles and formats that you can expect in the A2 assessment. The shorter structured questions test mainly knowledge and understanding of the topics, and the longer questions contain sections in which you may be required to interpret and analyse data. In the Core section of the paper, one question will require you to write an answer in continuous prose.

The question styles are essentially similar to those used in examinations prior to Curriculum 2000, so you can find extra practice questions on past papers set before January 2002. It should be noted, however, that the specifications for the Options are different and many past questions contain material that is not relevant to the current specification.

Chapter 1   Metabolic pathways

1 The diagram shows a summary of some of the steps in aerobic respiration.

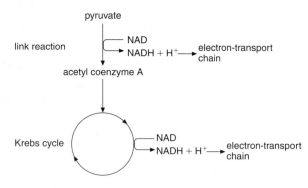

(a) State precisely where Krebs cycle takes place within a cell.   **[1]**

(b) Name the process that results in the production of ATP from ADP by the electron-transport chain.   **[1]**

(c) With reference to the diagram, explain why Krebs cycle can only take place when oxygen is available.   **[2]**

(Total 4 marks)
(Edexcel GCE Biology and Human Biology (6104, January 2002)

2 The diagram below shows a summary of glycolysis and two alternative pathways that may follow this process in anaerobic conditions.

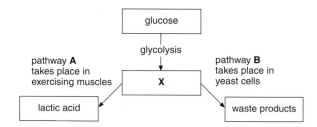

(a) Substance **X** is the final product of glycolysis. Name this substance.   **[1]**

(b) In glycolysis, NAD is converted to its reduced form (NADH + H$^+$). Describe how NAD is regenerated in pathway **A**.   **[2]**

(c) Name the waste products of pathway **B**.   **[1]**

(d) Describe the role of reduced NAD (NADH + H$^+$) when respiration takes place in aerobic conditions.   **[3]**

(Total 7 marks)
(Edexcel GCE Biology and Human Biology (6104, June 2002)

3 Triphenyl tetrazolium chloride (TTC) is a hydrogen acceptor that can be used as a redox indicator. TTC is colourless when oxidised and red when reduced.

Oxidised TTC $\rightleftharpoons$ Reduced TTC
   (colourless)   (red)

An investigation was carried out into the effect of temperature on oxidoreductase activity in yeast cells.

Four water baths were set up at 20 °C, 30 °C, 40 °C and 50 °C. A test tube containing 10 cm^3 of active yeast suspension was placed into each water bath. A test tube containing 1 cm^3 TTC was also placed into each water bath.

After 5 minutes, the TTC was poured into the yeast suspension at each temperature. The time taken for a red coloration to appear in each tube was recorded.

The results of this investigation are shown in the table.

Temperature / °C	Time for red coloration to appear / minutes
20	19
30	11
40	5
50	8

(a) Suggest why the tubes containing the yeast suspension and TTC were placed into the water baths 5 minutes before their contents were mixed. **[1]**

(b) Explain how the results indicate that the activity of the yeast cells involves (oxidoreductase) enzymes. **[4]**

(c) (i) Name a hydrogen acceptor that would be found in active yeast cells **[1]**

    (ii) Give an example of a metabolic pathway in which this hydrogen acceptor is involved. **[1]**

(Total 7 marks)

(Edexcel GCE Biology and Human Biology (6104, January 2003)

4 Give an account of the stages that take place in the mitochondrion, stating the location of each stage

(Total 10 marks)

(Edexcel GCE Biology and Human Biology (6104, January 2003)

Chapter 2 Regulation of the internal environment

1 The diagram shows part of a nephron from a mammalian kidney.

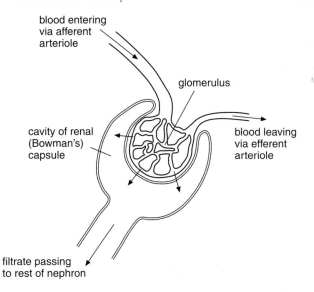

blood entering via afferent arteriole

glomerulus

cavity of renal (Bowman's) capsule

blood leaving via efferent arteriole

filtrate passing to rest of nephron

(a) Name the region of the kidney in which the renal capsules are found. **[1]**

(b) Describe and explain the process of ultrafiltration. **[4]**

(c) Name **one** substance, filtered from the blood, that would be completely reabsorbed as the filtrate passes through the nephron. **[1]**

(Total 6 marks)

(Edexcel GCE Biology and Human Biology (6104, January 2003)

2 Plants contain many pigments other than chlorophyll in their leaves. One of these pigments changes its form when exposed to different wavelenths of light. The diagram shows the interconversion between the two forms of this pigment.

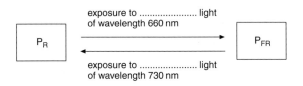

exposure to .... light of wavelength 660 nm

P_R

P_{FR}

exposure to .... light of wavelength 730 nm

(a) Name this pigment. **[1]**

(b) Complete the diagram by writing the colours of the light involved in each of the two spaces.

[1]

ASSESSMENT QUESTIONS

(c) Plants can respond to changes in the relative lengths of day and night. The interconversion of this pigment is involved in the control of these responses. Suggest one response that is controlled in this way. **[1]**

(d) Mammals also contain pigments that enable them to respond to light. Name one such pigment and state precisely where this pigment is found. **[2]**

(Total 5 marks)

(Edexcel GCE Biology and Human Biology (6104, January 2002)

3 The diagram below shows some of the effects that follow the secretion of FSH (follicle stimulating hormone).

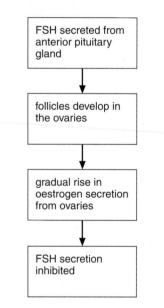

(a) State the type of mechanism, shown by the diagram, that controls the secretion of FSH and oestrogen. **[1]**

(b) Explain why hormones, such as FSH and oestrogen, only affect the activity of specific target organs. **[2]**

(c) With reference to the differences between nervous and hormonal coordination, suggest why the development of the follicles is coordinated by hormones and not by the nervous system. **[3]**

(Total 6 marks)

(Edexcel GCE Biology and Human Biology (6104, January 2003)

4 (a) The formation of the mammalian excretory product urea can be summarised by the following word equation.

Ammonia + Carbon dioxide → Urea + Water

(i) Name the organ in which urea is formed **[1]**

(ii) State how the ammonia is produced. **[2]**

(iii) Suggest how the carbon dioxide used in the formation of urea is produced. **[1]**

(b) In an investigation, a student compared the concentration of urea in her urine before and after taking a drink of water.

The student measured the concentration of urea in urine samples for a period of 5 days. Each day she took a urine sample within 15 minutes of waking after a night's sleep. She then drank 0.75 dm³ water. A second urine sample was then taken 30 minutes after drinking the water.

The results of this investigation are shown in the table.

Day	Urea concentraton before drinking /mol dm⁻³	Urea concentration after drinking /mol dm⁻³
1	1.1	0.2
2	1.3	0.3
3	1.1	0.3
4	1.0	0.1
5	1.5	0.3
Mean	1.2	0.2

(i) Calculate the mean percentage change in the urea concentration as a result of taking the drinking of water. Show your working. **[2]**

(ii) Explain how drink the water may have caused the reduction in urea concentration in the urine. **[4]**

(iii) Suggest why an estimate of the urea concentration in urine is not a reliable estimate of the total solute concentration of the urine. **[2]**

(Total 12 marks)

(Edexcel GCE Biology and Human Biology (6104, January 2002)

Chapter 3   Nervous coordination in mammals

1 The diagram below shows a section through a human brain.

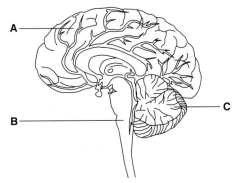

Complete the table below by writing in the letter and the name of the region of the brain that carries out each function.

Function	Letter	Name of region
Initiating and controlling voluntary muscle movement		
Coordinating skeletal muscle movement, balance and posture		
Controlling heart and breathing rate		

(Total 4 marks)
*(Edexcel GCE Biology and Human Biology
(6104, June 2002)*

2 The diagram shows a longitudinal section through part of the axon of a myelinated neurone.

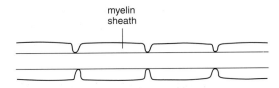

(a) Describe the structure of the myelin sheath
[2]

(b) The table shows the speed of conduction of an impulse along axons with different diameters. Data from both myelinated and non-myelinated neurones are included.

Type of neurone	Diameter of axon /μm	Speed of conduction / ms^{-1}
Non-myelinated	2	2
Non-myelinated	15	5
Non-myelinated	700	22
Myelinated	10	30
Myelinated	15	80

With reference to the data, describe and explain the effect that the myelin sheath has on the speed of conduction of a nerve impulse.
[5]

(Total 7 marks)
*(Edexcel GCE Biology and Human Biology
(6104, June 2002)*

3 The diagram shows the structure of a synapse.

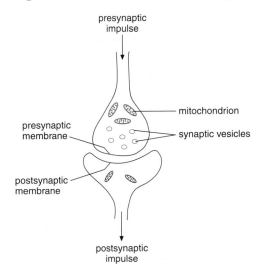

(a) Describe what would happen in the presynaptic neurone as a result of the arrival of an action potential. **[3]**

(b) The graphs below show the changes in membrane potential in the presynaptic neurone and the postsynaptic neurone as an impulse passes across a synapse.

ASSESSMENT QUESTIONS

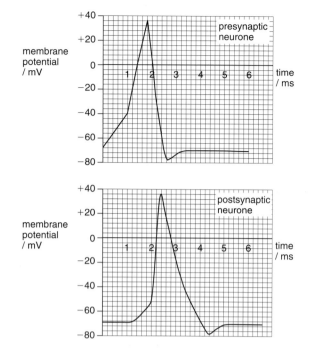

(i) On the graph for the postsynaptic neurone, indicate by using a letter S the point at which the sodium channels open, allowing an increased flow of sodium ions into the neurone. **[1]**

(ii) On the graph for the postsynaptic neurone, indicate by using a letter P the point at which the potassium channels open, allowing an increased flow of potassium ions out of the neurone. **[1]**

(iii) Calculate the delay between the arrival of the action potential at the presynaptic neurone and the production of an action potential in the postsynaptic neurone. Show your working. **[2]**

(iv) Explain the reason for this delay. **[2]**

(Total 9 marks)
(Edexcel GCE Biology and Human Biology
(6104, January 2002)

4 In an investigation into the effect of a drug on the nervous system, the reaction time of four volunteers was tested by timing how long it took for them to push a button after seeing a lamp light up.

Volunteer A drank 50 cm^3 of water. Volunteers B, C and D each drank 50 cm^3 of a solution containing different concentrations of the drug. The reaction time of each volunteer was then tested every ten minutes during the next hour.

(a) Suggest what the data indicate about the absorption of the drug into the bloodstream. Give a reason for your answer. **[2]**

(b) Describe the effects that the drug had upon the reaction times of the volunteers during the 60 minutes of the investigation. **[3]**

(c) This drug is known to affect synaptic transmission. Suggest how the drug might cause the effects you have described in (b). **[3]**

(d) Give **three** factors, other than the concentration of the drug, that would need to

Volunteer	Concentration of drug / arbitrary units	Reaction time/seconds						
		0 min	10 min	20 min	30 min	40 min	50 min	60 min
A	0	0.3	0.3	0.2	0.2	0.2	0.2	0.2
B	1	0.3	0.4	0.4	0.4	0.3	0.2	0.3
C	2	0.2	0.5	0.6	0.6	0.5	0.4	0.4
D	3	0.3	0.8	0.9	1.0	1.0	0.9	0.9

be taken into account in this investigation. **[3]**

(Total 11 marks)
(Edexcel GCE Biology and Human Biology
(6104, January 2003)

Option A Microbiology and biotechnology

1 The table refers to some features of three different viruses. Copy and complete the table by writing the appropriate word or words in the spaces.

Virus	Type of nucleic acid	Structure	Example of host cell
Tobacco mosaic virus (TMV)			Leaf cell in tobacco plant
λ (lambda) phage		Complex	Bacterium
Human immunodeficiency virus (HIV)			

(Total 6 marks)
(Edexcel GCE Biology and Human Biology
(6104, June 2002)

2 *(a)* Explain what is meant by the term **antibiotic**
[2]

(b) Describe the effect of penicillin on bacterial growth.
[3]

(Total 5 marks)
(Edexcel GCE Biology and Human Biology
(6104, June 2002)

3 An infection is caused when pathogenic microorganisms enter the tissues of the host organism and multiply. The symptoms of the infection may result from the production of toxins by the microorganism or from the destruction of host tissue.

(a) Food poisoning can be caused by a number of pathogenic bacteria, including *Salmonella* and *Staphylococcus*.

  (i) Name the type of toxin produced by *Salmonella*. **[1]**

  (ii) The symptoms of food poisoning caused by *Salmonella* occur 1–2 days after eating contaminated food. However the symptoms resulting from infection by

Staphylococcus occur within a few hours after infection.

Explain why this difference occurs. **[2]**

(b) *Salmonella* is Gram negative whereas *Staphylococcus* is Gram positive. Describe how the colour of these bacteria would differ after Gram staining had been carried out. **[2]**

(Total 5 marks)
(Edexcel GCE Biology and Human Biology
(6104, January 2003)

4 *Escherichia coli* were incubated for 24 hours in a culture medium containing 1% glucose and 1% lactose. Samples were removed every hour and a viable cell count made. The results of this experiment are presented in the graph below.

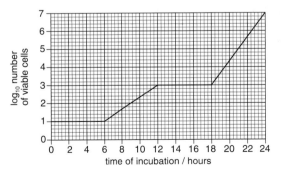

ASSESSMENT QUESTIONS

(a) Calculate the number of generations produced between 6 and 12 hours of incubation, using the formula:

$$n = \frac{\log_{10} N_1 - \log_{10} N_0}{\log_{10} 2}$$

where n = number of generations
N_0 = number of cells after 6 hours
N_1 = number of cells after 12 hours
$\log_{10} 2 = 0.301$

Show your working **[3]**

(b) Describe and explain the shape of the graph between 12 and 18 hours. **[5]**

(c) (i) Compare the rate of growth of the population between 18 and 24 hours with the rate between 6 and 12 hours. **[2]**

(ii) Suggest an explanation of the difference you have described. **[2]**

(Total 12 marks)
(Edexcel GCE Biology and Human Biology (6104, June 2002)

Option B: Food science

1 The table refers to foods that are produced by fermentation. Copy and complete the table by writing the appropriate word or words in the spaces.

Processed food product	Raw food material	Sugar(s) used as main substrate for fermentation
Sauerkraut		
Yoghurt	Milk	
	Grape juice	Glucose and fructose

(Total 4 marks)
(Edexcel GCE Biology and Human Biology (6104, June 2002)

2 Tomatoes on display in a supermarket can remain on the shelves for several days. During this time, it is important that they do not over-ripen. The diagram shows a section through a container used to display pre-packed tomatoes in a supermarket.

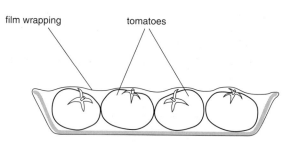

(a) Suggest **one** reason why it is important that the tomatoes do not become over-ripe on the supermarket shelf. **[1]**

(b) Explain why the material chosen for the film wrapping might help to prevent the tomatoes from becoming over-ripe if it is more permeable to carbon dioxide than it is to oxygen. **[3]**

(c) Explain why the permeability of the film to water vapour must be sufficient to maintain humidity without excessive condensation. **[2]**

(Total 6 marks)
(Edexcel GCE Biology and Human Biology (6104, January 2003)

3 A skinfold calliper was used to estimate the percentage body fat on a sixteen year old student. Three readings were taken at slightly different positions from the back of the upper arm. These readings are shown in the table.

Reading	Skinfold measurement / mm
1	10
2	12
3	10

The percentage body fat of the student was estimated by using the data in the table below.

Mean skinfold thickness /mm	Percentage body fat		
	Age 16–29	Age 30–49	Age 50+
7	12.5	20.2	22.9
8	13.9	21.5	24.6
9	15.2	22.6	26.2
10	16.4	23.6	27.6
11	17.4	24.5	28.8
12	18.4	25.3	30.0
13	19.3	26.1	31.1
14	20.1	26.8	32.1
15	20.9	27.5	33.0

(a) Estimate the percentage body fat of the student. Show your working. **[2]**

(b) Explain how you could use your answer to estimate the lean body mass of the student. **[2]**

(c) (i) Name a disorder which involves obsessive dieting. **[1]**

    (ii) Give **two** symptoms, other than the loss of subcutaneous fat, of this disorder. **[2]**

(Total 7 marks)

(Edexcel GCE Biology and Human Biology (6104, January 2003)

4 During the formation of the helical structure of the protein collagen, hydrogen bonds form between hydroxyproline residues. Hydroxyproline is synthesised in cells from the amino acid proline, as shown by the diagram.

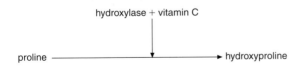

Collagen was extracted from mammals with a normal diet and from mammals fed on a diet deficient in vitamin C (ascorbic acid). An investigation was carried out to compare the effect of temperature upon these two forms of collagen. The effect was estimated by measuring the percentage of collagen that remained in the form of a triple helix.

The results of this investigation are shown in the table.

Temperature /°C	Percentage of collagen helix remaining as a triple helix	
	Normal diet	Vitamin C deficient diet
0	100	100
10	100	95
20	100	25
30	100	10
40	95	5
50	35	5
60	10	5

(a) Compare the effect of increasing temperature upon collagen from mammals fed on a normal diet with that from mammals fed on a diet deficient in vitamin C. **[3]**

(b) Suggest why the differences in the vitamin C content of the diet may lead to the differences you have described in part (a) **[4]**

(c) Name the disorder associated with a deficiency of vitamin C, and describe its symptoms. **[3]**

(d) Suggest how the results of this investigation indicate why a deficiency of vitamin C in the diet may lead to the disorder you have described in part *(c)*. **[2]**

(Total 12 marks)

(Edexcel GCE Biology and Human Biology (6104, January 2003)

ASSESSMENT QUESTIONS

Option C   Human health and fitness

1 The diagram below shows some cardiac muscle cells.

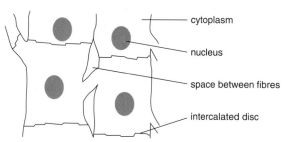

- cytoplasm
- nucleus
- space between fibres
- intercalated disc

(a) The cytoplasm of these muscle cells contains two types of filament.
Name the proteins that form these filaments. **[1]**

(b) State what is found in the spaces between the fibres. **[1]**

(c) State the function of the intercalated discs. **[1]**

(d) Copy and complete the table by describing **two** differences between the **structure** of cardiac muscle and skeletal muscle.

	Cardiac muscle	Skeletal muscle
1		
2		

[1]

(Total 5 marks)
(Edexcel GCE Biology and Human Biology
(6104, January 2003)

2 (a) Describe how tuberculosis (TB) is caused. **[3]**

(b) Describe how this disease is treated. **[2]**

(Total 5 marks)
(Edexcel GCE Biology and Human Biology
(6104, June 2002)

3 The flow chart summarises the response of lymphocytes in the blood to a bacterial infection.

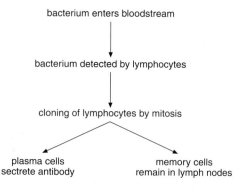

bacterium enters bloodstream

bacterium detected by lymphocytes

cloning of lymphocytes by mitosis

plasma cells
sectrete antibody

memory cells
remain in lymph nodes

(a) Explain what is meant by the term **antibody**. **[1]**

(b) Suggest why the cloning of lymphocytes by mitosis is important in the production of an antibody. **[2]**

(c) The process shown in the flow chart would lead to active immunity. Explain how active immunity differs from passive immunity. **[3]**

(Total 6 marks)
(Edexcel GCE Biology and Human Biology
(6104, June 2002)

4 Diagram A and diagram B below show recordings of the breathing patterns of a person. In diagram A the person is at rest. In diagram B the person has just finished a period of strenuous exercise.

(a) Calculate the mean tidal volume between 10 and 30 seconds when the person is at rest. Show your working. **[2]**

(b) The ventilation rate of a person can be calculated by multiplying the rate of breathing by the depth of breathing. Use diagram B to calculate the ventilation rate of the person during the first 10 seconds after exercise. Show your working. **[2]**

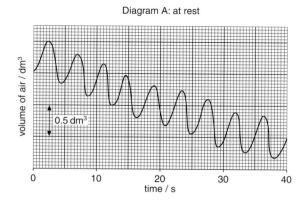

Diagram A: at rest

(c) Using the data in the recordings, compare the breathing patterns of this person before and after exercise. **[3]**

Diagram B: after exercise

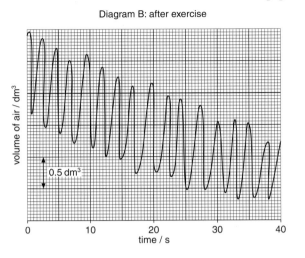

(d) This person then undertook a physical training programme.

(i) Describe and explain **two** differences that you would expect to see in the breathing patterns of this person following exercise as a result of the training programme. **[4]**

(ii) Suggest how the training programme might affect the cardiac output of the person. **[2]**

(Total 13 marks)
*(Edexcel GCE Biology and Human Biology
(6104, June 2002)*

Mark schemes

In the mark schemes the following symbols are used:
;   indicates separate marking points
/   indicates alternate marking points
eq. means correct equivalent points are accepted
{} indicate a list of alternatives

Unit 4

Chapter 1

1   *(a)* matrix of mitochondrion ;   **[1]**

   (b) oxidative phosphorylation ;   **[1]**

   (c) oxygen needed to accept, hydrogen / protons / electrons ;
          (if no oxygen then) oxidative phosphorylation / etc cannot take place / eq ;
          (so) NAD / electron carriers cannot be regenerated / reduced NAD is not oxidised ;   **[2]**

                                           (Total 4 marks)

2   *(a)* Pyruvate / pyruvic acid ;   **[1]**

   (b) Pyruvate / pyruvic acid / substance X, reduced / accepts hydrogen / protons / electrons (to form lactic acid) ;

          $NADH + H^+$ / reduced NAD/$NADH_2$ (used in this reduction is *oxidised* to NAD ;   **[2]**

   (c) Ethanol / ethyl alcohol, *and* carbon dioxide / CO_2 ;   **[1]**

   (d) Transfers electrons / H^+ / hydrogen (ions), to form electron transfer chain / FAD ;

          Reference to inner membrane of mitochondrion / cristae ;

          Oxidative phosphorylation ;

          Generation of ATP (from ADP) ;   **[3]**

                                           (Total 7 marks)

3   *(a)* {Equilibration / eq} / allow contents to reach temperature ;   **[1]**

   (b) {Red coloration / colour change} indicates reduction (of TTC) ;

          TTC reduced when it {accepts / eq} hydrogen ;

Hydrogen {released / removed} by dehydrogenation ;

Rate of reaction increases as temperature increases (up to 40 °C) ;

Rate slows above 40 °C ;

Indicating some denaturing of enzyme ;
[ignore references to optimum temperature   **[4]**

   (c) (i)   NAD / FAD / cytochrome oxidase / ethanal / oxygen ;   **[1]**

          (ii) Respiration / glycolysis / Krebs cycle / electron transfer chain / (alcoholic) fermentation ;

                [must be correct for the answer given in *(c)* (i)]   **[1]**

                                           (Total 7 marks)

4   Accept points in correct context only

   1. Pyruvate (from glycolysis) {passes / diffuses} into mitochondria ;

   2. Combines with {coenzyme A / coA} to form acetyl coenzyme A ;

   3. {NADH (+ H^+) / reduced NAD} and carbon dioxide formed ;

   4. {Acetate / acetyl / acetyl coenzyme A} combines with {4C compound / oxaloacetate} to form {6C / citrate} ;

   5. Reference to Krebs cycle in the matrix ;

   6. Reference to Krebs cycle (as series of reactions) regenerating {4C compound / oxaloacetate} ;

   7. Reference to enzyme control (at any point) ;

   8. (more) {NADH (+ H^+) / reduced NAD} and carbon dioxide formed ;

   9. ATP is produced (directly) ;

   10. {Electrons / hydrogen (ions)} from {NADH / FADH} pass on to {electron carriers / cytochromes / FAD} ;

   11. Reference to {cytochromes / electron carriers /

ETC / oxidative phosphorylation} in {inner (mitochondrial) membrane / cristae} ;

12. {H^+ / protons} pumped out (of matrix) into intermembranal space ;

13. ATP produced as {H^+ / protons} flow back (into matrix) ;

14. Through stalked particles ;

15. Water formed as electrons and {H^+ / protons} combine with oxygen ;

(Maximum 10 marks)

Chapter 2

1 (a) Cortex ;   **[1]**

   (b) Reference to high pressure {of blood / in glomerulus} ;

      Because afferent vessel wider than efferent vessel ;

      {Small molecules / molecules up to 70 000 MW} {forced / eq} out (through capillary wall) ;

      {Larger molecules / protein / cells} remain in blood ;

      Reference to basement membrane as a filter ;

      Reference to {fenestrations / large pores} in capillary walls ;

      Reference to {slits / pores} in {podocytes / cells lining capsule} ;   **[4]**

   (c) Glucose / amino acids ;   **[1]**

(Total 6 marks)

2 (a) phytochrome ;   **[1]**

   (b) red *and* far red ;   **[1]**

   (c) germination / breaking of dormancy (in seeds or buds) / (initiation of) flowering / fruit formation / leaf fall ;   **[1]**

   (d) rhodopsin / visual purple ;

      rod cells (in retina) ;

      or

      iodopsin ;

cone cells (in retina) ;

or

melanin ;

pigment cells / melanocytes (in skin) ;   **[2]**

(Total 5 marks)

3 (a) Negative feedback ;   **[1]**

   (b) {Ovary / (target) organs / cells} have receptor {sites / molecules / proteins} ;

      On cell surface / plasma membrane ;

      Hormone binds with (receptor) {site / molecule} / hormone–receptor complex forms ;   **[2]**

   (c) Follicles develop over time / eq ;

      Hormone levels in the blood gradually build up ;

      Hormones present in blood for period of time ;

      Hormone effect lasts long time ;

      Nervous system co-ordinates {short term / immediate} responses ;   **[3]**

(Total 6 marks)

4 (a) (i)   liver ;   **[1]**

      (ii) deamination / removal, of, amino / amine / NH_2 / NH_3^+, group ;

          of *excess*, amino acids / proteins ;   **[2]**

      (iii) by respiration / Krebs cycle ;   **[1]**

   (b) (i)   (1.2–0.2) × 100 ÷ 1.2 ;
          = 83.3 / 83 (%) ;   **[2]**

      (ii) reference to water absorbed into blood ;

         blood becomes more dilute / less concentrated / eq ;

         detected by hypothalamus ;

         release of ADH (into blood) stops / reduced ;

         from (posterior) pituitary ;

         (cells in) collecting duct / distal convoluted tubule become less permeable (to water) ;

less water reabsorbed (from renal
filtrate) ; **[4]**

(iii) there are other solutes / urea not the only
solute ;

named e.g. of other solute ;

concentration of these may be high even
when urea concentration is low ; **[2]**

(Total 12 marks)

Chapter 3

1

One main Function	Letter	Region
Initiating and controlling voluntary muscle movement	A ⎫	Cerebral hemispheres / cerebrum / cortex
Co-ordination of skeletal muscle movement, balance and posture	C ⎬ ;	Cerebellum ;
Contains centres controlling heart and breathing rate	B ⎭	Medulla (oblongata) / brain stem ;

1 mark only for correct letters ;

(Total 4 marks)

2 (a) Schwann cells ;

Wrap / fold / roll, around *axon* ;

Fatty / lipid / phospholipid, nature ;

Reference to nodes as, gaps in the sheath, /
naked / exposed / uncovered, axon ; **[2]**

(b) (myelination) increases speed of, conduction /
impulse ;

When diameters, same / both 15 μm,
myelinated faster than non-myelinated ;

(Both) myelinated speeds faster than non-
myelinated at 700 μm even though diameters
much smaller / eq ;

Correct manipulation of figures to compare the
effect of the myelin sheath on speed of
conduction ;

Myelin sheath prevents (initiation of), action
potential / depolarisation / acts as an
insulator ;

Action potential/ depolarisation, only possible
at nodes / gaps ;

Reference to, impulse jumping from node to
node / saltatory effect ;

No Na$^+$ channels except at nodes / reference
to inward movement Na$^+$ involved in action
potential ; **[5]**

(Total 7 marks)

3 (a) calcium channels open / membrane more
permeable to Ca ;

calcium (ions), diffuse / move in ;

vesicles move towards (presynaptic) membrane ;

vesicles, fuse / bind / eq, with membrane ;

transmitter / acetylcholine, released into,
(synaptic) cleft / gap ; **[3]**

(b) (i) S indicated at 1.2 ms ; **[1]**

(ii) P indicated at 2.4 ms ; **[1]**

(iii) 2.4 – 1.8 ;
= 0.6 ms ; **[2]**

(iv) release of, transmitter / acetylcholine ;
diffusion / movement, across cleft ;
time to, depolarise / form action potential
/ reference to Na channels opening ; **[2]**

(Total 9 marks)

4 (a) (absorption is) {very quick / within 10
minutes} / reference to absorbed through
stomach wall / eq ;

{Volunteers who had the drug / B, C & D} all
had slower reactions within 10 minutes ; **[2]**

(b) The drug increases reaction time ;

The greater the {quantity / concentration} of
the drug the greater the effect / eq ;

Calculation of relative increase for at least two
volunteers ;

The greater the {quantity / concentration} of
the drug the longer the recovery back to
normal ;

Volunteer B back to normal within 40 minutes
but {C / D} still not back to normal after
60 minutes ;

Reference to reaction time of A
decreasing ; **[3]**

(c) Reference to the drug slowing down (rate of
synaptic transmission) ;

(drug has) {similar shape / mimics}
{transmitter / acetylcholine} ;

{Blocks / eq} receptors on postsynaptic
membrane ;

May affect {permeability / ion channels / eq} of
(pre / post) synaptic membranes ;

May {affect / inhibit} release of
{neurotransmitter / acetylcholine} ;

May bind to {transmitter / acetylcholine} ;

Reference to effect on acetylcholinesterase ;
[3]

(d) Age ;

Gender ;

Weight / BMI / eq ;

Health / eyesight ;

Whether other drugs used / e.g. tobacco / eq ;

Previous exposure to this drug ;

Fitness ;

Time since eating / amount of food eaten ;

Time of day / reference to tiredness ; **[3]**

(Total 11 marks)

2 (a) Substance / chemical, that can, kill / inhibit
growth, of an organism ;

Produced by, microorganisms / fungi / other
organism ; **[2]**

(b) Reference to penicillin targeting cell wall ;

During growth of bacterial cell ;

By interfering with synthesis (of cell wall) ;

By preventing formation of, cross links / bonds,
between peptidoglycan molecules ;

Make bacteria more susceptible to osmotic
shock / eq ; **[3]**

(Total 5 marks)

3 (a) (i) Endotoxin ; **[1]**

(ii) *Salmonella* releases {endotoxin / toxin}
when it dies / eq ;

Staphylococcus releases exotoxins
immediately ;

Reference to endotoxins needed in high
concentrations ; **[2]**

(b) *Salmonella* would be {red / pink} ;

Staphylococcus would be {purple / dark blue /
violet} ; **[2]**

(Total 5 marks)

Option A

1

Name of virus	Type of nucleic acid	Structure	Example of host cell
TMV (Tobacco mosaic virus)	**RNA ;**	**Helical ;**	Leaf cells in tobacco plant
Lambda phage (λ)	**DNA ;**	Complex	Bacterium
HIV (Human immunodeficiency virus)	**RNA ;**	**Polyhedral ;**	**T-lymphocyte / T-cell / T4 / T-helper**

(Total 6 marks)

MARK SCHEMES

4 *(a)* $n = \dfrac{3.0 - 1.0}{0.301}$;

$= 6.64$;

Number of generations $= 6$;

Allow consequential error **[3]**

(b) Reference to the level line ;

No increase in number of cells / no growth / second lag phase / eq ;

No reproduction / death rate = birth rate ;

Glucose exhausted / eq ;

No available respiratory substrate ;

Bacteria synthesising, enzyme / lactase ;

(needed for) hydrolysis of lactose ;

Reference to diauxic growth ; **[5]**

(c) (i) Rate between 18–24 hours greater than that between 6–12 hours ;

Credit calculation of growth rates ; **[2]**

(ii) Using lactose ;

Two monosaccharides / glucose and galactose, available ;

Reference to greater concentration of substrates ; **[2]**

(Total 12 marks)

Option B

1

Processed food product	Raw food material	Sugar(s) used as main substrate for fermentation
Sauerkraut	**Cabbage ;**	**Glucose and fructose ;**
Yoghurt	Milk	**Lactose ;**
Wine / vinegar ;	Grape juice	Glucose and fructose

(Total 4 marks)

2 *(a)* Reference to (over ripe tomatoes) softer / more easily damaged (therefore less likely to be sold) / eq ; **[1]**

(b) Oxygen used up as tomatoes *respire* faster than it diffuses into container ;

{Anaerobic / low oxygen} conditions develop ;

That {inhibit / slow down} respiration ;

Reduces ethene production / ripening slowed down ;

Carbon dioxide produced by respiration can escape so that {pressure does not increase / container does not inflate} ; **[3]**

(c) (humidity needs to be maintained) to {slow down / reduce} water loss by {transpiration / evaporation} ;

To prevent tomatoes shrivelling up / eq ;

Condensation may encourage growth of microorganisms (that would spoil the tomatoes) ; **[2]**

(Total 6 marks)

3 *(a)* Mean thickness $= 10 + 12 + 10 \div 3 = 10.67$ / 10.7 mm OR mean of percentage body fat ;

% body fat (10.67 or 11 mm) = accept 16.9 to 17.4 ; **[2]**

(b) Find {mass / weight} of student ;

Calculate {mass / weight} of fat using percentage ;

Deduct (mass / weight of) fat from total body {mass / weight} ; **[2]**

(c) (i) Anorexia nervosa ; **[1]**

(ii) Amenorrhoea / no (menstrual) periods in girls / low blood pressure / downy hair / distorted perception of body size / muscle wasting ;;
[ANY TWO]

[If *(c)* (i) incorrect e.g. Bulimia, accept correct symptoms for *(c)* (ii)] **[2]**

(Total 7 marks)

4 *(a)* Increase in temperature has a {greater effect / eq} with Vitamin C deficient diet than with normal diet ;

Normal – no {effect / denaturation} 30 °C / 40 °C
Deficient – {effect / denaturation} occurs {below / at} 10 °C ;

Normal – still being denatured at 60 °C
Deficient – no further denaturation above 40 °C

Normal – largest {decrease / denaturation} between 40 °C and 50 °C
Deficient – largest {decrease / denaturation} between 10 °C and 20 °C ;

Both still have some collagen (not denatured) at 60 °C / eq ;

Both have no denaturation at 0 °C ;

Comparative manipulation of figures ; **[3]**

(b) Vitamin C {required for / eq} formation of hydroxyproline / less hydroxyproline formed if vitamin C deficient ;

As cofactor for {hydroxylase / hydroxylation} ;

(therefore) fewer hydrogen bonds in {collagen / triple helix} ;

(therefore) collagen structure {weaker / unstable} ;

(therefore) {denatures / eq} {more easily / at lower temperatures} ; **[4]**

(c) Scurvy ;

Bleeding gums / slow wound healing / painful joints / internal bleeding ;
[ANY TWO] **[3]**

(d) Reference to collagen (fibres) present in {connective / named} tissues ;

Lack of vitamin C {causes / leads to} weaker collagen (in connective tissues) ;

Symptoms associated with poor {formation / maintenance} (of connective tissue) ; **[2]**

(Total 12 marks)

Option C

1 *(a)* Actin and myosin ; **[1]**

(b) Connective tissue / elastic fibres / (blood) capillaries / tissue fluid / eq ; **[1]**

(c) {Speeds up / allows} transmission of {wave of excitation / action potential} OR transmit force of contraction / attach cells to each other ; **[1]**

(d)

Cardiac muscle	Skeletal muscle
one nucleus per cell	multinucleated ;
branched	not branched ;
intercalated discs / gap junctions	no intercalated discs / no gap junctions ;
more mitochondria	fewer mitochondria ;
has spaces	no spaces
less {endoplasmic/ sarcoplasmic} reticulum	more {endoplasmic / sarcoplasmic} reticulum ;

[ANY TWO PAIRS OF POINTS]
[2]

(Total 5 marks)

2 *(a)* Reference to *Mycobacterium tuberculosis* ;

Inhalation of droplets (containing *Mycobacterium tuberculosis* / bacteria) ;

Bacteria, live / reproduce / active, inside cells (in lungs) ;

Formation of, tubercles / plaques ;

Reference to destruction of, (lung) tissue / alveoli, / reference to lesions ; **[3]**

(b) Reference to use of, antibiotics / isoniazid / rifampin / ethambutol / pyranamide ;

In combination therapy / more than one drug needed ;

Two phases of treatment ;

Long period / several months / at least one month, of treatment ; **[2]**

(Total 5 marks)

MARK SCHEMES

3 *(a)* Protein / immunoglobulin / chemical / substance, produced in response / binds to antigen / foreign (glyco)protein ; **[1]**

(b) Large number of genetically-identical, lymphocytes / cells, produced ;

Which produce a large amount of antibody ;

Specific to, antigen / bacterium ; **[2]**

(c) Bacteium / antigen, triggers active and, no bacterium / antigen, in passive ;

Antibodies produced by infected individual in active, antibodies received from, mother / vaccination, in passive ;

Memory cells produced in active, no memory cells produced in passive ;

Active lasts longer than passive ; **[3]**

(Total 6 marks)

4 *(a)* $(0.60 + 0.65 + 0.65 + 0.65 + 0.75) \div 5$;
$= 0.66 \, dm^3$; **[2]**

(b) Breaths per minute = 4 or $5 \times 6 = 24/30$, volume of each breath = 1.25 to 1.5 ;

Ventilation rate = $24 / 30 \times 1.25$ to $1.5 = 30.0$ to 45.0 (depends on values used) $dm^3 \, min^{-1}$; **[2]**

(c) *Tidal volume* increases ;

Rate of breathing increases ;

Greater variation of volume ;

Credit comparative manipulation use of figures ; **[3]**

(d) (i) Increase in *tidal volume* after exercise not as great ;
Increase in ventilation rate after exercise not as great ;
Faster return to normal breathing pattern ;
Respiratory muscles stronger ;
Alveolar capillary network increased ;
Gaseous exchange more efficient ; **[4]**

(ii) (Because) volume pumped per beat / stroke volume, increased ;
Maximum / potential, cardiac output increased ; **[2]**

(Total 13 marks)

Index

Page references in italics refer to a table or an illustration.

INDEX

INDEX

INDEX

INDEX